Role Mining
in Business

Taming Role-Based Access
Control Administration

Role Mining
in Business
Taming Role-Based Access Control Administration

Alessandro Colantonio
Bay31 GmbH, Switzerland

Roberto Di Pietro
Università di Roma Tre, Italy

Alberto Ocello
CrossIdeas Srl, Italy

World Scientific

NEW JERSEY · LONDON · SINGAPORE · BEIJING · SHANGHAI · HONG KONG · TAIPEI · CHENNAI

Published by

World Scientific Publishing Co. Pte. Ltd.

5 Toh Tuck Link, Singapore 596224

USA office: 27 Warren Street, Suite 401-402, Hackensack, NJ 07601

UK office: 57 Shelton Street, Covent Garden, London WC2H 9HE

British Library Cataloguing-in-Publication Data
A catalogue record for this book is available from the British Library.

ROLE MINING IN BUSINESS
Taming Role-Based Access Control Administration

ISBN-13 978-981-4374-00-2
ISBN-10 981-4374-00-8

Printed in Singapore.

To Vittoria, amazing, lovely, and true.

— *A. Colantonio*

Preface

In computer security, *access control* represents the process of mediating requests to data and services, and determining whether the requests should be granted or denied. In recent years significant research has focused on providing formal representations of access control models. In this context, *role-based access control* (RBAC) has become the norm for managing entitlements within commercial applications. RBAC simplifies entitlement management by using *roles*. A role uniquely identifies a set of permissions, and users are assigned to appropriate roles based on their responsibilities and qualifications. When users change their job function, they are assigned new roles, and old roles are removed from their profile. This results in users' entitlements matching their actual job functions. While RBAC is not a panacea for all ills related to access control, it offers great benefits to users managers and administrators, especially non-technical people. First, RBAC helps business users define security policies, since the role concept can be easily understood by them even without the support of IT staff. Second, RBAC implements the security engineering principles that support risk reduction, such as separation of duty (SoD) and least privilege. Finally, roles minimize system administration effort by reducing the number of relationships among users and permissions. Indeed, when two or more users have similar permissions, we can reduce the number of administrative actions by just grouping those permissions.

Despite the widespread adoption of RBAC-oriented systems, organizations frequently implement them without due consideration of roles. To minimize deployment effort or to avoid project scope creep, organizations often neglect role definition in the initial part of the deployment project. Very often, organizations do not invest enough time to define roles in detail; rather, they define high-level roles that do not reflect actual business requirements. The result of this thoughtless role definition process is that deployed RBAC systems do not deliver the expected benefits. Additionally, it also leads to role misuse (e.g., roles incorrectly assigned due to their unclear meaning). This is the main reason why many organizations are still reluctant to adopt RBAC. The *role engineering* discipline addresses these problems. Its aim is to properly customize RBAC systems in order to capture the needs and functions of the organizations. Yet, choosing the best way to design a proper set of roles is still an open problem. Various approaches to role engineering have been proposed, which are usually classified as: *top-down* and *bottom-up*. Top-down requires a deep analysis of business processes to identify which access permissions are necessary to carry out specific tasks. Bottom-up seeks to identify *de facto* roles embedded in existing access control information. Since bottom-up approaches usually resort to data mining techniques, the term *role mining* is often used. In practice, top-down approaches may produce results that conflict with existing permissions, while bottom-up approaches may not consider the high-level business structure of an organization. For maximum benefits, a *hybrid* of top-down and bottom-up is often the most valid approach.

The bottom-up approach has recently attracted both researchers and practitioners, since it can be easily automated. Indeed, companies which plan to deploy RBAC-oriented systems usually find themselves migrating from several "conventional" access control systems. In this scenario, role mining uses data mining techniques to generate roles from the access control information of this collection of legacy and standard systems. Current role mining approaches, however, must deal with some practical issues:

Meaning of Roles   Automatically elicited roles often have no connection to business practice. Existing role mining algorithms can be classified in two different classes, both of which suffer from the same problem. The first class seeks to identify *complete RBAC states*—that is, minimal sets of roles to cover all existing access permissions—minimizing the resulting system complexity. It is dubious, however, that automated techniques can completely overcome and replace the cognitive capacity of humans. This is particularly true when complex security policies also allow for exceptions. As a result, organizations are unwilling to deploy automatically elicited roles that they cannot fully understand or trust. To gain greater flexibility, a second class of algorithms proposes a *complete list of roles*, so role designers can manually select the most relevant ones. However, there is the risk of missing the complete view of data due to the typically large number of candidate roles and unavoidable exceptions.

Algorithm Performance   Several works prove that the role mining problem is reducible to many other problems that are known to be intractable (i.e., $\mathcal{NP}$-hard), such as clique partition of graphs, binary matrix factorization, bi-clustering, and graph vertex coloring, to name a few. As a result, many role mining algorithms entail long running times and huge memory footprints. Moreover, when hundreds of thousands of existing user-permission assignments need to be analyzed, the number of candidate roles may be so high that trying to analyze them is often impractical.

Noise Within Data   The number of roles elicited by existing role mining approaches is often very large. This is mainly due to "noise" within the data, namely permissions exceptionally or accidentally granted or denied. In such a case, classical role mining algorithms elicit multiple small fragments of the true role. Recently, a number of methods have been proposed to discover approximate patterns in the presence of noise. However, they usually require tuning several parameters that can greatly affect algorithm performances and the quality of results. Another problem is that the adopted noise model may not fit real cases, mainly when exceptions are legitimate and cannot be avoided. Further, the number of exceptions may be so high to make it difficult to navigate and analyze them.

Problem Complexity   Introducing new users, permissions, or relationships between them into the access control system may require reassessing the role-set in use. In other words, the system could require a complete redesign of its roles in order to reduce the overall administration cost. Hence, it is important to design a proper set of roles that allows to effectively manage the unavoidable changes to which organizations incur. Another observation relates to the typically large number of candidate roles proposed by role mining algorithms, which hampers the selection of the most meaningful ones for the organization. Furthermore, matching top-down information with bottom-up results is often impracticable.

Risk of Unmanageable Roles   As stated before, a superficial application of standard data mining approaches often yields roles that are merely a set of permissions, with no connection to the business practices. It is difficult to incorporate such roles into an organization's risk management framework. Thus, poorly designed roles directly increase the risk of incorrectly authorized users.

Book Content

This book collects and harmonizes the most significant contributions in the literature to address the current issues related to role mining. To this aim, we divide existing approaches in five main areas—each of them covered by a part of this book—and we strive to provide a complete analysis of each of them. The purpose of the first part is to acquaint the reader with the prerequisite knowledge required to fully understand the content of this book. In turn, the subsequent four parts analyze different aspects of role mining. In particular, we first survey the state-of-the-art about *pattern identification* in users' entitlements. We describe how to efficiently enumerate interesting patterns among user-permission assignments via "classical" data mining approach or specific algorithms for role mining. Further, we report on several approaches to obtain a *minimal* set of roles, by also showing how to estimate the minimum number of roles required to cover all user-permission relationships. In turn, we generalize the role-finding problem by offering a *cost-based approach* that seeks to minimize the overall administration complexity of RBAC systems.

Second, we tackle the problem of *eliciting meaningful roles* by providing two useful approaches to solve it. One solution leverages the aforementioned cost-driven approach, as well as the modeling of business, to *evaluate the meaning of roles* during the entire role-finding process. Another solution is represented by a novel approach referred to as *visual role mining*. The key idea is that of adopting a visual representation of existing user-permission assignments, hence allowing for a quick analysis and elicitation of meaningful roles. We describe an algorithm that seeks to best represent user-permission relationships in a graphical form.

As for *role mining complexity*, we describe how to decompose the whole role mining problem into smaller and simpler sub-problems by restricting the analysis to sets of data that are homogeneous from an enterprise perspective. The approach also make it simpler for analysts to elicit meaningful roles. The key observation is that users sharing the same business attributes will essentially perform the same task within the organization. Consequently, it will be easier for an analyst to assign a business meaning to the roles elicited via bottom-up approaches. To apply this *divide-and-conquer* strategy, we describe how to choose the decomposition that most likely leads to roles with a tight business meaning. Additionally, we study the problem of identifying exceptionally/accidentally granted/denied permissions. We propose a methodology that allows role engineers to elicit *stable* candidate roles, namely roles that likely remains unchanged during their lifecycle. We introduce a strategy that avoids the generation of unstable roles during the application of any role mining algorithm. The dual problem of selecting assignments related to unstable roles is represented by the identification of *missing* assignments: those permissions that, if granted to certain users, would simplify the mining task. We describe a viable and effective approach to identify such missing values.

Finally, we confront the question of effectively managing the *risk derived from granting access* to resources. We discuss how a divide-and-conquer approach to role mining actually reduces the risk related to illegal accesses. In particular, we describe a risk model that assesses the risk related to entitling users to not expected operations, or hampering their jobs by not granting required permissions. Another solution is to highlight users and permissions that markedly deviate from those "similar" to them. That is, bringing out users that have a permission-set different from other users with the same business attributes (i.e., job title, department, cost center, etc.) since they are likely prone to error when roles are operating. Focusing on such users and permissions during the role definition process likely mitigates the risk of unauthorized accesses and role misuse.

Outline of the Book

The remainder of the book is organized as follows. Part 1 offers some preliminaries required for the subsequent chapters. Chapter 1 introduces Identity and Access Management (IAM) systems and basic access control concepts. A description of RBAC is then provided in Chap. 2. Subsequently, in Chap. 3 we briefly survey the state-of-the-art in role engineering. A viable role mining process is discussed in Chap. 4. Then, some mathematical background related to role mining is provided in Chap. 5. This background is required to formally describe all the mining algorithms offered by this book.

Part 2 surveys the most used techniques to enumerate candidate roles from existing user-permission assignments. Chapter 6 introduces the problem of enumerating all possible roles. In particular, we show the relationship between roles and frequent itemset mining, clustering, subset enumeration, and other well-know data mining strategies. The chapter also addresses the problem of providing a minimal set of roles. This problem is subsequently generalized in Chap. 7 by providing a metric to measure the "cost" of RBAC administration. Further, we describe an algorithm that leverages the cost metric to find candidate role-sets with the lowest possible administration cost.

Part 3 copes with the problem of assigning a business meaning to roles. To this aim, two different approaches are detailed. First, Chap. 8 introduces a metric to assess how "good" are roles from a business perspective, by measuring their "spreading" among business processes or the organization structure. Then, in Chap. 9 we offer a graphical way to visually identify meaningful roles within access control data.

Part 4 addresses the problem of reducing the role mining complexity in RBAC systems. In Chap. 10 we propose a methodology that helps analysts decompose the dataset into smaller subsets homogeneous from a business perspective. It describes some indices that estimate how easy is to perform a role mining analysis. Then, Chap. 11 proposes a three-steps methodology to identify and discard user-permission assignments that cannot belong to so-called "stable" roles. Furthermore, in Chap. 12 we also consider the possibility that analyzed data present some missing user-permission assignment. Thus, we propose an algorithm to efficiently impute such missing values.

Finally, Part 5 describes a risk model to analyze the proneness of RBAC configurations to allow for unauthorized access to resources. To measure the likelihood of having meaningless and unmanageable roles within the system, we recall the methodology described in Chap. 10, where data to analyze are decomposed into smaller subsets according to the provided business information. In particular, in Chap. 13 we show how this processing decreases the probability of making errors in role management, and consequently reduces the risk of role misuse. Moreover, Chap. 14 introduces an approach to highlight users and permissions that markedly deviate from others, and that might consequently be prone to error when roles are operating.

Intended Audience and How to Read this Book

This book focuses on recent developments for role mining, by covering the most relevant facets of existing techniques, as well as showing both antic-ipated and unanticipated positive effects on the overall cost of managing roles. To this objective, it couples a tight formalism when exposing the role mining problem, with both theoretical and experimental results. In partic-ular, it provides an optimal combination of theory (that can be of relevant interest to Academia) and practice (that can be of interest for the Industry). Therefore, IT professionals and researchers can benefit from reading this book, such as:

- computer science and IT researchers, students, and instructors, who want to gain a deep knowledge of role mining concepts;
- role-engineering consultants, who provide technical expertise during the role engineering phase of RBAC implementation;
- governance and compliance consultants, who help end users leverage RBAC to develop the processes of review and attestation necessary for regulatory compliance;
- system integrators, who integrate heterogeneous systems for the end user;
- target system developers, who incorporate access control enforcement into the target systems;
- IAM system developers, who create the suite of tools for end users to manage users' identities and permissions across heterogeneous systems; and,
- in-house developers, who design custom software for the end user.

To make a clear distinction between theoretical-oriented sections and the more general content of this book, we put the symbol "$\star$" in the chapter/section titles that can be more relevant for academic people, or that contain in-depth explanation of algorithms. Such parts can be skipped by more business-oriented people without missing the general meaning of each chapter.

Finally, notice that Part 1 contains some propaedeutic material required to understand all the subsequent chapters. In particular, reading chapters from 1 to 5 is suggested before going ahead. However, the subsequent chapters can be read in any order.

About the Authors

Alessandro Colantonio is Founder of Bay31. He brings more than 10 years of experience in IT security industry. He received a Ph.D. in Mathematics from the "Roma Tre" University, Italy, in 2011. He received a Master's Degree in Computer Engineering with specialization in IT Systems and Applications at University of Pisa, Italy, in 2001. He also received a Specialization Master in IT Security Management at "La Sapienza" University, Italy, in 2008. His main interests include Governance, Risk Management, and Compliance of RBAC-oriented Identity & Access Management systems.

Roberto Di Pietro is an Assistant Professor at the Department of Mathematics of "Roma Tre" University, Italy. He received the Ph.D. in Computer Science from "La Sapienza" University, Italy, in 2004. In 2004 he also received from the Department of Statistics of the same University a Specialization Diploma in Operating Research and Strategic Decisions. He received the Laurea degree in Computer Science from the University of Pisa, Italy, in 1994. His main research interests include: Role mining, security for mobile, ad-hoc, and underwater wireless networks, intrusion detection, security for distributed systems, secure multicast, applied cryptography, and computer forensics.

Alberto Ocello is Chief Executive Officer at CrossIdeas (formerly Engiweb Security). He holds a master in Electronic Engineering from the University of Rome, Italy and brings more than 25 years of experience in the security software industry. Alberto Ocello began his career at Page Europa (GTE Group) working in various roles in security application development, starting as Chief Product Architect and moving on to several product development groups in international military security projects. He then served as director of engineering, focusing on the application of PKI and new cryptographic technologies for enhancement of information security in electronic business scenarios.

Contents

Pattern Identification in Users' Entitlements   87

The Risk of Unmanageable Roles   **235**

PART 1

Fundamentals

The purpose of this part is to acquaint the reader with the prerequisite knowledge required to fully understand the content of this book. The first chapter starts with a brief overview of *Identity and Access Management* (IAM) systems, focusing on *access control*. The subsequent chapter describes the *Role-Based Access Control* (RBAC) model and other role-based concepts, followed by their formal description according to the ANSI/INCITS 359-2004 standard. In turn, we explain the way an organization can migrate from other access control models to RBAC through *role engineering* methodologies. The typical classification of the various role engineering approaches is presented. *Role mining* techniques, namely the automated part of role engineering, are also introduced. A typical role mining process is described, highlighting its related problems and solutions. For academic-oriented readers, we also offer the required mathematical formalism. In particular, we summarize a few concepts about *binary matrices* and *graph theory*, by showing the relationship with role mining.

Chapter 1

Managing Access Rights

Today's enterprises need to manage secure access to information and applications across multiple systems, delivering on-line services to employee, customer, and suppliers without compromising security. Companies must be able to trust the identities of users requiring access and easily administer user identities in a cost-effective way. *Identity and Access Management* (IAM) faces to this issue. This chapter thus offers an overview of IAM systems as well as general access control concepts for those readers that are not very familiar with this topic.

1.1 Challenges of Controlling Access

To do their business, enterprises have to "open" their networks, first to customers, but also to partners. More and more users and applications bring a critical concern to these enterprises, which is to ensure and maintain the security of assets and privacy protection, while identifying authorized parties [Linares (2005)]. The fast growth of the user population, as well as frequent job turn over, makes the task of managing users more complicated. Creation of new accounts with appropriate privileges to adequate resources, modifying privileges associated to users when their job roles change, and disabling outdated accounts for employees/contractors/partners/customers when these accounts are no longer needed, have to be performed efficiently and in a secure way. If not, this can result in an unmanageable number of permissions, loss of productivity, and might lead to major security issues.

Therefore, one of the most important features of today's systems is the protection of their resources (i.e., data and services) against unauthorized disclosure and intentional or accidental unauthorized changes, while at the same time ensuring their accessibility by authorized users whenever needed

Fig. 1.1: Main components of an Identity and Access Management system

[De Capitani Di Vimercati *et al.* (2007)]. The ability of an organization to rapidly search, identify, and verify who is accessing its information systems is considered a critical aspect of meeting security and compliance requirements for the organization. For this reason, there is an increasing interest in adopting *Identity and Access Management* (IAM) systems. IAM has become a key issue in information security in the last years [Matys *et al.* (2009)]. It encapsulates people, processes, and products to identify and manage the data required to authenticate users and then grant or deny access rights to system resources. Put another way, an IAM system represents the infrastructure that ensures people are who they say they are and provides users their appropriate level of access.

To provide the right access to the right people in order to protect information sources, a typical IAM relies on four main components: *authentication, authorization, user management*, and *central user repository* (see Fig. 1.1). The authentication and authorization parts of an IAM system represent what is usually referred to as *access control* in IT security (see Sec. 1.2.3). Specifically, access control is the process of mediating requests to data and services maintained by a system, and determining whether the requests should be granted or denied. Arguably, access control is one of the most important security services required to achieve data protection.

Besides IAM infrastructures, organizations also require *access control policies* to be defined. An access control policy is generally technology-independent, and it defines the (high-level) rules according to which access control must be regulated [De Capitani Di Vimercati *et al.* (2007)]. A policy may be general and apply to all departments in an organization, or it may be specific to the structure of a particular department. More generally, it is a response to the following requirements: *business requirements* (e.g., lowering the cost of managing employees' permissions); *security constraints* (e.g., ensuring information confidentiality, integrity, and availability); and, *regulations* (e.g., complying with regulations such as the Health Insurance Portability and Accountability Act (HIPAA) [Kennedy and Kassebaum (1996)] or the Sarbanes-Oxley Act [Sarbanes and Oxley (2002)])

In organizations with few users or few resources to protect, maintaining an access control policy may be as straightforward as directly granting access to users. However, for many organizations, especially medium and large ones, maintaining an access control policy requires a substantial dedication of resources because of the large number of users, objects, and systems. The more complex the policies become, the more likely it is that they will contain errors from changes in regulations, implementation of new systems and policies, interactions among policies, or human error [Ni *et al.* (2010)]. For this reason, it follows that technology that optimizes access control policies' effectiveness and efficiency offers substantial economic benefits. This book aims at describing some of such technologies.

1.2 Access Control Concepts

As mentioned earlier, among IAM system features, access control is likely to be the most relevant. Thus, the main objective of this section is to provide an overview of the main concepts related to access control. Those concepts are summarized in Fig. 1.2.

1.2.1 *Policies, Models, and Mechanisms*

When planning an access control system, three abstractions of controls should be considered: access control *policies*, *models*, and *mechanisms* [Hu

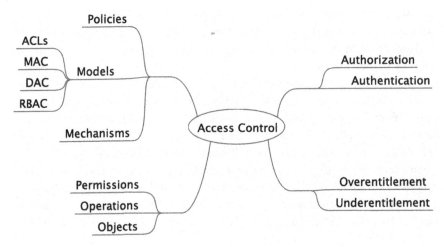

Fig. 1.2: Access control concepts

et al. (2006)]. *Access control policies* are high-level requirements that specify how access is managed and who, under what circumstances, may access what information. Access control policies can be application-specific—and thus taken into consideration by the application vendor—or they can pertain to user actions within the context of an organizational unit or across organizational boundaries. In general, policies are based on need-to-know, competence, authority, obligation, or conflict-of-interest factors.

Access control policies are enforced through a *mechanism* that translates user's access requests. This often happens in terms of structures provided by the access control system. There are a wide variety of structures; for example, a simple table lookup can be performed to grant or deny access. Although no well-accepted standard yet exists for determining their policy support, some access control mechanisms are direct implementations of formal access control policy concepts [Ferraiolo *et al.* (2007)].

Access control models are usually written to describe the security properties of an access control system. A model is a formal presentation of the security policy enforced by the system and is useful for proving theoretical limitations of a system. Access control models are of general interest to both users and vendors. They bridge the gap in abstraction between policy and mechanism. Access control mechanisms can be designed to adhere to the properties of the model. Users see an access control model as an unambiguous and precise expression of requirements. Vendors and system developers see access control models as design and implementation requirements. On one extreme, an access control model may be rigid in its implementation of a single policy. On the other extreme, a security model will allow for the expression and enforcement of a wide variety of policies and policy classes [Ferraiolo *et al.* (2007)]. Section 1.3 describes the most common access control models that can be found in the current literature.

1.2.2 *Permissions, Operations, and Objects*

In any access control system, *permissions*, sometimes referred to as *privileges* or *entitlements*, specify what *operations* a user may perform on a specific *resource* or *object*. Typical operations include read, write, delete, and execute, or complex transactions such as a money transfer. In a typical organization, objects are databases, applications, and files.

As for *databases*, objects are typically organized in *tables*. Users can create new tables, add new information to existing tables, or modify information that exists in the tables. A user may have permission to read a table within a database containing, for instance, sales information, but may not be granted permission to modify any of the entries in that table.

We refer to *applications* as the executable programs that individuals use. These include common office-automation applications, as well as communication applications such as e-mail, to name but a few. Please notice that, for many applications, there is only a single permission allowing a user to execute the application. As identity-aware applications have matured, however, more sophisticated access control policies can be implemented. One example of such applications is represented by workflow and collaborative systems [Tolone *et al.* (2005)].

Files within operating systems also have their use regulated through access control decisions. Similar to databases, users can create, modify, or delete files according to the security requirements of the organization.

1.2.3 *Authentication and Authorization*

Access control is an important component of identity and access management system. As mentioned earlier, there are two aspects related to access control: authorization and authentication. *Authentication* refers to determining whether users are who they say they are. The ways in which someone may be authenticated fall into (at least) three categories, based on what are known as the *factors of authentication* [Federal Financial Institutions Examination Council (2005)]: something you know, something you have, or something you are. For example, bank ATMs require the presence of both a bank card and the knowledge of a personal identification number to access bank accounts and perform transactions. For most organizations, the most common technique is to require a username and password pair to verify a user's identity. More advanced technologies are gaining popularity, such as biometric authentication, which uses retinal scans or fingerprints, and security tokens, which may change a portion of a password every 30 seconds and display that change to users.

Authorization refers to determining the permissions a user has and enforcing those permissions. In other words, while authentication permits users access to a system by validating or verifying their identity, authorization specifies what objects the user may access and what operations she may perform. This book focuses on the authorization part of IAM.

1.2.4   *User Life-Cycle Management and Provisioning*

We refer to *user life-cycle management* as the series of steps involved in managing a user's identity and permissions in order to comply with access control policies. When a new user joins an organization, he must be given all of the permissions necessary to perform his job. Likewise, if a user changes positions or responsibilities, additional permissions must be provisioned and the permissions that are no longer appropriate for his job function should be removed. The task of assigning and terminating users' permissions is referred to as *provisioning*.[1] The process by which access permissions are removed from users is referred to as "deprovisioning." When a user leaves the organization, all permissions must be terminated.

To identify which access control policies are applicable to a given user or resource, an organization must be able to easily *review* users' permissions. This involves not only verifying which permissions are currently possessed by users, but also understanding what these permissions allow these users to do. To properly deprovision, an organization must know what permissions a user currently has and which of the permissions are no longer appropriate

---

[1]The term "provisioning" has its origin in the telecommunications industry and dates to the 1960s. It referred to preparing networks and systems to accommodate the addition of a new user. In the IT industry, the term refers to the assignment of system resources and permissions to new users.

for the user's business function.[2]

Until the past decade, most permissions were assigned to users using *access control lists* (ACLs, see Sec. 1.3.1) because flexible access control models were not available. An IT administrator usually enforces a desired access control policy entirely by adding and removing permissions or users from an ACL. Maintaining all of the user permissions within a *central directory* (e.g., Lightweight Directory Access Protocol, LDAP [Koutsonikola and Vakali (2004)]) simplifies provisioning by assigning all of the permissions in one place. Thus, central directories are an important component of IAM systems. However, this still requires that all user-permission assignments are created directly and that they are removed when they are no longer needed. But, in addition to the significant time cost of provisioning and deprovisioning, reviewing the access control permissions for a single user requires the administrator to review all ACLs. Performing these reviews regularly for all users becomes an extremely costly review process.

1.2.5 *Overentitlement and Underentitlement*

An access control policy that strictly adheres to least privilege may be too costly to implement in practice. In this case, organizations must choose between implementing an access control policy that gives some users too many or too few permissions. In fact:

- An "overentitled" user presents a security risk. There is a greater chance that the user will have a so-called *toxic combination of permissions* that allow violation of intended policy.
- An "underentitled" user presents both a business risk and security risk. If a user has too few permissions to do his job effectively, then the organization will lose productivity. An underentitled user will also seek to circumvent the access control system to complete his job, for example, by using another user's account to access the necessary information. This poses a security risk by not having an accurate documentation of "who accessed what."

---

[2]An access control system includes administrative, system, and review functions [O'Connor and Loomis (2010)]. Administrative functions allow to assign and remove permissions from users. System functions make and enforce access control decisions. Review functions allow administrators to review the existing access control policy and potentially an auditable track of access to resources.

If deprovisioning does not occur, it may not affect a user's productivity, but it results in the user maintaining unnecessary or inappropriate permissions. This phenomenon is referred to as *permission drift* or *privilege accumulation*. Overentitled users may possess toxic combination of permissions, which would enable a user to break the law, violate rules of ethics, damage customers' trust, or even create the appearance of impropriety [Sinclair and Smith (2008)]. An example is *separation of duty* (SoD) [Colantonio *et al.* (2008a)]. Alternatively indicated as "conflict of interest" or "mutual exclusion", SoD usually refers to the identification of operations which should not be granted to an individual user. For instance, an employee acting as a financial manager may not be allowed to act as a financial auditor at the same time. SoD is further discussed in Chap. 2.

1.3   Access Control Models

As mentioned earlier, an *access control model* provides a formal representation of the access control security policy and its working. In other words, access control models are abstractions that incorporate the rules and parameters required to execute access control policies. Since multiple mechanisms can be constructed to support a particular access control policy, access control models provide a framework for policy implementation. Application of the model promotes consistent access control mechanisms across platforms, which lowers costs, increases security, and supports interoperability [O'Connor and Loomis (2010)].

Early access control models were developed for defense-related applications and began to be formalized mathematically in the 1960s and 1970s. Two important models for the military—*Discretionary Access Control* (DAC) and *Mandatory Access Control* (MAC)—were specified in detail with the 1983 release of *Trusted Computer System Evaluation Criteria* (TCSEC, [United States DoD (1983)]), also referred to as the *Orange Book*. ACLs, MAC, and DAC largely dominated access control theory and practice until RBAC was introduced in the 1990s.

In the following we provide a brief overview of these models. Figure 1.3 summarizes these models. RBAC is detailed in Chap. 2 and not further discussed in this chapter.

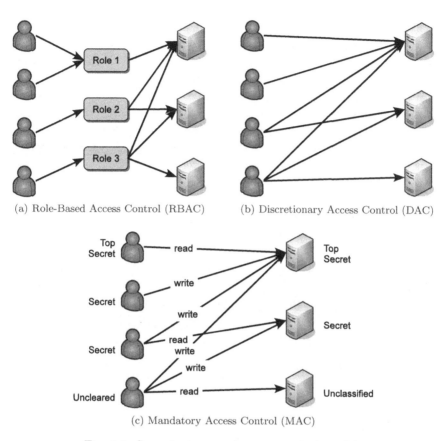

(a) Role-Based Access Control (RBAC) (b) Discretionary Access Control (DAC)

(c) Mandatory Access Control (MAC)

Fig. 1.3: Some instances of access control models

1.3.1 *Access Control Lists*

As mentioned earlier, *Access Control Lists* (ACLs, for short) are the most prevalent and simple form of access control. An ACL is a list of users, or groups of users, and their permissions associated with a specific resource. Any user trying to access the resource will only be entitled according to the parameters specified in the ACL. It is possible to enforce a specified access control policy by assigning users to ACLs, and many organizations rely on this approach. However, maintaining ACLs to reflect the desired access control policy is labor intensive. A user may eventually receive his necessary permissions by request, but requests to remove permissions are rarely made.

Manually applied rules are often used in combination with ACLs, where ACLs are the repository of authorized users and the rule specifies what the users listed in a given ACL are permitted to perform. Before the advent of more flexible models such as RBAC (see Chap. 2), rules and ACLs were the predominant method of managing access control. Systems that can enforce arbitrary rules at run time are often called *rule based* or *attribute based* access control systems (see also Sec. 1.3.4).

While ACLs are resource specific, *capability lists* are user specific. Capability lists are lists of resources and permissions associated with a specific user. Capability lists solve the problem of determining the resources a user has access to, but they make it difficult to determine what users have access to a specific resource.

Many systems provide a means of placing users into one or more *groups*, with permissions attached to both a group and individual users within the group. In some cases, this approach can be nearly equivalent to the most basic form of role-based access control model that will be detailed in Chap. 2 (without concepts such as hierarchies or separation of duty constraints, as will be explained in the next chapter), although the ability to attach permissions directly to users may lead to leaking privileges in unintended ways.

1.3.2   *Discretionary Access Control*

Discretionary Access Control (DAC) is not a fixed set of rules to determine access, but rather a mechanism for how permissions are assigned to users. It is defined by TCSEC "as a means of restricting access to objects based on the identity of subjects and/or groups to which they belong. The controls are discretionary in the sense that a subject with a certain access permission is capable of passing that permission (perhaps indirectly) on to any other subject (unless restrained by mandatory access control)." Generally speaking, the model dictates that the owner of a resource has the ability to grant (at their discretion) users access to the resource. Thus, because users can give away permissions, the access control policy enforced may deviate from the organization's desired access control policy. Administering access control using ACLs is one implementation of DAC. A straightforward example of DAC is the traditional Unix permissions with its system of users, groups, and read-write-execute permissions for objects (i.e., files and directories).

1.3.3   *Mandatory Access Control*

Mandatory Access Control (MAC), sometimes termed *non-discretionary access control*, is a policy-specific, non-discretionary access control model. MAC was developed to implement a *multilevel security* (MLS) access control policy, in which permissions are determined according to the user's clearance level (e.g., Classified, Secret, Top Secret). It is non-discretionary, meaning that the rules governing access are not subject to change at the discretion of system administrators. Thus, the desired access control policy is always the access control policy enforced. TCSEC defines MAC as "a means of restricting access to objects based on the sensitivity (as represented by a label) of the information contained in the objects and the formal authorization (i.e., clearance) of subjects to access information of such sensitivity." Examples of MAC models are those proposed by Bell and LaPadula (1976) and Biba (1977).

Although MAC is well suited for the military, most other organizations do not conform well to the MLS structure enforced with it. In fact, the diversity and complexity of commercial organizations require a useful access control model be policy independent. To maintain enforcement of the desired policy, a useful model would need to be non-discretionary. It is within this context that the formal RBAC model (see Chap. 2) was developed.

1.3.4   *Attribute-Based Access Control*

There is little consensus on what is meant by *attribute-based access control* (ABAC) [Kuhn *et al.* (2010)]; however, the basic concept is that each user and resource has a series of attributes that are known about them. Through a comparative assessment of situational data (i.e., time of day or persons logged on to the network) and known information about a user (i.e., job title and location), the access control system can make near-instantaneous decisions about whether a user is appropriately authorized to perform an operation on an object. The data elements analyzed are referred to as *attributes*. The advantage of ABAC is that it leverages known information about users and contextual information, thereby avoiding role engineering (i.e., the process of designing a role structure, see Chap. 3). The disadvantages are that attributes may not be defined consistently, the access control policy becomes more dynamic than would be preferable for audit and attestation, and it requires specifying a large number of rules, making analysis difficult.

1.4   Final Remarks

This chapter introduced Identity and Access Management systems, which allows private or public organizations to securely manage identities and access to their resources while meeting the requirements of today's business world. Besides the benefits described throughout the chapter, it is important to note that the implementation of a IAM solution—which can require multiple products from multiple vendors—is a real investment: money, time, as well as resources. It also results in business process change for organizations which need to define the right phases of IAM deployment and the key concerns that must be resolved through efficient project management. However, the return of investment is achieved through multiple factors: simplified centralized administration with a complete provisioning system, an access enforcement system, faster application development and deployment, less help-desk involvement, and a strong auditing capability [Linares (2005)].

We also pointed out that a fundamental part of IAM systems is represented by their access control capabilities. In addition to the authentication mechanism, access control is concerned with how authorizations are structured. In some cases, authorization may mirror the structure of the organization, while in others it may be based on the sensitivity level of various documents and the clearance level of the user accessing those documents. Organizations planning to implement an access control system should consider three abstractions: access control policies, models, and mechanisms. Access control policies are high-level requirements that specify how access is managed and who may access information under what circumstances. Policies are enforced through a mechanism that translates a user's access request, often in terms of a structure that a system provides.

Access control models bridge the gap in abstraction between policy and mechanism. Security models are formal presentations of the security policy enforced by the system and are useful for proving theoretical limitations of a system. Although only the most commonly used access models are discussed in this book, many extensions, combinations, and different mechanisms are possible. Trade-offs and limitations are involved with all mechanisms and access control designs, so it is the users responsibility to determine the best-fit access control mechanisms that work for their business functions and requirements.

Chapter 2

Role-Based Access Control

This chapter provides the foundation for the remainder of the book. It offers an overview of the so-called *Role-Based Access Control* (RBAC) model. In particular, the reader can find here a formal description of the RBAC model as well as a summarization of its administrative and cost advantages.

The large number of concepts covered, and its importance as a preparatory material for all that follows, is reflected by the extent of the chapter. Its content is sufficient to acquaint the reader with all the RBAC-related concepts required to master this book. Nonetheless, this chapter cannot be considered a comprehensive description of the state-of-the-art in this area. In case the reader requires an in-depth analysis of the RBAC model, they can refer to the book of Ferraiolo *et al.* (2007) and NIST's economic analysis [O'Connor and Loomis (2010)]. Conversely, the reader that already has a proper knowledge of RBAC can entirely skip this chapter.

2.1 RBAC Basics

Role-based access control (RBAC) [Ferraiolo *et al.* (2001, 2007)] is the next evolutionary step in access control. The RBAC model introduces a framework for using *roles* (i.e., sets of connected behaviors, rights, and obligations as conceptualized by actors in an organization) within access control systems. The fundamental concept of RBAC is that roles aggregate privileges. Users inherit permissions by being members of roles. Rather than assigning permissions directly to users, under RBAC, permissions are assigned to roles engineered in software systems and users are assigned the roles necessary to do their jobs (see Fig. 2.1). Permissions can be grouped into roles based on location, business function, department, or other attributes of users, for example. Assignment of permissions to a role and determining

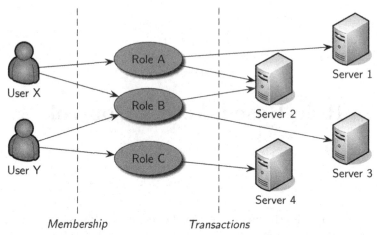

Fig. 2.1: Relations among users, roles, transactions, and resources in RBAC

membership of roles is supposed to be non-discretionary.

RBAC can be used by any organization, regardless of its size, to specify and administer access control policies. When permissions can be easily
grouped into roles based on business function, location of employee, department, or other attributes of employees, assigning roles to employees rather
than individual permissions will yield provisioning and productivity benefits. RBAC will yield the greatest provisioning and productivity benefits for
organizations with a large number of users occupying relatively stable roles
that experience regular turnover. For any organization that requires regular
certification of access control policies, aggregating permissions into roles will
simplify access control policy maintenance and certification. RBAC also allows access control to be managed more directly by the business managers.
This creates an important separation of duties, allowing IT professionals
to focus on information security design and business managers to govern
day-to-day operations [O'Connor and Loomis (2010)].

In 1975, Saltzer and Schroeder identified eight principles of design to
enhance security within computer systems. These principles are reported
in Table 2.1. The RBAC model specifically enables the achievement of
two of these principles, "least privilege" and "separation of privilege," and
contributes to the principles of "economy of mechanism" and "psychological
acceptability." The principle of *least privilege* states that users have only
the permissions necessary to perform their job functions. Least privilege
minimizes the impact of deliberate or accidental damage to a system, as
well as limits the chance that a toxic combination of permissions exists.

Table 2.1: Eight Principles of Secure Design for Computer Systems of Saltzer and Schroeder (1975)

Principle	Meaning
1. Economy of mechanism	The system should be as simple as possible.
2. Fail-safe defaults	The default is denial of access.
3. Complete mediation	Every access decision must be checked.
4. Open design	The design must be open to review.
5. Separation of privilege	Sensitive tasks should not be completed by a single individual.
6. Least privilege	Users should not possess extraneous privileges.
7. Least common mechanism	The fewer the number of users sharing a mechanism, the less problematic a user damaging the mechanism will be.
8. Psychological acceptability	The security interface must be easy to use, or it will not be used correctly.

Strict adherence to least privilege, however, is difficult to implement in practice. RBAC provides the best framework to achieve least privilege within complex organizations [O'Connor and Loomis (2010)].

The principle of *separation of privilege*, also known as *separation of duty* (SoD), refers to the identification of operations which should not be granted to an individual user. For instance, an employee acting as a financial manager may not be allowed to act as a financial auditor at the same time. RBAC can be used to enforce SoD within digital systems by identifying toxic combinations of permissions and rendering them mutually exclusive. The usage of roles as an abstraction layer between users and privileges simplifies management, contributing to economy of mechanism and making privilege assignment easier because roles reflect user jobs.

Although RBAC is not a panacea for all ills pertaining to access control, it enables greater shared responsibility, and more effective and efficient permissions management for IT and business operations. RBAC is recognized for simplifying access control administration and improving visibility of both the access control policy and the organizational structure [Gallaher *et al.* (2002); O'Connor and Loomis (2010)]. In fact, RBAC allows for:

- *More efficient access control policy maintenance and certification.* RBAC facilitates and, relative to other access control models, reduces costs associated with *governance, risk, and compliance* (GRC, [Tarantino (2008)]). It also ease: access control policy maintenance, attestation of access control policies in place, certification of regulated information systems, and access control policy audits conducted by internal and external auditors.
- *More efficient provisioning by network and systems administrators.* RBAC reduces the costs of administering and monitoring permissions relative to ACLs and other antecedent access control models. RBAC allows for greater automation while adhering to the specified access control policy. Changes to permissions are automated through role assignment rather than being manually assigned whenever a new user is hired, an existing user changes positions, or new applications or IT systems are adopted.
- *Reduction in new employee downtime from more efficient provisioning.* RBAC accelerates bringing "new" employees to full productivity. New employees are those that have been recently hired, or are existing employees placed in new positions within the organization. During this time period, these employees may be only marginally or partially productive because they are underentitled. These benefits greatly outweigh the benefits from greater efficiency in network and systems administrators' execution of provisioning tasks.
- *Automated deprovisioning.* That is, revoking permissions that no longer apply to the user's new position by just removing old roles. Moreover, if the organization upgrades a system, an IT administrator needs to only update the new permissions to the appropriate roles, and the permissions will be propagated to all relevant users via roles.
- *More effective review of the access control policies.* Indeed, roles already contain the user and permission information in a central location. Understanding the access control policy that is currently enforced within the organization is crucial to identify security threats and may aid in the attestation and auditing required by law.

2.2   RBAC Standards

The success of RBAC is witnessed by the large number of groups that have contributed, and continue to contribute, to improve role-based approaches to access control. Academic, government, and industry researchers develop and discuss cutting-edge research, such as models for distributed administration of RBAC and novel role-mining algorithms (see Chap. 3). Standardization groups bring together experts to codify these novel security technologies to support their adoption and interoperability with existing systems. For instance, in 2004 the *American National Standard and International Committee for Information Technology Standards* (ANSI/INCITS) approved an RBAC standard [ANSI/INCITS (2004)] that combined features of the models introduced by Ferraiolo and Kuhn (1992) and Sandhu *et al.* (1996). In addition to NIST's RBAC standards work, the *Organization for the Advancement of Structured Information Standards* (OASIS) has contributed standards to support the interoperability of IAM tools across heterogeneous target systems, such as the *Security Assertion Markup Language* (SAML) for authentication across target systems and the *eXtensible Access Control Markup Language* (XACML) for access control across target systems. OASIS has published a profile for implementing RBAC with XACML. *Health Level Seven* (HL7), an ANSI-accredited organization working to develop standards for exchanging clinical and administrative data, began a role-engineering effort to define standardized permissions and constraints for the health care industry.

In this book we only focus on the ANSI/INCITS standard. This standard defined four levels of RBAC with their respective administrative, system, and review functions. Depending on their needs, companies can choose to use one or more of them. These levels are: *Core* RBAC; *Hierarchical* RBAC; *Static Separation of Duties* (SSD) RBAC; and, *Dynamic Separation of Duties* (DSD) RBAC. The following are more details about each level. Only the concepts strictly required by this book are described. Moreover, the exposition is simplified when compared to standard definition. For an in-depth analysis of the ANSI RBAC standard, please refer to [ANSI/INCITS (2004)].

2.2.1   *Core RBAC*⋆

Core RBAC delineates the basic elements and functions that are contained in each level described in the RBAC standard. This means that every RBAC-compliant system should implement all the functions envisaged by Core RBAC. The basic elements are *users*, *roles*, and *operations* and *objects* that combine to form *permissions*. Core RBAC functions can be disaggregated into:

- *administrative functions*, which include creating and deleting users and roles and creating and modifying user-to-role assignments and permission-to-role assignments;
- *system functions*, which include creating a user session that activates the user's roles and determining access decisions based on the user's roles;
- *mandatory review functions*, which include reviewing users assigned to a given role and roles assigned to a given user; and
- *optional review functions*, which include reviewing permissions assigned to a given role and permissions assigned to a given user.

As for Core RBAC formal description, in the following we only summarize the entities of interest for the present book:

- *PERMS*, the set of all possible access permissions;
- *USERS*, the set of all system users;
- *ROLES*, the set of all roles;
- $UA \subseteq USERS \times ROLES$, the set of user-role assignments;
- $PA \subseteq PERMS \times ROLES$, the set of permission-role assignments.

The following functions are also provided by the standard:

- ass_users: $ROLES \rightarrow 2^{USERS}$ to identify users assigned to a role and, in case of Hierarchical RBAC described in the next section, to none of its senior roles.[1]
- ass_perms: $ROLES \rightarrow 2^{PERMS}$ to identify permissions assigned to a role and, in case of Hierarchical RBAC described in the next section, to none of its senior roles.[2]

Figure 2.2 depicts all the above entities. For the sake of simplicity, we do not discuss in details other concepts provided by the standard such as *sessions*. Sessions allows to dynamically activate roles. In other words, you must "activate" one or more of your roles before the access management system can figure out what you can and cannot do. However, sessions are irrelevant for most of the commercial role management tools.[3]

---

[1]The RBAC standard does not make a clear distinction between base and derived relations [Li *et al.* (2007)]. We therefore consider the functions *ass_users* as derived from *UA*, that is $ass\_users(r) = \{u \in USERS \mid \langle u, r \rangle \in UA\}$. We also assume that users assigned to a role are not assigned to its seniors.

[2]Analogous to *ass_users*, we consider the function *ass_perms* as derived from *PA*, that is $ass\_perms(r) = \{p \in PERMS \mid \langle p, r \rangle \in PA\}$. We also assume that permissions assigned to a role are not assigned to its juniors.

[3]The basic concept of RBAC is that permissions are assigned to roles, and users obtain such permissions by being assigned to roles. This simple concept, with or without fea-

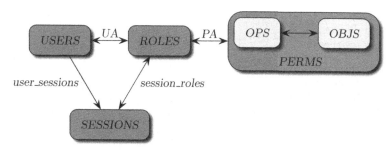

Fig. 2.2: Core RBAC

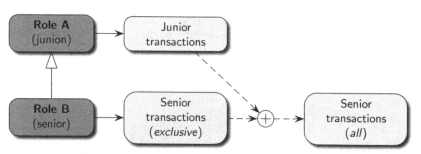

Fig. 2.3: Role hierarchy

2.2.2 *Hierarchical RBAC*★

Hierarchical RBAC provides for the establishment of role hierarchies, with *senior* roles adopting all of the permissions within *junior* roles. Figure 2.3 depicts this concept, while Fig. 2.4 shows a possible example for health care. Role hierarchy has the potential to simplify RBAC administration by streamlining the number of roles to which permissions and users are assigned. To realize these benefits, however, an organization must be structured hierarchically. Where this is not the case, Hierarchical RBAC may add complexity that outweighs the benefits of simplified administration.

Administrative functions within Hierarchical RBAC include those within core RBAC as well as functions to establish inheritance relationships between junior and senior roles. System functions are the same as

---

tures such as sessions, has demonstrated to provide powerful and useful access control systems [Li *et al.* (2007)]. Given a definition of Core RBAC that requires support for sessions and role activation, most of role management products on the market cannot claim to support ANSI RBAC. For this reason, we do not further discuss about sessions—even considering that they are not strictly required by the rest of the book.

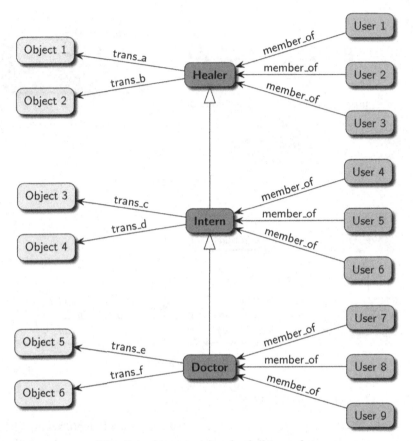

Fig. 2.4: An example of role hierarchy

in Core RBAC, with the addition of activating all junior roles to a user's roles. Review functions are the same as in Core RBAC; however, these functions must take into account the hierarchy of roles when reviewing the access policy.

More formally, hierarchical relationships are defined through the set $RH \subseteq ROLES \times ROLES$, namely the set of hierarchically related pairs of roles. Figure 2.5 graphically shows this set. RH derives from the partial order [Davey and Priestley (2002)] based on permission-set inclusion.[4] Hence,

---

[4]RBAC papers that mention role hierarchy most often treat it as a partial order. By maintaining only a partial order it is not possible to distinguish role dominance relationships explicitly added from those implied [Li *et al.* (2007)]. Since consensus (on this matter) has yet to be reached among researchers, we only consider hierarchical relationships derived from permission-set inclusion.

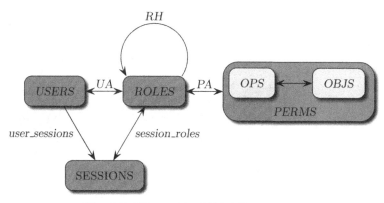

Fig. 2.5: Hierarchical RBAC

$\langle r_1, r_2 \rangle \in RH$ indicates that all the permissions assigned to r_1 are also assigned to r_2, and some more permissions are assigned to r_2. The symbol '$\succeq$' indicates the ordering operator. If $r_1 \succeq r_2$, then r_1 is referred to as the *senior* (or *child*) of r_2, namely r_1 adds certain permissions to those of r_2. Conversely, r_2 is the *junior* (or *parent*) of r_1. Additionally, the symbol '$>$' also indicates the ordering operator, but there is no intermediate elements between operands. In other words,

$$\forall r_1, r_2 \in ROLES \, : \, r_1 > r_2 \implies$$
$$\nexists r' \in ROLES \, : \, r' \neq r_1 \, \wedge \, r' \neq r_2 \, \wedge \, r_1 \succeq r' \, \wedge \, r' \succeq r_2.$$

If $r_1 > r_2$ then r_1 is referred to as an *immediate senior* of r_2, while r_2 is referred to as an *immediate junior* of r_1.

The following functions are also provided by the ANSI standard:

- *auth_users*: $ROLES \to 2^{USERS}$ to identify users assigned to a role or to at least one of its seniors (see also *ass_users* in Sec. 2.2.1);
- *auth_perms*: $ROLES \to 2^{PERMS}$ to identify permissions assigned to a role or to at least one of its seniors (see also *ass_perms* in Sec. 2.2.1).

The following relation holds true:

$$\forall r_1, r_2 \in ROLES : r_1 \succeq r_2 \implies auth\_users(r_1) \subseteq auth\_users(r_2) \, \wedge$$
$$auth\_perms(r_1) \supseteq auth\_perms(r_2). \quad (2.1)$$

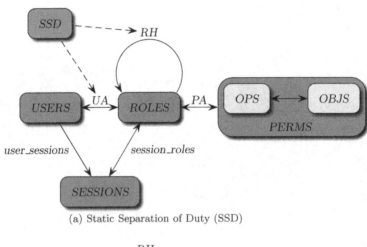

(a) Static Separation of Duty (SSD)

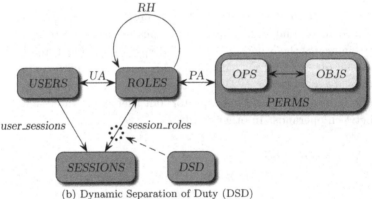

(b) Dynamic Separation of Duty (DSD)

Fig. 2.6: Constrained RBAC

2.2.3 *Static Separation of Duties (SSD) RBAC*⋆

SSD RBAC allows for the creation of sets of mutually exclusive roles that, together, would allow users to possess a toxic combination of permissions (a set of permissions that would allow a single person to perform a critical operation—see Sec. 1.2.5). "Static" means that SoD constraints are enforced at user-role assignment, rather than dynamically based on previous user actions.

Figure 2.6a formalize the previous concepts. Administrative functions include all those associated with Core RBAC, as well as creating, deleting, and modifying an SSD relation, as well as setting the cardinality of the SSD role set. The cardinality determines the number of users to whom the entire set of SSD roles could be assigned, thus violating SSD, but in a known and limited way. Since the SoD constraint is enforced at the user-role assignment stage, SSD RBAC system functions are the same as core RBAC. Additional review functions for SSD RBAC allow for a review of the current SSD relations, the set of roles within a particular SSD relation, and the cardinality of an SSD role set.

Since SSD RBAC is not strictly required by the remainder of this book, it is not further discussed.

2.2.4 Dynamic Separation of Duties (DSD) RBAC⋆

DSD RBAC, as in SSD, allows for the creation of sets of mutually exclusive roles that, together, would allow users to possess a toxic combination of permissions. The difference is that users may be assigned to mutually exclusive roles; however, users will not be able to activate both roles simultaneously. For instance, a user may be able to request and approve purchases, but he would not be able to perform both duties on any purchase.

Figure 2.6b formalize the previous concepts. Administrative functions include creating, deleting, and modifying a DSD relation, as well as setting the cardinality of the DSD role set. Additional system functions include enforcing the specified DSD constraints during a user session. Upon activating a user session, a user must not be assigned all authorized roles because some are mutually exclusive. Rather, the user will add active roles throughout the session, and the permission to add authorized roles will enforce DSD constraints. Review functions include reviewing established DSD relations, the set of roles within a particular DSD relation, and the cardinality of a DSD role set.

Since DSD RBAC is not strictly required by the remainder of this book, it is not further discussed.

2.3 Advantages of RBAC

This section enumerates some of the RBAC's principal advantages that should lead organizations to migrate to this model. We redirect to [O'Connor and Loomis (2010)] for more details.

2.3.1 *Efficient Policy Maintenance and Certification*

In an era of increased regulation of internal controls, RBAC facilitates and, relative to other approaches, reduces costs associated with *governance, risk, and compliance* (GRC) activities. Indeed, it offers greater visibility of permissions assigned to users and easier verification of internal controls, hence simplifying: access control policy maintenance; attestation of access control policies in place; certification of regulated information systems; and, access control policy audits conducted by internal and external auditors.

Although information security is addressed in many regulations, the requirements mandated by HIPAA [Kennedy and Kassebaum (1996)], Graham-Leech-Bliley Act of 1999 (GLBA) [Gramm *et al.* (1999)], and Sarbanes-Oxley [Sarbanes and Oxley (2002)] are the most relevant for access control systems. These acts explicitly dictate minimum standards for access control policies and information security. These recommendations are best met using an RBAC-enabled IAM systems [O'Connor and Loomis (2010)].

2.3.2 *Efficient Provisioning*

RBAC reduces the costs of administering and monitoring permissions when compared to other antecedent access control models. RBAC allows for greater automation, while adhering to the specified access control policy. The key concept is the following: rather than manually assigning permissions whenever a new user is hired, an existing user changes positions, or new applications or IT systems are adopted, these changes are automated through role assignment.

By assigning a predetermined role to the user, the labor expense of assigning permissions is significantly reduced, thus freeing resources for other tasks. Several attributes influence the magnitude of the expected cost decrease:

- The greater employee turnover or the number of people changing roles, the greater the cost savings of RBAC relative to other access control systems.
- Some firms or organizations are very dynamic, and user roles and permissions change quickly. In these environments, RBAC is more efficient in moving users in and out of static roles and changing the permissions of given roles than competing access control systems.
- RBAC reduces the provisioning decisions managers need to make. In

alternative access control approaches, upper management is integrally involved in determining individual privileges and authorizing access for each new employee. RBAC supports the automation of this process.

- RBAC is scalable, meaning that the model can work as well in large environments covering several offices and classes of users as it can in one-office environments. Roles matching job positions can be determined in a central office, but the actual assignment of roles to or change of roles for new employees can occur at each branch office by an administrator.

2.3.3 *Reduction in New Employee Downtime*

RBAC accelerates bringing new company joiners to full productivity. This also includes existing employees placed in new positions within the organization. During this time period, these employees may only be marginally or partially productive because they are underentitled. These benefits greatly outweigh the benefits from greater efficiency in network and systems administrators' execution of provisioning tasks.

2.3.4 *Enhanced System Security*

RBAC is designed to discourage the accumulation of a toxic combination of permissions by lowering the cost of administration and enabling the creation of SoD constraints. Using RBAC generally lowers both the probability and cost of access control breaches.

Costs due to inadequate access control policies can be extreme. Recall the example in which a trader at Société Générale was able to circumvent their internal controls to execute fraudulent trades because of "entitlement creep." Back-office permissions allowing him to perpetrate the crime had never been removed from his account, costing the bank billions [PriceWaterhouseCoopers (2008)]. National security-related examples include the WikiLeaks release of classified information in 2010. To prevent future leaks, the vice-chair of the Joint Chiefs of Staff recommended "moving to both identity- and role-based models so we know who's doing what and that they have the right credentials" [Reilly (2010)].

Roles offer improved security and audit trails over alternative methods. RBAC reduces the impact from security violations in two ways: first, it decreases the likelihood that a security violation occurs; and second, if a security violation occurs, RBAC can limit the damage from the violation. Since privileges are not assigned to each user manually, it is less likely that the security administrator will make an error and inadvertently grant a user access to information or applications to which she would otherwise be prohibited.

2.3.5   *Enhanced Organizational Productivity*

A major objective of devising the RBAC model has been to enhance security of information systems while not compromising system productivity. In fact, RBAC provides the underlying structure to streamline workflow management for organizations and user groups that are well-defined, such as that within a large grocery-store chain's retail operations or a call center. Because of the greater flexibility associated with RBAC, the model can be adapted to mirror the organizational structure. This creates the potential for new and innovative ways of structuring the organization, altering the routing of information, or changing the organization's production processes [Kampman and Purdue (2006)].

In particular, RBAC introduces the following enhancements:

- Within workflow management systems, work is broken up into its components, some of which may need to be performed by different job functions. RBAC allow anyone of a particular role to execute the next portion of a task, avoiding bottlenecks associated with individuals in the process.
- RBAC makes visible the impacts of business decisions. For instance, if an enterprise is considering adopting a new application, it can use the access control system to discover precisely how many licenses would be required in adopting the application.
- Finally, RBAC lowers the frictional cost of transition within and between enterprises. Businesses using RBAC can transition to new and better technologies and easily incorporate them into their access control policies through roles.

2.4   Obstacles to Migrating to RBAC

After having pointed out RBAC advantages, we now focus on possible barriers that can hinder a migration process to RBAC. In an ideal scenario, an organization will establish and design operations processes and then create an infrastructure that would execute those processes, providing to each member only the tools needed to perform his function. Information

Fig. 2.7: Balance between pros and cons of migrating to RBAC

systems would be designed and built to support the roles that correspond to these processes. Each role would be assigned a series of permissions defined by their position and function within the organization. Ideally, the system would be clearly defined and agile, making the addition of new applications, roles, and employees as efficient as possible.

However, the ideal scenario rarely occurs. Business processes and employee positions, both formal and informal, are preexisting and entrenched, impeding turn-key implementation of new approaches to access control. Aligning RBAC roles with workflow and positions may be very expensive, difficult, and time consuming. RBAC is a tool that supports a correctly defined administrative policy. Actually, RBAC will cost an organization more in the long run if the policy for that organization is not realistic in terms of operational requirements for RBAC or fails to even define RBAC and its use throughout the organization.

The following sections enumerates some of the main issues that can hinder a beneficial implementation of RBAC-oriented systems. Figure 2.7 summarizes both pros and cons of adopting RBAC.

2.4.1   *Role Engineering*

We refer to *role engineering* as the process of defining and implementing roles. More details about role engineering issues will be provided in Chap. 3. In this section we only point out that role engineering can be a contentious and time-consuming process, but it is integral to RBAC's success. Role engineering entails defining the roles that will determine which employees have access to which data and to which applications, as well as roles' relationships to one another, role hierarchy, and role constraints. As this process progresses, implementers may see benefits in rethinking how work is allocated and completed within the organization.

Role-engineering expense has decreased over time because of the development of new software tools and increased familiarity with the process of defining and assigning roles. Several companies have developed or are in the process of developing software tools that help automatically define roles using existing patterns of access permissions gleaned from user databases. These tools reduce the labor expense of manually defining and creating all roles—showing how these tool actually work is the main objective of the remainder of this book. Furthermore, as companies and consultants become familiar with the implementation process, a learning curve effect has emerged. However, the extent of these two developments' impact on role engineering is not clear. The relative ease or difficulty of the role definition process depends on an entity's organizational and administrative structure—an attribute that varies widely among firms.

2.4.2   *Migration Costs*

Any time a new information system is installed, an organization accrues costs. This is especially true if the decision is to implement a new access control system. The costs of migrating to RBAC includes: salaries and consultants' fees, software purchases and licensing agreements, computing resources and infrastructure, and customization costs. These costs may differ depending on the scope of the package being installed, the size of the firm or the number of licenses, and the migration complexity.

A large cost component of installing an RBAC system is the salaries

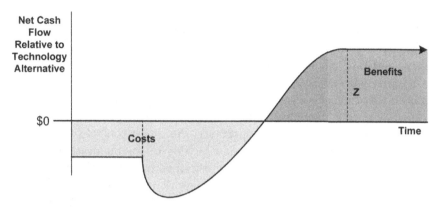

Fig. 2.8: RBAC adoption cost and operating benefits over the time. Source: [O'Connor and Loomis (2010)]

of the team tasked with its implementation. Tasks include not only the implementation and migration of the software system purchased, but also the staff training, software package selection, and the customization process. In addition to staff labor expenses, consultants may be hired to either implement the systems migration completely, or to offer their expertise on some component therein. External consultants may also be hired to customize a prepackaged system or help with role definition.

Figure 2.8 illustrates how, over time, the organization moves from an early planning period through a deployment period characterized by increased expenditures for software and services followed by a gradual increase in benefits, net of costs. Although there are routine role maintenance and management requirements, RBAC demonstrates net benefits over other access control models. In reality, it is more likely that firms would have a step-wise net benefit curve that may swing intermittently positive and negative. Moreover, even in well-defined job positions where roles are largely static, such as bank teller, not all permissions can be managed via roles. Roles might be used for some application and business, but not all.

2.4.3 Systems Structure and Interoperability

As new beneficial access control systems are deployed, administrators may have to rectify years of inefficiencies, such as informal access grants, disorganized systems, and different organization structures among divisions. The move toward disciplined, centralized systems often means realigning these systems and creating a more cohesive structure. Because of the time and cost involved, it is likely that a large organization will adopt RBAC at an incremental pace. By spreading out implementation over a period of time, companies avoid the risk-prone full rollout.

Security features need to be effective across sectors of the firm or organization without being overly intrusive to the user. Interoperability—that is, the ability to communicate and transfer data or information across different platforms—is of utmost importance. An access control system that displays perfect interoperability would be able to communicate with the security and administrative network across an entire firm without any disruptions or complications. Without a framework or architecture to address interoperability problem, firms may be unable to implement RBAC and benefit from reduced administrative costs and improved security.

2.4.4   *Product Acceptance and Comparison*

Buyers of software products usually gather information about the various potential products before making a decision. Characteristics being compared could include: cost, quality, reliability, and capacity. For this process to be effective, consumers must have an understanding of what they are getting from a product, and producers must be able to prove that they are delivering what the consumer wants.

Prior to the ANSI/INCITS RBAC standard, no commonly agreed-upon definition of RBAC existed. For example, some systems used the term "role" as a synonym for groups, and some had ad hoc implementations with a few hard-coded roles such as "manager" or "teller." Without a definition, firms that were interested in either upgrading their existing access control system or purchasing new access control systems had difficulty obtaining generic RBAC solutions and might have been unable to compare attributes across commercial products using roles.

2.5   Final Remarks

This chapter introduced the RBAC model, one of the principal approaches for managing users' access to information technology resources. We pointed out pros and cons of the model when compared to other access control approaches. In particular, we shown that RBAC is the ideal solution for most organizations, where networks, data, applications, and hardware and software systems are shared resources that users access to perform their duties. As a matter of fact, with access comes the risk of intentional or unintentional misuse of or changes to systems and data, thereby threatening the integrity, confidentiality, and availability of an organization's information and its infrastructure. This chapter discussed how RBAC effectively can address this issue.

As for real applications of RBAC, it is interesting to note that, according to a recent survey [O'Connor and Loomis (2010)], the use of roles has grown steadily since 1994, with the rate of RBAC adoption accelerating in 2004 and again in 2008. For 1995 the authors estimated just under a 4% penetration rate, growing to about 11% in 2002, 13% in 2004, and 41% in 2009. In 2010, just over 50% of users at organizations with more than 500 employees are expected to have at least some of their permissions managed via roles. Over 80% of respondents reported that using roles improved the efficiency of maintaining their organization's access control policy. It is important to note that almost all organizations reported that they adopted a hybrid approach, using either roles as the primary mechanism and ACLs as the secondary one, or ACLs as primary followed by roles as secondary. The same survey also demonstrated that, although roles do not eliminate the policy review and attestation process, they do make it easier to accomplish, especially when large numbers of employees fall within well-defined job functions for which roles are a particularly effective and efficient access control mechanism.

Finally, notice that the most significant expense related to migrating to RBAC-compliant systems was role engineering—the topic of this book. Survey results about the costs of implementing RBAC varied significantly, with some organizations spending millions of dollars on custom systems, initiatives related to large-scale ERP implementations, and extensive systems integration services. In contrast, other organizations made use of native role capabilities within systems they were currently using. The typical time required for implementation averaged about 18 months.

Chapter 3

Role Engineering

As previously mentioned in Chap. 2, we refer to *role engineering* as the discipline, art, skill, and profession of designing roles to maximize the benefits introduced by adopting RBAC-oriented IAM systems. Defining roles has been recognized as one of the costliest parts of migrating to an RBAC implementation. Therefore, any improvement to a methodology which can reduce the cost of RBAC system creation will further increase the effectiveness of RBAC and accelerate its adoption. This chapter thus aims at describing role engineering challenges, summarizing existing approaches, and introducing the *role mining* concept.

3.1 Modeling Roles

As organizations start deploying RBAC-oriented access control solutions, it is becoming increasingly important to devise a common set of roles that can be reused and easily maintained over the time. One of the challenges often faced is that, if defined incorrectly, roles are ineffective and fail to meet the organization's requirements [Colantonio *et al.* (2009a)]. Roles can be defined at an abstract level from a business perspective, or context-specific to an application or system from a technology perspective. Whether an organization looks at defining roles either abstract or specific to a context, the requirements to define roles are important and role definition is a critical step in deploying any RBAC system.

Role engineering [Coyne (1995); Coyne and Davis (2007)] is the process of defining roles and related information, such as permissions, constraints, and role hierarchies, as they pertain to the user's functional use of systems, applications, and business processes. The value of role engineering is widely recognized by firms and IT security experts. Yet, organizations often implement RBAC systems without much consideration for roles. To minimize deployment effort, role definition is often not considered as a part of the deployment project. Organizations frequently do not invest enough time to define roles in sufficient detail; rather, they tend to define high-level roles that do not reflect actual organizational job functions. Permissions mapped to high-level roles are usually generic in nature. The result of this "random" process is that additional efforts are required to manage job-specific permissions manually, outside the RBAC system. Hence, without exploiting all the RBAC benefits.

Several issues have to be faced when conducting a role engineering task. First, the process of defining roles should be based on a complete analysis of the given organization, including the input from a wide spectrum of users such as business line managers and human resources. Traditionally, user access has been defined by technical roles (provisioning roles, application roles, etc.). These roles generally make sense in a specific technical context, but are often confusing when applied to a broader business context. For example, one may have access to the "Approve Purchase Order" function, but that specific entitlement says nothing about user's functional role in the organization. The business context that is missing would tell an auditor why the user has this particular access. A more meaningful business role, such as "Accounts Payable Clerk" provides the necessary clarity to then understand if the entitlements are appropriate for the functional or process role. In general, role definition and management requires *alignment between business and IT*. It requires a strong commitment and cooperation among the business units, as a role engineering initiative could transcend the enterprise.

Another problem relative to a lack of business alignment during the role engineering task is that elicited roles often are no more than a set of permissions with no connection to the business practice [Colantonio *et al.* (2009a)]. Frequently, the main objective of most of the role engineering approaches (and "role mining" in particular, as described in the next section) is only to reduce the number of roles or to simplify the access control administration from a system perspective. But organizations are unwilling to deploy roles they cannot understand, even though such roles are limited in number. For instance, when the objective of role engineering is just reducing the number of roles, unmanageable solutions can be obtained. Figure 3.1 shows a simple case. In this trivial example, the objective is managing the user-permission assignments depicted in Fig. 3.1a through the adoption of roles. Despite both Fig. 3.1b and Fig. 3.1c show the same number of roles

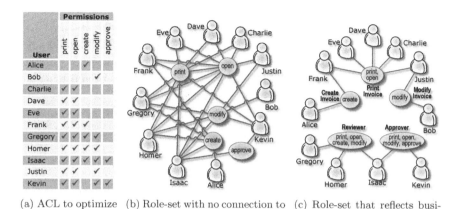

(a) ACL to optimize   (b) Role-set with no connection to   (c) Role-set that reflects busi-
                      business practice   ness functions

Fig. 3.1: Two minimal sets of roles with different business meaning

(represented as ellipses in the picture), the solution of Fig. 3.1c contains
more meaningful roles and requires less user-to-role relationships.

An important observation also relates to role hierarchy. Several vendors
of RBAC systems implements the Hierarchical RBAC described in Sec. 2.2.2
and advertise this feature as a necessary characteristic. Other approaches
strive to minimize the number of role-to-role relationships [Zhang *et al.*
(2007); Guo *et al.* (2008)]. However, due care should be exercised to not
utilize hierarchical roles when they are not warranted. For example, purchasing managers would require several entitlements, including the ability
to create purchase orders. If there is only one specific purchasing manager in Rome who also requires the ability to accept deliveries, it is not
necessary—and actually less efficient—to create a sub-role. To account for
unique situations such as this one, out-of-role entitlements should be used
instead. In general, role hierarchies present several challenges, including being counter-intuitive and being subject to high complexity. The semantics
of a role hierarchy can often be implemented in a flat structure—e.g., by
grouping together common access rights into an additional specially crafted
role and then assigning this role separately to the users of the intended parent roles.

Finally, it is also important to notice that there is a general temptation
to translate all access in the confines of a role. Out-of-role entitlements
are not necessarily a bad thing, and can be used to keep simplicity in the
overall model while still accounting for discrepancies as they are relevant

[Colantonio *et al.* (2010d); Frank *et al.* (2008)]. For example, when an application developer from one business unit is temporarily assigned to another business unit, out-of-role entitlements can be granted. It would not make much sense creating a specific role for this scenario as it is temporary in nature. Using out-of-role entitlements to manage access requirements that are out-of-constraint is the right approach.

3.2 Role Engineering Approaches

Despite the role engineering discipline dates back to 1995 [Coyne (1995)], choosing the best approach to model roles is still an open problem. Various approaches can be found in the current literature, which are usually classified as: *top-down* and *bottom-up*. The former requires a deep analysis of business processes to identify which access permissions are necessary to carry out specific tasks. The latter seeks to identify *de facto* roles embedded in existing access control information. Since bottom-up approaches usually resort to data mining techniques, the term *role mining* [Kuhlmann *et al.* (2003)] is often used as a synonym for bottom-up. Both top-down and bottom-up approaches have pros and cons. To maximize benefits, bottom-up should be used in conjunction with top-down, leading to an *hybrid* approach (see Fig. 3.2). As a matter of fact, top-down may ignore existing permissions and exceptions, whereas bottom-up may not consider the business functions of an organization [Kern *et al.* (2002)]. Hence, hybrid approaches leverage normalized roles derived from role mining and align them to job functions, with the involvement of the business staff. In the following, we summarize the state-of-the-art for both top-down and bottom-up approaches.

3.2.1 *Top-Down*

This approach is primarily business-driven, and roles are defined based on the responsibilities of a given job function. For roles to be effective, a strong alignment between business and IT objectives is of utmost importance. Roles are defined by reviewing organizational business and job functions and mapping the permissions for each job function. This approach provides business oversight and alignment of roles with business functions and reusability.

Top-down role engineering was first illustrated by Coyne (1995). He

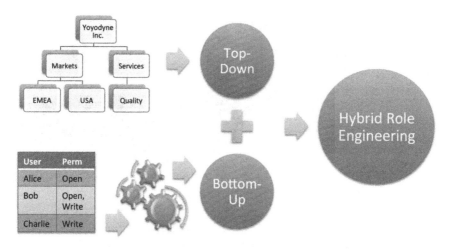

Fig. 3.2: Hybrid approach to role engineering

places system users' activities as high-level information for role identification; this approach is only conceptual, thus it lacks technical details. Fernandez and Hawkins (1997) propose a similar approach where use-cases are used to determine the needed permissions. Röckle *et al.* (2000) propose a process-oriented approach that analyzes business processes to deduce roles. The *role-finding* concept is introduced to deduce roles from business needs or functions. Information is organized in three different layers: process layer, role layer, and access rights layer. Crook *et al.* (2002) leverage organizational theory to elicit role-based security policies. Neumann and Strembeck (2002) present a more concrete approach to derive roles from business processes. They offer a scenario-based approach where a usage scenario is the basic semantic unit to analyze. Work-patterns involving roles are analyzed and decomposed into smaller units. Such smaller units are consequently mapped with system permissions. Shin *et al.* (2003) use a system-centric approach supported by the UML language to conduct top-down role engineering. Role engineering is discussed from the perspective of systems to be protected, assisting with the general understanding of RBAC roles and permissions in conjunction with business processes. Epstein and Sandhu (2001) also use UML to address role engineering. Kern *et al.* (2002) propose an iterative and incremental approach based on the role life-cycle, pertaining to analysis, design, management, and maintenance.

The primary intent of this book is providing an in-depth analysis of automated approaches to role engineering, mainly from a bottom-up

Fig. 3.3: Before migrating to RBAC, users already possess needed permissions—usually even more!

perspective. Hence, we do not further discuss top-down approaches. The book of Coyne and Davis (2007) is a practical reference that helps assess some of the previously cited role engineering approaches.

3.2.2 *Bottom-Up*

This approach is based on performing role-mining/discovery by exploring existing user permissions in current applications and systems. Once roles has been elicited, the next step is to perform role normalization and rationalization. One of the challenges of this approach is that it requires viable tools to perform role mining. An alternate approach is to select a set of representative users and extract the entitlements that best describe the job function. If the user population is significant, it would be ideal to sample a certain percentage of the population to validate the accuracy of the results. One of the outcomes of this approach is that users often accumulate entitlements based on their previous job functions performed over a period of time (see Fig. 3.3); it can become too daunting to validate roles without the business involvement. This is a key aspect of role rationalization to be considered as part of a bottom-up approach.

Kuhlmann *et al.* (2003) first introduced the term "role mining", trying to apply existing data mining techniques to elicit roles from existing access data. Indeed, role mining can be seen as a particular application of *Market Basket Analysis* (MBA, also known as *association-rule mining*), a method of discovering customer purchasing patterns by extracting associations or co-occurrences from transactional store databases. This translation can be done by simply considering permissions, roles and users instead of products, transactions and customers, respectively. Among all possible algorithms used in this area, Apriori [Agrawal and Srikant (1994)] is the most common. After the first proposal, the community started to identify specific algorithms to solve this particular problem instead of using existing approaches. The first algorithm explicitly designed for role engineering was ORCA [Schlegelmilch and Steffens (2005)] which applies hierarchical clustering techniques on permissions. However, this approach does not allow for permission overlapping among roles that are not hierarchically related. Vaidya *et al.* (2006) applied subset enumeration techniques to generate a set of candidate roles, computing all possible intersections among permissions possessed by users. Subset enumeration techniques had been advocated earlier by Rymon (2003). More recently, the same authors of [Vaidya *et al.* (2006)] also studied the problem of finding the minimum number of roles that cover all permissions possessed by users [Vaidya *et al.* (2007, 2008)]. By leveraging binary integer programming, Lu *et al.* (2008) presented a unified framework for modeling the role number minimization problem. Ene *et al.* (2008) offered yet another alternative model to minimize the number of roles, reducing it to the well-known problem of the minimum biclique covering. Zhang *et al.* (2007) provide an attempt to contextually minimize the number of user-role, permission-role, and role-role relationships. Frank *et al.* (2008) model the probability of user-permission relationships, thus allowing to infer the role-user and role-permission assignments so that the direct assignments become more likely. The authors offer a sampling algorithm that can be used to infer their model parameters. Several works prove that the role mining problem is reducible to many other well-known $\mathcal{NP}$-hard problems, such as clique partition, binary matrix factorization, bi-clustering, and graph vertex coloring [Colantonio *et al.* (2009c)] to cite a few. Recently, Frank *et al.* (2010) provided a detailed analysis of the requirements for role mining as well as the methods used to assess results. They also proposed a novel definition of the role mining problem that fulfills the requirements that real-world enterprises typically have.

The main limitation of all the cited role mining approaches is that they do not always lead to the optimal set of roles from a business perspective. The work of [Colantonio *et al.* (2008b)] represents the first proposal to allow for the discovery of roles with business meanings through a role mining algorithm—this approach is further discussed in Chap. 7. A similar approach has also been provided by Molloy *et al.* (2008). It tackles the problem in two settings. When only user-permission relations are available, the authors propose to discover roles by resorting to *formal concept analysis* (FCA). FCA is a theory of data analysis which identifies conceptual structures among data sets. If user attributes are additionally available, they utilize user attributes to provide a measurement of the RBAC state complexity, called "weighted structural complexity."

The following chapters detail the major results that can be found in the literature about various aspects of automating role engineering.

3.3   Parts of a Role Engineering Task

This section points out the main parts that make up a typical role engineering approach. Here we present a generic description of typical role engineering tasks. Chapter 4 will provide a more structured process to implement a bottom-up approach. Hence, this section can be considered a complement for Chapter 4. In particular, the envisaged activities are:

Permission Engineering   The first step in any role engineering project is to assess and label all IT permissions that are to be managed through access control policy. Since permissions can be considered the building blocks of roles, it is important to label them using terms that are easily understood by "analysts"—i.e., those in charge of conducting role engineering tasks such as subject matter experts, HR staff, management, and IT professionals. This activity should be performed before starting any role modeling exercise.

Top-Down Role Engineering   As mentioned earlier, top-down role engineering refers to developing roles, by both business and IT professionals, to conform to a particular business requirements and, in particular, to high-level access control policies. For example, a typical top-down approach entails subject matter experts determining the steps involved in a particular task, and IT professionals determining the permissions necessary to execute those steps and assign them to a role [Neumann and Strembeck (2002); Strembeck (2010)]. Although this process is labor intensive, it ensures that the roles created in the role-engineering process are understood and will be used appropriately. Top-down activities are also worth doing since their outcomes can be used in hybrid approaches to role engineering— more details can be found in chapters of Part 3.

Bottom-Up Role Engineering   Bottom-up role engineering refers to developing roles based on information used in the existing access control system, also referred to as "role mining." Role mining involves scouring the permissions contained within system ACLs and directories and using

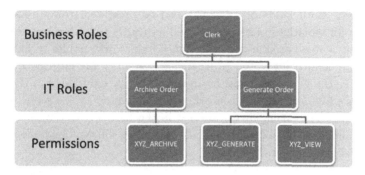

Fig. 3.4: An example of business roles and IT roles

algorithms to group these permissions into roles. This process will succeed in creating roles that reflect access control policies in place and improve provisioning of such policies. However, this process will unlikely generate roles that are transparent and easily understood across the enterprise. In addition, if the access control policy in place is not the desired access control policy, then this process alone will simply turn an incorrect access control policy into an incorrect access control policy administered with roles. The remaining chapters of this book strive to address these role mining issues.

Role Classification   One important concept that has emerged is the necessity to successfully translate sets of permissions into roles that are easily understood across business units. This understanding is necessary to attest to what access control policy is actually in place. There may be a conflict between IT-oriented roles and business functions (e.g., a "Clerk" and "Loan Officer" may need the same set of permissions; however, defining a role made up of these permissions and labeled as "Clerk" would make review of the access control policy not straightforward, since a Clerk is not a Loan Officer).

To face this problem, several RBAC-oriented IAM systems advocate a two-level hierarchy of roles: roles defined at the highest level called *business roles*, and roles at the lowest level referred to as *IT roles* [Kampman (2007)]. Business roles define operations that have business meaning within the organization, whereas IT roles supports technology functions (see Fig. 3.4). Business roles will mostly be presented to line-of-business managers (e.g., to assign to new recruits, to re-certify as part of compliance processes, and so forth). Conversely, IT roles will likely be used by resource owners and administrators, and their names should capture the distinct functions that they allow. Both kinds of roles will also be presented to auditors when they look for violations of separation of duty (SoD) and other business process rules. A role-based access governance framework enables technical IT roles to be defined for a user provisioning system, while layering business roles above the IT roles. Thus, business context is maintained in the business roles while provisioning context, which is limited by the scope of user provisioning deployment, is maintained in the IT role. As a result, access change management becomes seamless and more efficient and the overall role model is easy to maintain.

Roles may be developed in various subject domains, such as business, finance, administration, and security, and may be either *structural* or *functional*. Structural roles have permissions that permit connection or access to a gross level IT resource, such as a network, server, workflow, or device. A structural role might control access to an application's entry point, whereby a user could only open that application if he or she had been assigned to a structural role that grants that access. Functional roles have permissions that control finer-grained accesses within an IT resource. They are typically defined as controlling access to resources within applications. Since structural roles tend to be simpler that functional roles, it is advisable to define structural roles before defining functional roles. This approach can provide some RBAC advantages early on in the role engineering process.

Role Life-Cycle Analysis   A good role engineering process should also take into consideration the *life-cycle* of elicited roles. As a matter of fact, roles will need to be continually maintained to ensure compliance with the desired access control policy. As with users, permission drift can occur in roles if unnecessary permissions are not removed over the life of the role. In this case, users may still accumulate a toxic combination of permissions, however, now with the efficiency of roles. Proper maintenance of roles is necessary for correct adherence to a desired access control policy.

3.4   Guidelines

This section offers a guidance for role engineers to get started efficiently and keep their effort on the right track. The content of the section is mainly derived from the book of Coyne and Davis (2007) to which we redirect for further details. These guidelines should be taken into consideration before implementing any role engineering process, like the one described in Chap. 4. Figure 3.5 summarizes the tasks that are detailed in the following.

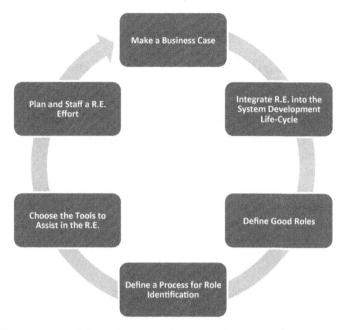

Fig. 3.5: Guidelines for a productive role engineering process

Make a Business Case Similar to other IT security projects, in order
to get commitment of resources to allow for a role engineering effort, it
might be necessary to make a business case. The business case for role
engineering is actually part of the business case for RBAC itself. In other
words, when justifying the adoption of RBAC, the costs and benefits for
role engineering must be factored into the RBAC business case. Obtaining
data on both costs and benefits is a challenge, although benefits tend to be
more of a challenge to determine than costs. This is because benefits tend
to include intangible items such as avoiding difficulties and conforming to
mandates. Security requirements are also needed to establish the security
policy that roles will support. These security requirements can be the
result of risk analysis, mandates from government or other authorities, or
may be industry best practices whose implementation may be considered
as performing due diligence with regard to IT security.

Return on Investment (ROI) also need to be evaluated. To estimate
the ROI of a role engineering effort, it is necessary to estimate the costs
of conducting the effort and to weigh these against the anticipated benefit.
Some rules of thumb for making the cost estimate are provided in Sec. 2.3.

Any way, as role engineering project goes on, it will be possible to refine estimates based on experience.

Integrate Role Engineering into the System Development Life-Cycle   As organization's applications are developed, there could be several role engineering efforts undertaken to provide the role definitions needed by the specific applications. In general, a role engineering effort may be undertaken as an independent effort at the enterprise level or as part of a system development project. When it is undertaken within a project, there must be a means of generalizing the results to the enterprise as a whole. The results of role engineering will benefit the whole enterprise, provided that each project-oriented effort is conducted with an eye toward achieving an enterprise-level result. This presupposes an enterprise model and a repository of role definitions. Then, each project can add its individual updates to the repository in a consistent manner.

Define Good Roles   Roles can be considered "good" when they have characteristics that make the roles easier to manage and also support the access control policy effectively. One example is when their *names* are readily recognized by administrative personnel and have permissions, constraints, and hierarchies that accurately reflect the access control policy. To define role names, it is necessary to understand the differences in permissions from one role to another. If two roles will have the same set of permissions assigned to them, it may not make sense to have two distinct roles. Of course, if it is anticipated that at some time in the future the two roles' permissions may differ, the two role definitions may be advantageous. Similarly, if two roles with the same permission sets will be assigned to two different types of users, perhaps the two roles should be maintained with different role names.

Furthermore, there must be a balance between roles with excessive numbers of permissions, which can violate the security principle of least privilege, and roles with too few privileges, which can obviate the advantage of RBAC that the number of roles is much less that the number of privileges. As mentioned earlier, out-of-role permissions are not necessarily a bad thing. The access control policy may not be entirely supported by RBAC. One example of this would be where access permissions must be assigned to an individual by name, perhaps because this person uniquely possesses a restricted authorization. In this case, the security policy would include the direct assignment of the permission to the designated individual. To know whether the number of roles is excessive, consider the line-of-business manager that is required to approve role definitions and role assignments. In particular, they should not deal with more than 20–50 roles on average. Organizations usually defend fewer roles with less coverage than needed. As a rule of thumb, role definitions shall cover 80% of the overall privileges, covering more than just the most common privileges.

One issue related to out-of-role permissions is deciding to what extent they are acceptable, that is understanding when the set of elicited roles can be considered sufficient. One indication is whether all of the access control policy has been covered by the role structure. Each element of the policy can be mapped to a role and verified as to its accuracy and completeness. Another indication is whether all job functions identified in the work flow analysis are reflected in the role structure. There will probably not be a one-to-one mapping between job functions and roles because different roles with the same sets of permissions may have been combined.

If two or more (sometimes many) roles are only distinguished by a few permissions, and if these permissions are not too sensitive, consider merging them into a single role. You will be granting some users a few more privileges than they really need, but the administrative gains will be substantial. Automated tools can easily identify these situations and guide you through the decision.

Finally, another aspect to take into consideration is the use of hierarchy. Whether or not to use hierarchies is not highly dependent on the access control policy, but the use of hierarchies should be considered early on in the role engineering process. In the role engineering process, any role in the hierarchy can be subdivided as to its permissions, and the permissions removed from the role can be assigned to roles lower in the hierarchy. Then the senior role can inherit the removed permissions from the junior roles.

Define a Process for Role Identification The role engineering process revolves around the enterprise job functions, responsibilities, organizational positions, and authorities that are considered to be relevant for access control. To avoid wasted effort and creating inadequate role structures, a defined process should be used to identify role names and associated permissions. This process may use a top-down, bottom-up, or combined approach. There are pros and cons to either approach.

With the top-down approach, we start from requirements and successively refine the definitions to result in role names, permissions, and roles. For instance, Strembeck (2010) proposes to analyze IT scenarios, which are depictions of real-world sequences of activities in which various computer users (agents) carry out their job functions in a typical setting. The main advantage to the top-down approach is that a global view of the organization is used, with the likelihood that the resulting roles will be globally valid within the organization. Possibly the primary disadvantage of the top-down approach is that it tends to be time-consuming and requires the time of subject matter experts, which might be difficult to secure for this purpose.

With the bottom-up approach, we examine existing information systems and extract implicit role definitions from such items as screen contents, user profiles, and access control lists—typical steps for the bottom-up approach are described in Chap. 4. A degree of creativity is needed to abstract role name and permissions from the available artifacts. It is by no means a process that can be followed without analytical skills to recognize role names and permissions. Once roles have been identified using a bottom-up approach, it is still necessary to normalize the results and transform the results into meaningful roles for the organization. The main advantage of the bottom-up approach is that it capitalizes on existing work products and potentially avoids some current work to develop the same results. Possibly the primary disadvantage of the bottom-up approach is that it still requires a degree of work to accomplish and it is not likely that the results will reflect a valid global view of the organization. Also, it will be necessary to reconcile the role data obtained from the bottom-up approach with other role data, including that obtained from a top-down approach—hence leading to a hybrid approach.

Choose the Tools to Assist in the Role Engineering There exist some software tools that can facilitate the overall role engineering process. Generic tools, such as spreadsheet and database products, are the minimum level of tools that should be available to a role engineering effort. Beyond these generic types of tools, more specialized role engineering tools are available in the marketplace—to understand how they actually work is one of the objective of this book.

Tools can assist the role engineering process but cannot fully automate it. Human skill and judgment are still needed. Acquisition of role engineering tools should be done on the same cost-effectiveness basis as for other acquisitions. Tools expressly designed to perform role engineering functions tend to follow the bottom-up approach, although some of them do perform top-down functions.

Plan and Staff a Role Engineering Effort Generally speaking, *planning* can be considered a combination of forecasting and controlling the future. Forecasting entails the gathering of data on the performance of previous projects. Planning can help prepare a good plan, and following the plan can help minimize uncertainty in the project and to communicate essential information to all concerned with the project.

As for role engineering, planning also means justifying and securing management approval for it. Therefore, the proposed effort must be described and its return on investment must be estimated. Cost-benefit analysis should be conducted, and this implies that costs and benefits can be quantified or at least characterized. Risks must be identified and their mitigation anticipated. Additional requirements include establishing goals, adopting strategies and methods, accomplishing staffing, and setting up control mechanisms for use as the effort is carried out. A communication plan should be part of the project plan. It will identify how the project team members will interact with one another to interchange data, review work items, and to discuss topics and action items.

Two basic approaches may be taken for conducting a role engineering effort. One approach is to conduct an independent role engineering effort at the *enterprise level*. The other approach is to include role engineering within a *system implementation* effort. It would be unlikely for a single implementation effort to result in a complete definition of roles for the enterprise, so it will to be necessary to perform role engineering on several system implementation projects before a complete set of enterprise roles is defined. The role engineering results from each of these individual implementation projects will have to reflect a common set of goals and expectations, and the results from the projects will need to be coordinated.

Another aspect of utmost importance is *staffing*. A successful role engineering effort depends on the availability of a team of qualified individuals with effective leadership of the team's efforts. In general, four options can be delineated:

(1) For an in-house, top-down effort, the appropriateness of the selected staff members is of paramount importance. The team leader must be experienced or well qualified.
(2) For an outsourced, top-down effort, effectiveness comes into play with the selection of a firm that will provide sufficient and appropriate staff members and an effective team leader.
(3) For an outsourced, bottom-up effort, the focus should be on the

selection of a firm that will provide sufficient staffing and leadership. As for the bottom-up process, a role mining tools should be adopted.

(4) For an effort that includes both in-house and outsourced staff and both top-down and bottom-up processes, a dual staffing situation will be the case, with the need for making available in-house staff and obtaining other staff from a vendor. Team leadership can come from either the enterprise or the outsourced vendor.

3.5   Final Remarks

Although RBAC can reduce provisioning costs by managing users and permissions with roles, it does not reduce the administration costs to zero. Implementing RBAC within an IAM system requires an up-front cost of creating the roles to be used, referred to as "role engineering." Once created, roles must be maintained to reflect changes to the access control policy and to the underlying information systems. This maintenance is referred to as "role life-cycle management."

The RBAC standard envisions all permission assignments and access control decisions to be mediated by roles. This would achieve "completeness" of the security system and ensure that no permissions granted outside of roles would be created that violate the desired access control policy. Managing all user permissions through roles, however, is not done in practice. Rather, a hybrid approach is taken, in which approximately some proportion of permissions are managed through roles, while the remaining proportion are managed through other means. Even the most exhaustive role-engineering efforts should not incorporate every permission into a role. In fact, it is important to set concrete, achievable goals.

A successful role-engineering project will bring together the IAM stakeholders within the organization, primarily human resources, management, and IT administrators. These individuals possess the tacit knowledge of the organizational and technological infrastructure that role engineering makes explicit and transparent.

Perhaps the most fundamental clue for a successful effort would be to strive for simplicity. It is always preferable to have a small success than to have a large failure. And, of course, an effort with limited scope can be expanded later, once success has been secured.

Chapter 4

A Step-to-Step Methodology for Role Mining

In this chapter we describe a possible *role mining process*. Before one attempts to automatically elicit roles from legacy access control systems, it is important to understand the overall approach. We first point out the importance of *data preparation* task. Real-world access control databases are highly susceptible to noise (i.e., permissions exceptionally or accidentally granted or denied) and inconsistent data. Moreover, in some cases there might be large number of objects to analyze (i.e., thousands of users and hundreds of thousands of resources) that likely originate from multiple, heterogenous sources. Consequently, role engineering activities should be performed after a proper data preparation phase. In turn, the proposed methodology reflects the importance of both bottom-up and top-down analysis. By combining both techniques, administrators can leverage the speed advantages of bottom-up role mining with the increased confidence provided by the top-down approaches.

4.1 Role Mining Steps

Arguably, one of the biggest barrier for manually defining and creating roles is the massive amount of data, as well as the complexity of access control policies. When organizations have to manage thousands of users, they can easily have millions of resources for which access must be controlled. In Chap. 3 we introduced role engineering. If properly applied, role engineering can help organization to effectively manage these numbers. In particular, *role mining*—that is, automatic elicitation of roles based on information within existing access control systems—can definitely smooth the way for devising useful roles in large organizations.

To be effective, however, role mining techniques requires to be applied

through a structured approach. Similar to any other data mining problem
[Cios *et al.* (2007); Han and Kamber (2006)], simply knowing many role
mining algorithms is not sufficient for a successful role engineering project.
Therefore, we need to identify a *role mining process* that leads to finding
useful roles through the application of role mining techniques. The process
defines a sequence of steps that should be followed to discover knowledge
(e.g., candidate roles) in access control data. Each step is usually realized
with the help of available commercial or open-source software tools—which,
in turn, may implement the role mining algorithm described in this book.

Striving for the definition of a good role mining process actually helps
organizations to better understand the required activities. Further, it provides a roadmap to follow while planning and executing the role engineering
project. This in turn results in cost and time savings, better understanding, and acceptance of the results of such projects—see barriers to RBAC
in Sec. 2.4. Organizations need to understand that a role mining process
is nontrivial and involve multiple steps, reviews of partial results, possibly
several iterations, and interactions with the data owners, IT administrators,
line-of-business managers, and user managers. There are several reasons to
structure a role mining process:

- An unstructured application of role mining techniques frequently pro-
  duces meaningless results, i.e., candidate roles that, while interesting,
  does not contribute to solving the role engineering problem [Colantonio
  et al. (2009a, 2010c)]. This result ultimately leads to the failure of the
  entire role engineering project.
- A well-defined role mining process can help decision-makers understand
  the need, value, and mechanics behind the process itself. As a matter of
  fact, business people often fail to grasp the potential knowledge available
  in large amounts of data. They prefer to rely on the skills and experience
  of domain experts, delegating data analysis to them [Cios *et al.* (2007)].
  Nonetheless, they want to be comfortable with the technology applied.
- A role mining project requires a significant project management effort
  that needs to be grounded in a solid framework. Similar to most data
  mining projects, it involves teamwork and thus requires careful planning
  and scheduling.

As a follow-on from the aforementioned issues, we now introduce a possible, viable role mining process. It derives from the hybrid data mining
model introduced by Cios *et al.* (2007), i.e., a model that combines aspects
of both academic and industrial data mining processes. In particular, the

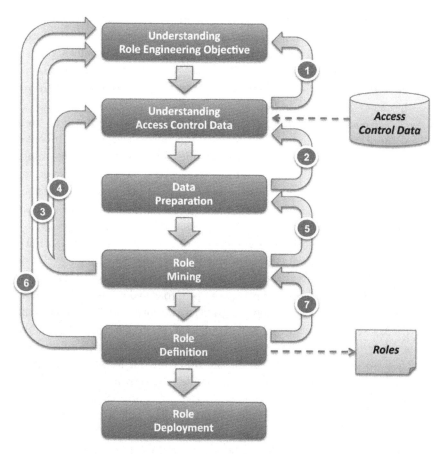

Fig. 4.1: Role mining steps

process envisages six steps (see Fig. 4.1):

(i) *Understanding Role Engineering Objective.* This initial step involves working closely with domain experts to define the problem and determine the project goals, identifying key people, and learning about current solutions to the problem. It also involves learning domain-specific terminology. A description of the problem, including its restrictions, is prepared. Finally, project goals are translated into role mining goals, and the initial selection of role mining tools to be used later in the process is performed. Following the guidelines provided in Sec. 3.4 is a good way to set up a role engineering process.

(ii) *Understanding Access Control Data.* This step includes collecting

sample data and deciding which data, including format and size, will
be needed. Background knowledge can be used to guide these efforts.
Data are checked for completeness, redundancy, missing values, plausi-
bility of attribute values, etc. Finally, the step includes verification of
the usefulness of the data with respect to the role mining goals. More
details can be found in Sec. 4.2.

(iii) *Data Preparation.* This step concerns deciding which data will be used
as input for role mining algorithms in the subsequent step. It involves
sampling, running correlation and significance tests, and data cleaning,
which includes checking the completeness of data records, removing or
correcting for noise and missing values, etc.. The cleaned data may
be further processed by feature selection and extraction algorithms
(to reduce dimensionality), by derivation of new attributes (say, by
discretization), and by summarization of data (data granularization).
Data preparation is further described in Sec. 4.3

(iv) *Role Mining.* Here the role engineers use various role mining algorithms to derive candidate roles from preprocessed access control data.
The result of mining can be provided in two forms. One form is a full
RBAC state: a suggested set of roles, a role hierarchy and possibly
a set of user-permission assignments not covered by these roles since
they do not fit the criteria. In the other output form, mining finds
patterns in user-permission assignments and returns candidate roles
one at a time until some portion of the user-permission assignments
is covered. Hybrid role engineering approaches can also be adopted as
described in Sec. 3.2.

(v) *Role Definition.* This step includes: understanding the results, checking whether the discovered roles are interesting, interpretation of the
results by domain experts, and checking the impact of deploying the
discovered roles. Only approved roles are retained, and the entire process is revisited to identify which alternative actions could have been
taken to improve the results. A list of errors made in the process is
prepared. This step is further described in Sec. 4.4.

(vi) *Role Deployment.* This final step consists of planning how to use
elicited roles. A plan to monitor the implementation of discovered
roles is created and the entire project documented. Finally, discovered
roles are deployed.

The previous tasks need not necessarily be applied in the given order. The model allows for an *iterative process*, identifying and describing explicit feedback loops. These loops, also enumerated in Fig. 4.1, are:

(1) from "Understanding Access Control Data" to "Understanding Role Engineering Objective." This loop is based on the need for additional domain knowledge to better understand and gather the required access control data—see Sec. 4.2.

(2) from "Data Preparation" to "Understanding Access Control Data." This loop is caused by the need for additional or more specific information in order to guide the choice of specific data preprocessing algorithms—see Sec. 4.3.

(3) from "Role Mining" to "Understanding Role Engineering Objective." The reason for this loop could be unsatisfactory results generated by the selected role mining methods, requiring modification of the project's goals.

(4) from "Role Mining" to "Understanding Access Control Data." The most common reason for this loop is poor understanding of the data, which results in incorrect selection of a role mining method and its subsequent failure.

(5) from "Role Mining" to "Data Preparation." This loop is caused by the need to improve data preparation, which often results from the specific requirements of the role mining method used, since these requirements may not have been known during the preparation of the data step.

(6) from "Role Definition" to "Understanding Role Engineering Objective." The most common cause for this loop is invalidity of elicited roles. Several possible reasons include incorrect understanding or interpretation of the domain and incorrect design or understanding of problem restrictions, requirements, or goals. In these cases, the entire role mining process must be repeated.

(7) from "Role Definition" to "Role Mining." This loop is executed when discovered roles are not novel, interesting, or useful. The least expensive solution is to choose a different role mining tool and repeat the role mining step—see Sec. 4.4.

In the following sections we provide additional details about some of the above steps.

4.2   Understanding Access Control Data

Of course, before starting any role mining activity, it is necessary to gather access control data from various IAM systems. The data collected can be classified into: *access control data*; and, *organizational data*. The basic access control data comprises users, permissions and user-permission assignments. Users and permissions may have *attributes* associated with them, and such attributes may further help in assigning meaning to user-permission assignments. For example, the cost center (i.e., the division that adds to the cost of an organization) to which the user belongs to, or the geographic location of a user's office, may explain permissions assigned to that user. Attributes are leveraged by all the techniques described in Part 3, Part 4, and Part 5.

Typically, all the access control and organizational data are automatically imported from configuration files, directories, and other databases into the role modeling system since they are available electronically. Besides this data, there are other facts that can be collected through a more manual process, in particular through *interviews* [Giblin *et al.* (2010)]. In an interview, the role engineer queries a person, such as a business process owner or system administrator, for insight into the known or intended users of systems, processes or applications. Possible questions relates to: the systems the interviewee is in charge of; a list of job functions in his area; for each job function, the list systems to be accessed. In this way, interviews help establish the business context of user-permission assignments. Although coarse-grained, this information can also be used to check the validity of user-to-permission assignments and determine whether data cleansing is needed. Interviews can be conducted through a variety of means such as: face-to-face meeting, phone conversation, web-based questionnaire, email, etc.. Notice that the outcome of interviews may contain ambiguities that must be resolved by role engineers. For example, one interviewee might refer to the "Payroll Accounting" system, while another interviewee might refer to the same system as "PA."

4.3   Data Preparation

In a general data mining process, the data preparation step is by far the most time-consuming task [Cios *et al.* (2007)]. We also advocate the importance of data preparation in a role mining project. After collecting data, the role engineer needs to assess the quality of the different sources. Data quality is an important factor in determining the role engineering strategy, as roles derived from bad data have questionable value. It is widely recognized that low-quality data will lead to low-quality mining results [Han and Kamber (2006)]. In particular, it is common to find incomplete or outdated data which may lead to inconsistencies. To assess data quality, role engineers explore data at various points in the process, formulate queries that return statistical summaries. Visualization (see Chap. 9) is an effective way to enhance the exploration of data, revealing patterns relevant to role design. Visual representations should be easily understood by both security and non-security professionals.

As anticipated in Sec. 4.2, another aspect to take into consideration is the availability of *attributes* of users and permissions. Indeed, role engineers gather evidence from the data to justify the creation of a role from the user-permission assignments. Since user-permission assignments are created to support the organization, one should expect much of the data can be compressed into roles that should be supported with evidence from both the business and IT sides. For example, a set of user-permission assignments where all users with the "surgeon" job title share the "sign surgical report" permission provides both business and IT evidence for creating a "Surgeon" role. Chapter 8 offers a viable technique to evaluate business meaning by leveraging attributes.

Besides evaluating the business meaning of roles, organizational or administrative attributes for users and permissions can be used to lead to a *data partition*. As stated in Chap. 10, we can leverage attributes to restrict the analysis to sets of data that are homogeneous from an enterprise perspective. Moreover, an organization may enforce a constraint whereby roles are not allowed to cross divisional or geographic boundaries. A further reason for partitioning the data relates to scalability. Partitioning data introduces benefits in terms of execution time of role mining algorithms. Large datasets in general pose problems when attempting to inspect, visualize, or mine data. This partition can be based on a combination of clustering results and attribute based partitions. Finally, how access control enforcement is performed may also influence the partitioning of data. For example, a role may contain a set of permissions which, at the implementation level, spans more than one system. While at a high level, these permissions may by grouped together, at an operational level, they are treated as distinct sets of permissions, since no mechanism is in place to provide the enforcement across applications. In this case, the data may best be partitioned along system boundaries.

Finally, notice that one of the main benefits of RBAC is reducing the number of relationships to manage. In particular, if n users share m permissions, instead of dealing with $n \times m$ user-permission assignments, a role is introduced requiring a total of $n + m$ assignments [Colantonio *et al.* (2008b, 2009b)]. However, it is not clear that introducing a role will help in the administration when n or m are small. Typically, role mining algorithms behave badly when there are patterns made up of small sets of user-permission assignments. Small patterns (i.e., small n and m) may be exceptional or out-of-role permissions as described in 3.1. These assignments may also be mistakes due to errors in the data. Part 4 discuss how to identify and isolate exceptional and wrong user-permission assignments. Generally speaking, to simplify the role engineering task, practitioners frequently use an 80/20 rule whereby roughly 80% of the user-permission assignments are covered by roles and the remaining 20% is treated as exceptions—see Chap. 3. Data cleansing techniques described in Part 4 help select the most appropriate 80% of the data for role engineering.

4.4 Role Definition

By using the outcome of role mining algorithms, the creation of roles can start. Role classification described in Sec. 3.3 should be applied. Some roles may be directly mandated by an organization's policies or by regulations and therefore easily predefined. Additionally, role engineers can take the suggested mined roles and incorporate them as system roles if they are considered appropriate. In this step, role engineers may reject automatically elicited roles, modify roles, or merge and split roles. Also, appropriate role names need to be assigned to mined roles. Particular attention must be paid to roles which were manually defined and passed to the role mining as predefined roles. These roles could have been modified, in some cases even ignored, necessitating a human decision. One important feature that role mining tools should offer is the ability to elicit candidate roles with respect to a predefined set of roles. With the ability to compare roles, roles can be mined according to different criteria to find similarities and differences between multiple mining runs.

Another observation is that a good role should be resilient to change: if users move within the organization or leave the organization or new users join, the roles, defined as a collection of permissions, do not need to change.

Thus, we are interested in stable roles—see Chap. 11. One possible way to verify role stability is to partition the user-permission assignment randomly, run role mining in the different partitions and check that roles keep reappearing.

4.5 Final Remarks

In this chapter we introduced a role mining process to find new candidate roles within existing access control data. It consists of many steps—one of which is the actual role mining task—each aiming to complete a particular discovery task, and accomplished by the application of a discovery method. These steps are executed in a sequence. The subsequent step is initiated upon successful completion of the previous step and requires results generated by the previous step as its inputs. It is highly iterative, and includes many feedback loops and repetitions, which are triggered by revision processes.

The main reason for introducing a role mining process is to formalize role mining projects within a common framework, a goal that will result in cost and time savings, and will improve understanding, success rates, and acceptance of such projects. The models emphasize independence from specific role mining tools and vendors.

A very important consideration in the role mining process is the relative time spent to complete each step. In general, we acknowledge that the data preparation step is by far the most time-consuming part of the role mining task. This is why we dedicated most of this book to solve this problem, i.e., Part 3 and Part 4.

Chapter 5

The Hidden Structure of Roles

In this chapter we provide the basic formalism required to illustrate algorithms and techniques introduced in the subsequent chapters. The symbol "⋆" in all the section titles clearly states that this chapter is only relevant for academic people, or for system developers that need to implement the algorithms described in this book. Consequently, this chapter can be skipped by more business-oriented people without missing the general meaning of the book.

The chapter is organized as follows. First, we supply a mathematical description of the role mining problem. Then, we show how the role mining problem is equivalent to several graph-related problems, such as *biclique cover*, *clique partition*, and *vertex coloring*. Finally, we also demonstrate that the role mining problem can be reduced to the *factorization of binary matrices*. In this chapter we also present *pseudo-roles*, a concept that will be extensively used in the reminder of the book.

5.1 Formalization of the Role Mining Problem ⋆

In the following we present some concepts required to formally describe role mining approaches in the subsequent chapters. In particular, in addition to RBAC concepts introduced in Sec. 2.2, this book introduces the following entities:

- $UP \subseteq USERS \times PERMS$, the set of the existing user-permission assignments to be analyzed;
- $perms: USERS \to 2^{PERMS}$, the function that identifies permissions assigned to a user. Given $u \in USERS$, it is defined as $perms(u) = \{p \in PERMS \mid \langle u, p \rangle \in UP\}$.

- users: $PERMS \rightarrow 2^{USERS}$, the function that identifies users that have been granted a given permission. Given $p \in PERMS$, it is defined as $users(p) = \{u \in USERS \mid \langle u, p \rangle \in UP\}$.

After having introduced the entities above, we can formally define the main objective of role mining. In particular, the outcome of any role mining tool is a set of *candidate roles*, that is roles which requires an attestation by business people, according to the observations of Chap. 4. More formally:

Definition 5.1 (System Configuration). *Given an access control system, we refer to its configuration as the tuple* $\varphi = \langle USERS, PERMS, UP \rangle$, *that is the set of all existing users, permissions, and the corresponding relationships between them within the system.*

A system configuration is the users' authorization state before migrating to RBAC, or the authorizations derivable from the current RBAC system.

Definition 5.2 (RBAC State). *An RBAC state is represented by tuple* $\psi = \langle ROLES, UA, PA, RH \rangle$, *namely an instance of all the sets that characterize the RBAC model.*

An RBAC state is used to obtain a system configuration. When the given RBAC system does not support the role hierarchy (see Sec. 2.2.2), a RBAC state can be also indicated as $\psi = \langle ROLES, UA, PA \rangle$. Moreover, we do not consider the possibility to have out-of-role permissions (see Sec. 3.1). Put another way, we seek to cover all possible user-permission assignment with at least one role. Part 4 is entirely devoted to identifying user-permission assignments that should not be managed through roles.

Having defined the RBAC state, the role engineering goal becomes *finding a state that correctly describes a given configuration*. In particular we are interested in the following:

Definition 5.3 (Candidate Role-Set). *Given a system configuration* φ, *a* candidate role-set *is the set of roles of a given RBAC state* ψ *that "covers" all possible combinations of permissions possessed by users according to* φ, *namely a set of roles whose union of authorized permissions matches exactly with the permissions possessed by system users. Formally:*

$$\forall u \in USERS, \exists R \subseteq ROLES :$$

$$\bigcup_{r \in R} auth\_perms(r) = \{p \in PERMS \mid \langle u, p \rangle \in UP\}.$$

Table 5.1: Example of roles built from $USERS = \{A, B, C, D, E, F, G\}$ and $PERMS = \{1, 2, 3, 4, 5\}$, and their support values

(a) UP

User	Permissions
A	$\{1, 2\}$
B	$\{1, 2, 3\}$
C	$\{1, 2, 4\}$
D	$\{1, 2, 5\}$
E	$\{2, 5\}$
F	$\{1, 3, 5\}$
G	$\{1, 2, 4, 5\}$

(b) Roles and their and supports

Role	Permissions	Support
r_1	$\{1\}$	$85{,}71\% = 6/7$
r_2	$\{2\}$	$85{,}71\% = 6/7$
r_3	$\{1, 2\}$	$71{,}43\% = 5/7$
r_4	$\{5\}$	$57{,}14\% = 4/7$
r_5	$\{2, 5\}$	$42{,}86\% = 3/7$
r_6	$\{1, 5\}$	$42{,}86\% = 3/7$
r_7	$\{2, 4\}$	$28{,}57\% = 2/7$
r_8	$\{1, 2, 4\}$	$28{,}57\% = 2/7$
r_9	$\{1, 2, 5\}$	$28{,}57\% = 2/7$
r_{10}	$\{3\}$	$28{,}57\% = 2/7$
r_{11}	$\{4\}$	$28{,}57\% = 2/7$
r_{12}	$\{1, 3\}$	$28{,}57\% = 2/7$
r_{13}	$\{1, 4\}$	$28{,}57\% = 2/7$
r_{14}	$\{3, 5\}$	$14{,}29\% = 1/7$
r_{15}	$\{4, 5\}$	$14{,}29\% = 1/7$
r_{16}	$\{2, 3\}$	$14{,}29\% = 1/7$
r_{17}	$\{1, 2, 3\}$	$14{,}29\% = 1/7$
r_{18}	$\{1, 3, 5\}$	$14{,}29\% = 1/7$
r_{19}	$\{1, 4, 5\}$	$14{,}29\% = 1/7$
r_{20}	$\{2, 4, 5\}$	$14{,}29\% = 1/7$
r_{21}	$\{1, 2, 4, 5\}$	$14{,}29\% = 1/7$

Please also note that every system configuration may allow for multiple candidate role sets. In Chap. 7 we will explain how to select the "best" one according to organization requirements.

Definition 5.4 (Support of a Role). *Given a role $r \in ROLES$, its* support *indicates the percentage of users possessing all permissions assigned to that role, that is* $support(r) = |auth\_users(r)|/|USERS|$.

Definition 5.5 (Degree of a Role). *The* degree *of a candidate role indicates the number of permissions assigned to it, that is* $degree(r) = |auth\_perms(r)|$.

Definition 5.6 (Confidence Between Roles). *Given a pair of hierarchically related candidate roles,* confidence *is the percentage of users possessing permissions assigned to both senior and junior roles, that is*

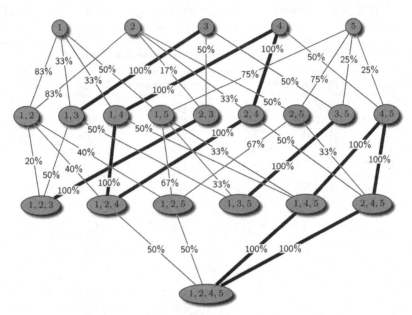

Fig. 5.1: Candidate roles listed in Table 5.1 and pertaining confidence values between immediate hierarchical relationships. Thicker lines indicate a confidence of 100%—see Lemma 5.4. Confidence between any pair of hierarchically-related roles can be computed through Lemma 5.2. For instance, the confidence between $\{1\}$ and $\{1,2,3\}$ can be derived from any path between them, such as $\{1,2,3\} \to \{1,2\} \to \{1\}$ or $\{1,2,3\} \to \{1,3\} \to \{1\}$. In both cases, the confidence is $83\% \times 20\% = 33\% \times 50\% = 17\%$

$$confidence(r_2 \succeq r_1) = |auth\_users(r_2)|/|auth\_users(r_1)|.$$

Table 5.1 and Fig. 5.1 provide some examples of the previous concepts. Additionally, in [Colantonio *et al.* (2008c)] the following lemmas are provided and proven:

Lemma 5.1. *Given* $r_1, r_2 \in ROLES$ *such that* $r_2 \succeq r_1$, *the confidence between* r_1, r_2 *is given by the ratio between supports of child and parent roles:*

$$confidence(r_2 \succeq r_1) = support(r_2)/support(r_1).$$

Lemma 5.2. *Given* $r_1, r_2, \ldots, r_{n-1}, r_n \in ROLES$ *such that* $r_n \succeq r_{n-1} \succeq \ldots \succeq r_2 \succeq r_1$, *the confidence between* r_1, r_n *is equal to the product of*

confidences between intermediate roles of the given hierarchical path between
those two roles:

$$\text{confidence}(r_n \succeq r_1) = \prod_{i=2}^{n} \text{confidence}(r_i \succeq r_{i-1}).$$

Let us consider Eq. (2.1) at page 23. Given two roles $r_1, r_2 \in ROLES$
such that $r_2 \succeq r_1$, if $r_1 \neq r_2$ then the role r_2 adds permissions to role r_1.
Instead, the users possessing the permissions assigned to role r_2 can be the
same as those possessing the permissions assigned to role r_1. Moreover, we
can have the following case:

Definition 5.7 (Role-Role Equivalence). *Given the roles* $r_1, r_2 \in$
ROLES, we say that they are equivalent, *and indicate this with* $r_1 \equiv r_2$, *if*
$auth\_users(r_1) = auth\_users(r_2)$.

In [Colantonio *et al.* (2008c)] the following lemmas are provided and
proven:

Lemma 5.3. *The equivalence relation is transitive, meaning that:*

$$\forall r_1, r_2, r_3 \in ROLES : r_1 \equiv r_2 \;\wedge\; r_2 \equiv r_3 \implies r_1 \equiv r_3.$$

Lemma 5.4. *Given* $r_1, r_2 \in ROLES : r_1 \succeq r_2$, *if* $\text{confidence}(r_1 \succeq r_2) = 1$
then $r_1 \equiv r_2$.

In addition to the equivalence between a role pair, referred to as "1:1",
it is possible to consider an equivalence relationship between a role and a
set of roles, that is "1:n." In particular:

Definition 5.8 (Role-Roleset Equivalence). *Given a role* $r \in ROLES$
and a set of roles $\{r_1, \ldots, r_n\} \subseteq ROLES$ *they are* equivalent, *and thus*
indicated as $r \equiv \{r_1, \ldots, r_n\}$, *when*

$$auth\_users(r) = \bigcup_{i=1}^{n} auth\_users(r_i).$$

5.2 Graph-Based Approach ⋆

After having formally introduced the role mining problem, we now illustrate
a mapping between role mining and some graph-related problems. This
allows to borrow well-known solutions from *graph theory* in order to solve
role mining problems. Indeed, the development of algorithms to handle
graphs has been of major interest in computer science for several years,
thus leading to very interesting and efficient solutions to graph-structured

problems. These algorithms can thus be reused for role mining. To show the link between graphs and role mining, we first summarize the main concepts of graph theory (see Sec. 5.2.1). Then, we describe a graph-based approach to role mining (see Sec. 5.2.2).

5.2.1   *Graph Theory Basics* ⋆

In mathematics and computer science, *graph theory* [Diestel (2005)] is the study of *graphs*, mathematical structures used to model pairwise relations between objects from a certain collection. More formally, a *graph* G is an ordered pair $G = \langle V, E \rangle$, where V is the set of *vertices*, and E is a set of unordered *pairs of vertices* (or *edges*). The *endpoints* of an edge $\langle v, w \rangle \in E$ are the two vertices $v, w \in V$. Two vertices in V are *neighbors* if they are endpoints of an edge in E. We refer to the set of all neighbors of a given vertex $v \in V$ as $N(v)$, namely $N(v) = \{v' \in V \mid \langle v, v' \rangle \in E\}$. The *degree* of a vertex $v \in V$ is indicated with $d(v)$ and represents the number of neighbors of v, that is $d(v) = |N(v)|$. The degree of a graph $G = \langle V, E \rangle$ is the maximum degree of its vertices, namely $\Delta(G) = \max_{v \in V}\{d(v)\}$.

Given a set $S \subseteq V$, the subgraph *induced* by S is the graph whose vertex set is S, and whose edges are the members of E such that the corresponding endpoints are both in S. We denote with $G[S]$ the subgraph induced by S. A *bipartite graph* $G = \langle V_1 \cup V_2, E \rangle$ is a graph where the vertex set can be partitioned into two subsets V_1 and V_2, such that for every edge $\langle v_1, v_2 \rangle \in E$, $v_1 \in V_1$ and $v_2 \in V_2$. A *clique* is a subset S of V such that the graph $G[S]$ is a complete graph, namely for every two vertices in S an edge connecting the two exists. A *biclique* in a bipartite graph, also called *bipartite clique*, is a pair of vertex sets $B_1 \subseteq V_1$ and $B_2 \subseteq V_2$ such that $\langle b_1, b_2 \rangle \in E$ for all $b_1 \in B_1$ and $b_2 \in B_2$. In the rest of the chapter we will say that a set of vertices S induces a biclique in a graph G if $G[S]$ is a complete bipartite graph. In the same way, we will say that a set of edges induces a biclique if their endpoints induce a biclique. A *maximal* (bi)clique is a set of vertices that induces a complete (bipartite) subgraph and is not a subset of the vertices of any larger complete (bipartite) subgraph. Among all maximal (bi)cliques, the largest one is the *maximum* (bi)clique. The problem of enumerating all maximal cliques in a graph is usually referred to as the *(maximal) clique enumeration problem*. As for maximal biclique, Zaki and Ogihara (1998) showed that there exists a one-to-one correspondence among maximal bicliques and several other well-known concepts in computer science, such as *closed itemsets* (maximal sets of items shared by a given set of transactions [Yahia *et al.* (2006)]) and *formal concepts* (maximal sets of attributes shared by a given set of objects [Ganter and Wille (1999)]). Indeed, many existing approaches to role mining have reference to these concepts [Vaidya *et al.* (2006); Molloy *et al.* (2008); Lu *et al.* (2008); Ene *et al.* (2008); Colantonio *et al.* (2011b)]. The application of closed itemsets in role mining is further discussed in Chap. 6.

A *clique partition* of $G = (V, E)$ is a collection of cliques $C_1, \ldots, C_k$ such that each vertex $v \in C$ is a member of exactly one clique. It is a partition of the vertices into cliques. A *minimum clique partition* (MCP) of a graph is the smallest collection of cliques such that each vertex is a member of exactly one clique. A *biclique cover* of G is a collection of biclique $B_1, \ldots, B_k$ such that for each edge $\langle u, v \rangle \in E$ there is some B_i that contains both u and v. We say that B_i covers $\langle u, v \rangle \in E$ if B_i contains both u and v. Thus, in a biclique cover, each edge of G is covered at least by one biclique. A *minimum biclique cover* (MBC) is the smallest collection of bicliques that covers the edges of a given bipartite graph. The minimum biclique cover problem can be reduced to many other $\mathcal{NP}$-complete problems, like binary matrices factorization [Siewert (2000); Lu *et al.* (2008)] and tiling database [Geerts *et al.* (2004)] to cite a few. Several role mining approaches leverage these concepts [Ene *et al.* (2008); Vaidya *et al.* (2007); Lu *et al.* (2008); Colantonio *et al.* (2011a, 2009c,b, 2010d)].

5.2.2 *Role Mining and Graph-Related Problems*⋆

We now describe a possible mapping between role mining and graph-related problems. In particular, we demonstrate that the role mining problem can be reduced to other well-known problems such as: *biclique cover, clique partition*, and *vertex coloring* [Diestel (2005)]. As mentioned earlier in Sec. 5.1, we do not consider the possibility to have out-of-role permissions. That is, we strive for covering each possible user-permission assignment with at least one role.

If we do not consider role hierarchy, it is possible to represent a given configuration $\varphi = \langle USERS, PERMS, UP \rangle$ through a bipartite graph

$$G = \langle V_1 \cup V_2, E \rangle = \langle USERS \cup PERMS, UP \rangle, \qquad (5.1)$$

where two vertices $u \in USERS$ and $p \in PERMS$ are connected by an edge if the user u is granted permission p, namely $\langle u, p \rangle \in UP$. A biclique cover of the graph G univocally identifies a candidate role-set $\psi = \langle ROLES, UA, PA \rangle$ for the configuration φ. Indeed, every biclique identifies a role, and the vertices of the biclique identify the users and the permissions assigned to this role [Ene *et al.* (2008); Colantonio *et al.* (2011a, 2009c,b, 2010d)]

By starting from the bipartite graph G, it is possible to construct an undirected unipartite graph G' in the following way: each edge in G (i.e., an assignment of UP) becomes a vertex in G', and two vertices in G' are connected by an edge if and only if the endpoints of the corresponding edges of G induce a biclique. To ease the exposition, we define the function $\mathcal{B}: UP \to 2^{UP}$ that indicates all edges in UP which induces a biclique together with the given edge, namely:

$$\mathcal{B}(\langle u, p \rangle) = \left\{ \langle u', p' \rangle \in UP \mid \langle u, p' \rangle, \langle u', p \rangle \in UP \ \wedge \ \langle u, p \rangle \neq \langle u', p' \rangle \right\}. \quad (5.2)$$

Note that two edges $\omega_1 = \langle u_1, p_1 \rangle$ and $\omega_2 = \langle u_2, p_2 \rangle$ of UP that share the same user (that is, $u_1 = u_2$) or the same permission (that is, $p_1 = p_2$) induce a biclique. Also, $\langle u_1, p_1 \rangle$ and $\langle u_2, p_2 \rangle$ induce a biclique if the pair $\langle u_1, p_2 \rangle, \langle u_2, p_1 \rangle \in UP$ exist. Moreover, given $\omega_1, \omega_2 \in UP$, it can be easily verified that $\omega_1 \in \mathcal{B}(\omega_2) \iff \omega_2 \in \mathcal{B}(\omega_1)$ and $\omega_1 \in \mathcal{B}(\omega_2) \implies \omega_1 \neq \omega_2$. Therefore, the undirected unipartite graph G' induced from G can be formally defined as:

$$G' = \langle V', E' \rangle = \left\langle UP, \ \left\{ \langle \omega_1, \omega_2 \rangle \in UP \times UP \mid \omega_1 \in \mathcal{B}(\omega_2) \right\} \right\rangle \quad (5.3)$$

In this way, the edges covered by a biclique of G induce a clique in G'. Thus, every biclique cover of G corresponds to a collection of cliques of G' such that their union contains all of the vertices of G'. From such a collection, a clique partition of G' can be obtained by removing any redundantly covered vertex from all but one of the cliques it belongs to. Similarly, any clique partition of G' corresponds to a biclique cover of G.

To clarify this concept, Fig. 5.2 shows a simple example, where $USERS = \{A, B, C, D\}$, $PERMS = \{1, 2, 3, 4\}$, and $UP = \big\{ \langle A, 1 \rangle, \langle A, 2 \rangle,$ $\langle A, 3 \rangle, \langle B, 1 \rangle, \langle B, 2 \rangle, \langle B, 3 \rangle, \langle C, 3 \rangle, \langle C, 4 \rangle, \langle D, 4 \rangle \big\}$. In the figure, the assignment $\langle B, 2 \rangle$ represents an edge in the bipartite graph (Fig. 5.2a) and a vertex in the unipartite graph (Fig. 5.2b). The figures show with thicker lines all the assignments that induce a biclique with $\langle B, 2 \rangle$, according to Eq. (5.2); for example, $\langle B, 3 \rangle$ share the same user of $\langle B, 2 \rangle$, while $\langle A, 1 \rangle$ induce a biclique with $\langle B, 2 \rangle$ since the assignments $\langle B, 1 \rangle$ and $\langle A, 2 \rangle$ exist.

It is known that finding a clique partition of a graph is equivalent to finding a coloring of its complement [Colantonio *et al.* (2010d)]. To this aim, let $\overline{G}'$ be the graph made up of the same vertices of G', but edges of $\overline{G}'$ are the complement of edges of G'. Given an assignment $\omega \in UP$, we

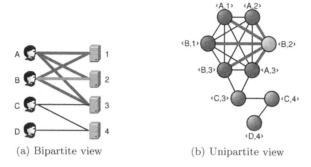

| (a) Bipartite view | (b) Unipartite view |

Fig. 5.2: An assignment (i.e., $\langle B, 2 \rangle$) and those that induce a biclique with it (i.e., $\langle A, 1 \rangle$, $\langle A, 2 \rangle$, $\langle A, 3 \rangle$, $\langle B, 1 \rangle$, $\langle B, 3 \rangle$), in both graph G and G'

indicate with $\overline{\mathcal{B}}(\omega)$ the assignments that do *not* induce a biclique together with ω, namely

$$\overline{\mathcal{B}}(\omega) = (UP \setminus \{\omega\}) \setminus \mathcal{B}(\omega). \tag{5.4}$$

Hence, the graph $\overline{G}'$ can be formally defined as:

$$\overline{G}' = \langle \overline{V}', \overline{E}' \rangle = \langle UP, \{\langle \omega_1, \omega_2 \rangle \in UP \times UP \mid \omega_1 \in \overline{\mathcal{B}}(\omega_2)\} \rangle \tag{5.5}$$

Any coloring of the graph $\overline{G}'$ identifies a candidate role-set of the given system configuration $\varphi = \langle USERS, PERMS, UP \rangle$, from which we have generated G. Thus, finding a proper coloring for $\overline{G}'$ means finding a candidate role-set that covers all possible combinations of permissions possessed by users according to φ; namely, a set of roles such that the union of related permissions matches exactly with the permissions possessed by the users.

The aforementioned properties are graphically depicted in Fig. 5.3. In particular, Fig. 5.3a shows a possible biclique cover. This cover is composed by 3 different bicliques: $\{\langle A, 1 \rangle, \langle A, 2 \rangle, \langle A, 3 \rangle, \langle B, 1 \rangle, \langle B, 2 \rangle, \langle B, 3 \rangle\}$, $\{\langle B, 4 \rangle\}$, and $\{\langle C, 4 \rangle, \langle C, 5 \rangle, \langle C, 6 \rangle, \langle D, 4 \rangle, \langle D, 5 \rangle, \langle D, 6 \rangle\}$. Figure 5.3b represents the same information in the unipartite view in terms of clique partition. Figure 5.3c demonstrates that the same information represents a vertex coloring in the complement of the unipartite graph. Edges in G belonging to the same biclique have the same color, and vertices in G' and $\overline{G}'$ have the same color of their corresponding edges in G. Moreover, vertices in G' that belong to the same clique are connected with an edge with the same color of their vertices, while dashed lines indicate that their endpoints do not belong to any clique of the chosen partition.

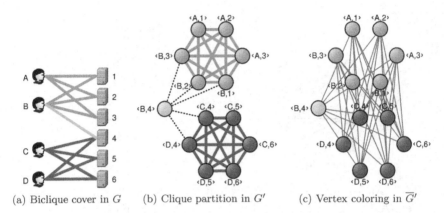

(a) Biclique cover in G (b) Clique partition in G' (c) Vertex coloring in $\overline{G'}$

Fig. 5.3: Relationship among biclique cover, clique partition, and vertex coloring

5.3   Matrix-Based Approach ⋆

Similar to Sec. 5.2, this section illustrates a mapping between role mining and some matrix-related problems. In particular, we will adopt *binary matrices*, that is matrices with entries from the Boolean domain $\{0, 1\}$. Such matrices can be used to represent binary relations between pairs of finite sets. Binary matrices abound in a large variety of fields: market basket data analysis [Agrawal *et al.* (1993)], ecology and paleontology [Puolamäki *et al.* (2006)], just to cite a few. In particular, they have been largely studied in genetic [Armin *et al.* (2000); Kim *et al.* (2000); Shmulevich and Zhang (2002)]. As for role mining, we demonstrate that it is equivalent to factorizing binary matrices.

Additionally, we introduce a concept that was born in the role mining community: *pseudo-roles*. Pseudo-roles are defined upon binary matrices, and they are the foundation for several methodologies described in this book. We also provide a fast algorithm, called EXTRACT, to efficiently enumerate pseudo-roles even in large datasets.

5.3.1   *Role Mining and Binary Matrix Factorization⋆*

As described in [Zhang *et al.* (2007); Vaidya *et al.* (2007); Lu *et al.* (2008); Colantonio *et al.* (2008b); Frank *et al.* (2010)], the problem of finding a candidate role-set can be mathematically expressed as the solution of the equation $A = B \otimes C$, where A, B, C are *binary matrices*, such that:

- $A \in \{0,1\}^{n \times m}$ is the matrix representation of *UP*, where $n = |USERS|$, $m = |PERMS|$, and $a_{ij} = 1$ when the ith user of *USERS* has the jth permission of *PERMS* granted;
- $B \in \{0,1\}^{n \times k}$ is the matrix representation of *UA*, where $n = |USERS|$, $k = |ROLES|$, and $b_{i\ell} = 1$ when the ith user of *USERS* is assigned to the ℓth role of *ROLES*;
- $C \in \{0,1\}^{k \times m}$ is the matrix representation of *PA*, where $k = |ROLES|$, $m = |PERMS|$, and $c_{\ell j} = 1$ when the ℓth role of *ROLES* has the jth permission of *PERMS* assigned;
- the operator "$\otimes$" is such that $a_{ij} = \bigvee_{\ell=1}^{k}(b_{i\ell} \wedge c_{\ell j})$.

The set *RH* can be represented by decomposing the matrix C. For instance, if there is a two-level hierarchy of roles, two matrices C' and C'' can be identified such that $C = C' \otimes C''$.

Having multiple candidate role-sets for a given system configuration equals to stating that several values for B and C are solution of the equation $A = B \otimes C$. According to Definition 5.3, the goal is to identify candidate role-sets such that it is always possible to select a suitable subset of roles whose union of permissions matches exactly with the permissions possessed by each user. This is equivalent to find a decomposition $B \otimes C$ in order to exactly have the given matrix A. Similar to Sec. 5.2, we do not consider out-of-role permissions, namely we seek to cover each user-permission assignment with at least one role.

5.3.2 *Pseudo-Roles* ⋆

We now introduce a fundamental tool for most of the approaches described in this book. This tool, referred to as *pseudo-role*, has been introduced and used in several works [Colantonio *et al.* (2010a,c,d, 2011b)], most of which can be exploited in the data exploration phase of a role mining process—see Sec. 4.1.

Let A be a $n \times m$ binary matrix that represents the set *UP* of user-permission assignments, similar to the previous Sec. 5.3.1. We denote with $[n] = \{i \in \mathbb{N} \mid 1 \leq i \leq n\}$ the indices of the rows of A, and with $[m] = \{j \in \mathbb{N} \mid 1 \leq j \leq m\}$ the column indices. Moreover, we denote the ith row of A with a_{i*}, the jth column of A with a_{*j}, and the element that is intersection of the ith row with the jth column with a_{ij}, and we write $a_{ij} \in A$. The *cardinality* of A is the number of elements equal to 1, and it is indicated by $|A| = |\{a_{ij} \in A \mid a_{ij} = 1\}|$. In other words, $|A| = |UP|$.

We now define what is an RBAC role in this matrix representation of the set UP.

Definition 5.9 (Role). *Given a matrix A, a role R is a pair $\langle U, P \rangle : U \subseteq [n]$, $P \subseteq [m]$ such that the submatrix of A identified by selecting only the rows U and the columns P is completely filled by 1's, namely:*

$$\forall i \in U, \ \forall j \in P \ : \ a_{ij} = 1.$$

Definition 5.10 (Maximal Role). *Let $R = \langle U, P \rangle$ be a role in the matrix A. It is also a* maximal role *if:*

$$\nexists \ a \ role \ R' = \langle U', P' \rangle \ : \ U \times P \subset U' \times P'.$$

Informally, a maximal role is "representative" for all contained roles, that is all its possible subsets of rows (or columns) that are filled by 1's for a given subset of columns (or rows). In RBAC terms, a maximal role is the largest set of permissions shared by a given set of users, such that no other user can have the same set of permissions. The key observations behind adopting maximal roles are summarized in the following [Colantonio *et al.* (2008c)]:

- *If two access permissions always occur together among users, these should simultaneously belong to the same candidate roles.* Without further access data semantics, a bottom-up approach cannot differentiate between a role made up of two permissions and two roles containing individual permissions.
- *If no user possesses a given combination of access permissions, it makes no sense to define a role containing such combination.* Similar to the previous point, if no user actually performs a task for which a certain permission set is necessary, it is usually better not to define a role containing such an unassignable set.
- *It is quite common within an organization to have many users possessing the same set of access permissions.* This is one of the main justifications that brought about the RBAC model. The creation of a role in connection with a set of co-occurring permissions is typically more advantageous since the number of relationships to be managed is reduced.

In data mining applications, what we refer to as maximal role is also known as *closed itemset* [Zaki and Hsiao (2005)]. Applications of closed itemsets include the discovery of association rules, strong rules, correlations,

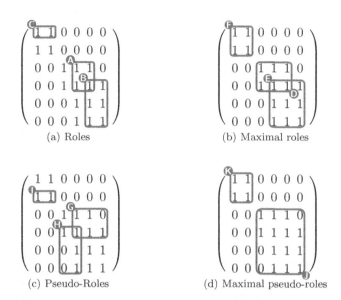

Fig. 5.4: Some examples of data patterns

sequential rules, episodes, multidimensional patterns, and many other important discovery tasks [Han and Kamber (2006)]. Chapter 6 discusses how closed itemsets can be adopted to solve the role minimization problem

Fig. 5.4a shows an example of binary matrix and also highlights some of the roles that can be identified within it. For example, the last three rows and last two columns—the cell grouping denoted by 'B' in the figure—contains cells filled by 1's. Hence, they represent a role. However, they do not represent a maximal role, because the third from last column also contains 1's in the last three rows. Indeed, the cells denoted by 'E' in Fig. 5.4b represent a maximal role: 'E' cannot be "expanded" by adding other rows and/or column. Further, the maximal role 'E' contains the role 'B'.

In the following we extend the role concept given in Definitions 5.9 and 5.10 by introducing a new concept:

Definition 5.11 (Pseudo-Role). *Given a matrix A, a pseudo-role R is a pair $\langle U, P \rangle : U \subseteq [n], P \subseteq [m]$ that has at least one row and one column filled by 1's, formally:*

$$\exists i \in U, \exists j \in P, \forall \ell \in U, \forall k \in P : a_{ik} = 1, a_{\ell j} = 1.$$

For ease of exposition, for a given pseudo-role $R = \langle U, P \rangle$ we also denote with $\hat{U} \subseteq U$ the set of rows filled by 1's, and with $\hat{P} \subseteq P$ the set of columns filled by 1's, that is:

$$\forall i \in \hat{U}, \forall j \in P : a_{ij} = 1,$$

$$\forall j \in \hat{P}, \forall i \in U : a_{ij} = 1.$$

Definition 5.12 (Maximal Pseudo-Role). *Let $R = \langle U, P \rangle$ be a pseudo-role in the matrix A. It is also a maximal pseudo-role if does not exists any pseudo-role $R' = \langle U', P' \rangle$ such that $\hat{U} \times \hat{P} \subset \hat{U}' \times \hat{P}'$.*

A maximal pseudo-role is a pseudo-role such that its rows and columns filled by 1's cannot be "expanded" by adding additional columns and rows. Figure 5.4c shows some examples of pseudo-roles. In particular, the matrix portion denoted by 'H' has all cells equal to 1 for the fourth row and the fourth column of the matrix. However, it is not a maximal pseudo-role, since the fourth row and the fourth column contain other cells equal to 1 that are not contained within 'H'. Hence, the pseudo-role 'H' can be "expanded" to the area denoted by 'J' in Fig. 5.4d, which represents a maximal pseudo-role. Note that, in this case, there is more than one column filled by 1's.

The following lemma relates roles to pseudo-roles (see [Colantonio *et al.* (2010a)] for the proof):

Lemma 5.5. *If $R = \langle U, P \rangle$ is a role, it is also a pseudo-role.*

Definition 5.13 (Maximal Pseudo-Role Generator). *An element $a_{ij} \in A$ is referred to as a generator of the maximal pseudo-role $R = \langle U, P \rangle$ if $U = \{\ell \in [n] \mid a_{\ell j} = 1\}$ and $P = \{k \in [m] \mid a_{ik} = 1\}$. If $a_{ij} \in A$ is a generator of R, we will also say that R is the maximal pseudo-role generated by a_{ij}, and we indicate it as $R_{a_{ij}}$.*

The key idea behind the generator concept is that, given a cell $a_{ij} \in A$, we can easily identify the role generated from it by just selecting all the 1's in the same row and the same column. In RBAC terms:

Definition 5.14. Given a user-permission assignment $\langle u, p \rangle \in UP$, the *pseudo-role generated by $\langle u, p \rangle$*, and referred to as $R_{\langle u,p \rangle}$, is a role represented by all users having the permission p granted and all permissions granted to the user u, namely ass_users$(R_{\langle u,p \rangle}) = $ users(p) and ass_perms$(R_{\langle u,p \rangle}) = $ perms(u).

If we consider the sub-matrix made up of rows and columns involved by a pseudo-role, there may also be some user-permission assignments that are not granted in the analyzed dataset—this is the reason for the "pseudo" prefix. Since a pseudo-role R is *not* an actual role, with abuse of notation we refer to its users as *ass_users*(R) and to its permissions as *ass_perms*(R).

Further, the generators of a maximal pseudo-role R all belong to rows/columns that have 1's in the same columns/rows, as is shown in the following theorem [Colantonio *et al.* (2010a)]:

Theorem 5.1. *All the generators of a maximal pseudo-role $R = \langle U, P \rangle$ belong to rows and columns that have 1's in the same positions, formally:*

$$\forall a_{ij}, a_{\ell k} \in A \ : \ a_{ij}, a_{\ell k} \text{ generate } R \implies$$
$$\forall t \in \hat{P}, \ \forall s \in \hat{U} \ : \ a_{it} = 1, \ a_{\ell t} = 1, \ a_{sj} = 1, \ a_{sk} = 1$$

Note that each cell that intersects a row and a column both filled by 1's is definitely a generator. Further, every pseudo-role has at least one generator, since a pseudo-role has at least one row and one column filled by 1's by definition. For instance, in Fig. 5.4d the maximal pseudo-role denoted by 'J' has two columns (the fourth and the fifth) and one row (the fourth) completely filled by 1's. Thus, cells a_{44} and a_{45} are generators of 'J'. Note that an element a_{ij} *generates exactly one* maximal pseudo-role, but a maximal pseudo-role can be generated by several elements $a_{ij} \in A$. In particular [Colantonio *et al.* (2010a)]:

Lemma 5.6. *Let MPR be the set of all the maximal pseudo-roles that exist within the matrix A. Then, $|MPR| \leq |A|$.*

5.3.3 Relevance of Maximal Pseudo-Roles ⋆

We now introduce a metric to measure the *relevance* of a maximal pseudo-role as a pattern for the role mining methodologies described in this book. Our analysis is mainly based upon two considerations. First, the more a maximal pseudo-role R is *close to being a maximal role*—namely, it is "almost" filled by 1's—, the more the pattern represented by R correctly describes the available data. The second consideration is that the more a maximal pseudo-role R has a *large area*—that is, a large number of involved cells—, the more it should be considered a significant pattern, and subsequently it should have a higher relevance. In more details:

(1) We prefer maximal pseudo-roles that are close to being maximal roles because, in this way, the rows and the columns of the matrix A that are involved in the maximal pseudo-roles are likely to be more similar.

(2) We prefer maximal pseudo-roles with a large area because they identify patterns that involve many rows and many columns.

The following index captures both points described above:

Definition 5.15 (Relevance of a Maximal Pseudo-Role). *Let MPR be the set of all maximal pseudo-role existing in a matrix A, and $R \in MPR$. The* relevance *of R is defined as:*

$$\varrho(R) = |\{a_{ij} \in A \mid a_{ij} \text{ is a generator of } R\}| = \sum_{a_{ij} \in A} \gamma(a_{ij}, R),$$

where

$$\gamma(a_{ij}, R) = \begin{cases} 1, & a_{ij} \text{ generates } R; \\ 0, & \text{otherwise.} \end{cases}$$

The index $\varrho(R)$ counts the number of generators of the maximal pseudo-role R. Informally, this index implicitly considers both the number of involved cells and the closeness of R to be a maximal role. As for the area, the generators a_{ij} of $R = \langle U, P \rangle$ are definitely elements of R. Thus, if the area $|U| \times |P|$ is small, the value of $\varrho(R)$ cannot be high. As for closeness, notice that generators are the intersection of rows and columns filled by 1's—see Theorem 5.1 in the previous section. Hence, the more rows and columns belonging to R are similar, the higher $\varrho(R)$ is. In particular [Colantonio et al. (2010a)]:

Theorem 5.2. *If a maximal pseudo-roles $R = \langle U, P \rangle$ is a maximal role, then $\varrho(R) = |U| \times |P|$.*

As stated before, the value of $\varrho(R)$ is related to the area of the maximal pseudo-roles $R = \langle U, P \rangle$ and its closeness to being a maximal role. According to Theorem 5.2, when R is a maximal role, $\varrho(R)$ is exactly equal to its area. Otherwise, $\varrho(R) < |U| \times |P|$. Indeed, some elements of R are set to 0—otherwise, R would be a maximal role. This means that there are rows and columns belonging to R that are not equal to each other, and thus, because of Theorem 5.1, not all the elements of R will be its generators. Subsequently, $\varrho(R) < |U| \times |P|$.

We will now introduce another relevance index for each element $a_{ij} \in A$ that is based on the relevance of maximal pseudo-roles.

Definition 5.16 (Relevance of a User-Permission Assignment).
Given a user-permission assignment represented by an element $a_{ij} \in A$, and let MPR be the set of all existing maximal pseudo-biclusters within the matrix A, the relevance of a_{ij} is the sum of the indices $\varrho(R)$ for all the maximal pseudo-roles R which a_{ij} belongs to. Formally:

$$\sigma(a_{ij}) = \sum_{R \in MPR: a_{ij} \in R} \varrho(R),$$

where $a_{ij} \in R = \langle U, P \rangle$ means that $i \in U$ and $j \in P$.

Finally, maximal pseudo-roles are related to the function $\mathcal{B}(\cdot)$ described in Eq. (5.2) (see Sec. 5.2.2). Indeed, the relevance of a user-permission assignment equals the number of neighbors of the corresponding node in the unipartite graph G' as defined in Eq. (5.3). In other words, we can discuss pseudo-roles from a graph theory perspective: pseudo-roles can be leveraged to identify those user-permission assignments that can be managed together with a given assignment through a single role. In particular [Colantonio *et al.* (2011b)]:

Theorem 5.3. *Let Σ_{UP} be the set of all possible RBAC states that cover all the user-permission assignments of UP, that is all tuples $\langle ROLES, UA, PA \rangle \in \Sigma_{UP}$ such that $\forall \langle u, p \rangle \in UP \implies \exists r \in ROLES : \langle u, r \rangle \in UA, \langle p, r \rangle \in PA$. Given a user-permission assignment $\langle u, p \rangle \in UP$, the set*

$$UP_{\langle u,p \rangle} = (\text{users}(p) \times \text{perms}(u)) \cap UP$$

corresponds to the set of all possible user-assignment relationships that can be managed together with the roles to which $\langle u, p \rangle$ belongs, namely

$$\forall \langle ROLES, UA, PA \rangle \in \Sigma_{UP}, \ \forall \langle u, p \rangle \in UP, \ \forall r \in ROLES :$$
$$\langle u, p \rangle \in \text{ass\_users}(r) \times \text{ass\_perms}(r) \implies$$
$$\text{ass\_users}(r) \times \text{ass\_perms}(r) \subseteq UP_{\langle u,p \rangle}.$$

The previous theorem states that the area covered by a pseudo-role $R_{\langle u,p \rangle}$ "contains" all possible roles that can be designed to manage the assignment $\langle u, p \rangle$. Note also that pseudo-roles can be thought of as a particular case of *approximate frequent itemsets* [Gupta *et al.* (2008)], where at least one transaction contains all items, and at least one item is contained in all transactions.

Finally, Fig. 5.5 depicts all the pseudo-roles that can be identified in a simple case which numbers 8 users, 11 permissions, and 70 user-permission

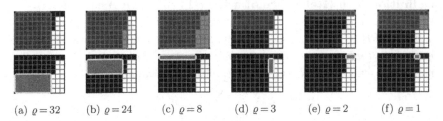

(a) $\varrho=32$ (b) $\varrho=24$ (c) $\varrho=8$ (d) $\varrho=3$ (e) $\varrho=2$ (f) $\varrho=1$

Fig. 5.5: Pseudo-roles (top figures) and corresponding generators (bottom figures)

assignments. Each figure from Fig. 5.5a to Fig. 5.5f shows a different pseudo-role. At the top of each figure, a binary matrix shows all the user-permission assignments covered by the pseudo-role (lighter cells are existing assignments covered by the pseudo-role). At the bottom, another matrix shows the assignments that generate the pseudo-role (lighter cells). Notice that when the pseudo-role relevance is high (e.g., Fig. 5.5a and Fig. 5.5b), it likely contains a role for managing most of the assignments. Conversely, less relevant pseudo-roles (e.g., Fig. 5.5e and Fig. 5.5f) identify assignment sets that are not worth investigating due to the reduced number of assignments that can be managed by a single role.

5.3.4 *Fast Computation of Maximal Pseudo-Roles* ⋆

Based on Definition 5.14, a naïve approach to generate all pseudo-roles is to scan all assignments in $\langle u, p \rangle \in UP$ and identifying the corresponding pseudo-role by computing $users(p)$ and $perms(u)$. During the scanning, whenever we generate an already existing pseudo-role, we update its relevance. This intuitive and simple algorithm has a running time $\mathcal{O}(|UP| \log |UP|)$. Assuming that UP is ordered, the search for all the users possessing p and all the permissions assigned to u can be executed in $\mathcal{O}(\log |UP|)$, and this must be done for all assignments in UP. In the worst case we generate $|UP|$ pseudo-roles—i.e., a different pseudo-role for each assignment. Hence, searching and updating the relevance requires $\mathcal{O}(\log |UP|)$, for instance by storing pseudo-roles in a self-balancing binary search tree.

Although this algorithm is quite efficient, we can still obtain better results. In particular, in the following we present a very fast randomized algorithm to generate pseudo-roles called EXTRACT (*EXception-Tolerant*

```
 1: procedure EXTRACT(UP, k)
 2:     P-ROLES, P-UA, P-PA ← ∅
 3:     for i = 1 ... k do
 4:         {Identify the current pseudo-role}
 5:         Pick ⟨u, p⟩ ∈ UP uniformly at random
 6:         U ← users(p)
 7:         P ← perms(u)

 8:         {Check if the pseudo-role has been previously generated}
 9:         if ∃R ∈ P-ROLES : ass_users(R) = U ∧ ass_perms(R) = P then
10:             {Update the relevance of the existing pseudo-role}
11:             R ← existing pseudo-role
12:             count[R] ← count[R] + 1
13:         else
14:             {Add a new pseudo-role to P-ROLES}
15:             R ← new pseudo-role
16:             P-ROLES ← P-ROLES ∪ {R}
17:             P-UA ← P-UA ∪ (U × {R})
18:             P-PA ← P-PA ∪ (P × {R})
19:             count[R] ← 1
20:         end if
21:     end for
22:     return P-ROLES, P-UA, P-PA, count[·]
23: end procedure
```

Fig. 5.6: The algorithm EXTRACT

Role ACTualizer, [Colantonio *et al.* (2011b)]). The key idea is that of *approximating* the relevance of pseudo-roles by sampling k times a relationship in UP uniformly at random, and then generating the corresponding pseudo-role. In turn, for each pseudo-role we count how many times it has been generated. Figure 5.6 summarizes this approach. The computational cost of EXTRACT is $\mathcal{O}(k \log |UP|)$. Indeed, the main loop (lines 3–21) is executed k times. The random selection of $\langle u, p \rangle$ (Line 5) is supposed to be executed in $\mathcal{O}(1)$. Moreover, searching all the users possessing p and all the permissions assigned to u (lines 6–7) can be executed in $\mathcal{O}(\log |UP|)$. Line 9 can be executed in $\mathcal{O}(\log |UP|)$. All the remaining statements can be performed in $\mathcal{O}(1)$. Hence, the overall computational complexity is $\mathcal{O}(k \log |UP|)$.

The following theorem gives a bound on the approximation introduced by this sampling approach [Colantonio *et al.* (2011b)]:

Theorem 5.4. *Let k be the number of the randomly chosen user-permission assignments by* **EXTRACT**. *Given a pseudo-role R, let $\tilde{\varrho}(R)$ be the actual number of times the pseudo-role has been generated by the algorithm. Hence,*

$$\Pr\left(\left|\frac{\tilde{\varrho}(R)}{k} - \frac{\varrho(R)}{|UP|}\right| \geq \varepsilon\right) \leq 2\exp\left(-2k\varepsilon^2\right). \tag{5.6}$$

Theorem 5.4 proves that there exists a value k such that the matrix permutation obtained by adopting sampled frequencies is, with a given probability, almost the same as using exact frequencies—the absolute difference between the two results is bounded. Both the absolute difference and the given probability are tunable parameters depending on k.

For practical applications of the algorithm **EXTRACT**, it is possible to calculate the number of samples needed to obtain an expected error less than ε with a probability greater than p. The following equation directly derives from Theorem 5.4:

$$k > -\frac{1}{2\varepsilon^2}\ln\left(\frac{1-p}{2}\right). \tag{5.7}$$

For example, if we want an error $\varepsilon < 0.05$ with probability greater than 98.6%, it is enough to choose $k \geq 993$.

5.4   Permission-Powerset Lattice ⋆

In this section we shall investigate the relationship among candidate role-sets and permission powerset. Moreover, we shall formally prove some interesting properties about the lattice of such a powerset.

5.4.1   *Posets, Lattices, Hasse Diagrams, and Graphs* ⋆

In computer science and mathematics, a *directed acyclic graph* (DAG) is a directed graph with no directed cycles. For any vertex v, there is no non-empty directed path starting and ending on v, thus DAG "flows" in a single direction. Each DAG provides a *partial order* to its vertices. We write $u \succeq v$ when there exists a directed path from v to u. The *transitive closure* is the reachability order "$\succeq$." A *partially ordered set* (or *poset*) formalizes the concept of element ordering [Davey and Priestley (2002)]. A poset $\langle S, \succeq \rangle$ consists of a set S and a binary relation "$\succeq$" that indicates, for certain element pairs in the set, which element precedes the other. A partial order differs from a total order in that some pairs of elements may not be comparable. The symbol "$\succeq$" often indicates a *non-strict* (or *reflexive*) partial order. A *strict* (or *irreflexive*) partial order "$\succ$" is a binary relation that is irreflexive and transitive, and therefore asymmetric. If "$\succeq$" is a non-strict partial order, then the corresponding strict partial order "$\succ$" is the reflexive reduction given by: $a \succ b \iff a \succeq b \wedge a \neq b$. Conversely, if "$\succ$" is a strict partial order, then the corresponding non-strict partial order "$\succeq$" is the reflexive closure given by: $a \succeq b \iff a \succ b \vee a = b$. An *antichain* of $\langle S, \succeq \rangle$ is a subset $A \subseteq S$ such that $\forall x, y \in A : x \succeq y \implies x = y$. We write $x \parallel y$ if $x \not\succeq y \wedge y \not\succeq x$. A *chain* is a subset $C \subseteq S$ such that $\forall x, y \in C : x \succeq y \vee y \succeq x$. Given a poset $\langle S, \succeq \rangle$, the *down-set* of $x \in S$ is $\downarrow x = \{y \in S \mid x \succeq y\}$, while the *up-set* of $x \in S$ is $\uparrow x = \{y \in S \mid y \succeq x\}$. Given $a \succeq b$, the interval $[a, b]$ is the set of points x satisfying $a \succeq x \wedge x \succeq b$. Similarly, the interval (a, b) is set of points x satisfying $a \succ x \wedge x \succ b$.

The *transitive reduction* of a binary relation R on a set S is the smallest relation R' on S such that the transitive closure of R' is the same as the transitive closure of R. If the transitive closure of R is antisymmetric and finite, then R' is unique. Given a graph where R is the set of arcs and S the set of vertices, its transitive reduction is referred to as its *minimal representation*. The transitive reduction of a finite acyclic graph is unique and algorithms for finding it have the same time complexity as algorithms for transitive closure [Aho *et al.* (1972)]. A *Hasse diagram* is a picture of a poset, representing the transitive reduction of the partial order. Each element of S is a vertex. A line from x to y is drawn if $y \succ x$, and there is no z such that $y \succ z \succ x$. In this case, we say y *covers* x, or y is an *immediate successor* of x, also written $y \gtrdot x$. A *lattice* is a poset in which every pair of elements has a unique *join* (the least upper bound, or *lub*) and a *meet* (the greatest lower bound, or *glb*). The name "lattice" is suggested by the Hasse diagram depicting it. Given a poset $\langle L, \succeq \rangle$, L is a lattice if $\forall x, y \in L$ the element pair has both a join, denoted by $x \curlyvee y$, and a meet, denoted by $x \curlywedge y$ within L. Let $\langle L, \succeq, \curlyvee, \curlywedge \rangle$ be a lattice. We say that $\langle \Lambda, \succeq, \curlyvee, \curlywedge \rangle : \Lambda \subseteq L$ is a *sublattice* if and only if $\forall x, y \in \Lambda : x \curlyvee y \in \Lambda \wedge x \curlywedge y \in \Lambda$. In general, we define:

- $\curlyvee \Lambda = \{x \in L \mid \forall \ell \in L, \forall \lambda \in \Lambda : \ell \succeq \lambda \implies \ell \succeq x\}$, the join of Λ (lub);
- $\curlywedge \Lambda = \{x \in L \mid \forall \ell \in L, \forall \lambda \in \Lambda : \lambda \succeq \ell \implies x \succeq \ell\}$, the meet of Λ (glb).

In particular, $x \curlyvee y = \curlyvee \{x, y\}$ and $x \curlywedge y = \curlywedge \{x, y\}$. Both $\curlyvee \Lambda$ and $\curlywedge \Lambda$ are unique.

5.4.2   *Mapping Permission Patterns to Roles* ★

We now introduce the model on which the following analysis is based. Consider the powerset of a set S (the set of all subsets of S) written as 2^S. The set 2^S can easily be ordered via subset inclusion "$\supseteq$." It can be demonstrated that $\langle 2^S, \supseteq, \cup, \cap \rangle$ is a lattice [Davey and Priestley (2002)]. Setting $S = PERMS$ makes it possible to build an RBAC model based on all derivable roles from a given permission set. As the operator "$\succeq$" (see Sec. 2) is based on the inclusion operator "$\supseteq$" applied to permissions assigned to roles, it is thus natural to map the operators "$\curlyvee$" to "$\cup$" (the join of two roles represented by the union of all assigned permissions) and "$\curlywedge$" to "$\cap$" (the meet of two roles represented by shared permissions). Every permission combination of the lattice $\langle 2^{PERMS}, \succeq, \curlyvee, \curlywedge \rangle$ identifies the following: 1) an element of $ROLES$, 2) its corresponding relationships in PA to such permissions, 3) all permission inclusions in RH which involve the role and 4) all relationships in UA to users possessing such combination. RH is defined to represent the transitive reduction of the graph associated to the lattice. Moreover, if a user is assigned to a role r, then UA will contain relationships between r, its juniors and users assigned to them, namely $\forall r \in ROLES, \forall j \in \downarrow r : ass\_users(r) \subseteq ass\_users(j)$.

For simplicity sake, from now on the lattice $\langle 2^{PERMS}, \succeq, \curlyvee, \curlywedge \rangle$ is identified only with the set $ROLES$.

5.4.3   *Finding Redundancies* ★

Several role mining techniques proposed to date seek to derive candidate roles through the identification of data patterns in existing access rights. Despite important differences among the various techniques, almost all can take advantage of some common principles summarized by the following [Colantonio *et al.* (2008c)]:

- *If two access permissions always occur together among users, these should simultaneously belong to the same candidate roles.* Without further access data semantics, a bottom-up approach cannot differentiate between a role made up of two permissions and two roles containing individual permissions [Vaidya *et al.* (2006)]. Moreover, defining roles made up of as many permissions as possible minimizes the administration cost by reducing the number of role-user assignments (see Chap. 7).
- *If no user possesses a given combination of access permissions, it makes no sense to define a role containing such combination.* Similar to the

Table 5.2: An example for *UP*

User	Perms	User	Perms	User	Perms	User	Perms	User	Perms
u_1	$\{1\}$	u_8	$\{1,3\}$	u_{15}	$\{3,6\}$	u_{22}	$\{1,3,5\}$	u_{29}	$\{2,4,6\}$
u_2	$\{2\}$	u_9	$\{1,4\}$	u_{16}	$\{4,5\}$	u_{23}	$\{1,3,6\}$	u_{30}	$\{1,2,3,5\}$
u_3	$\{3\}$	u_{10}	$\{1,5\}$	u_{17}	$\{4,6\}$	u_{24}	$\{1,4,5\}$	u_{31}	$\{1,2,3,6\}$
u_4	$\{4\}$	u_{11}	$\{1,6\}$	u_{18}	$\{1,2,3\}$	u_{25}	$\{1,4,6\}$	u_{32}	$\{1,2,4,5\}$
u_5	$\{5\}$	u_{12}	$\{2,5\}$	u_{19}	$\{1,2,4\}$	u_{26}	$\{2,3,5\}$	u_{33}	$\{1,2,4,6\}$
u_6	$\{6\}$	u_{13}	$\{2,6\}$	u_{20}	$\{1,2,5\}$	u_{27}	$\{2,3,6\}$	u_{34}	$\{2,3,4,5,6\}$
u_7	$\{1,2\}$	u_{14}	$\{3,5\}$	u_{21}	$\{1,2,6\}$	u_{28}	$\{2,4,5\}$	u_{35}	$\{1,2,3,4,5,6\}$

previous point, if no user actually performs a task for which a certain permission set is necessary, it is usually better not to define a role containing such an unassignable set.

- *It is quite common within an organization to have many users possessing the same set of access permissions.* This is one of the main justifications that brought about the RBAC model. The creation of a role in connection with a set of co-occurring permissions is typically more advantageous since the number of relationships to be managed is reduced.

The following example clarifies the assertions just made, particularly that of the first point presented. If of the given four permissions p_1, p_2, p_3, p_4, the pair p_1, p_2 is always found together with p_3, p_4, it is advisable not to define two distinct roles $\{p_1, p_2\}$ and $\{p_3, p_4\}$ but, rather, a single role $\{p_1, p_2, p_3, p_4\}$. This is different from saying that no user possesses only p_1, p_2 without also having some other permission. Suppose some users possess only p_3, others only p_4, others p_1, p_2, p_3 and still others p_1, p_2, p_4. In this case, even if p_1, p_2 never occur "by themselves", it could be convenient to define the role $\{p_1, p_2\}$ since roles $\{p_3\}$ and $\{p_4\}$ will certainly already exist individually. Thus, avoiding roles $\{p_1, p_2, p_3\}$ and $\{p_1, p_2, p_4\}$.

The above mentioned redundancies can be identified by applying the lattice theory on permission powerset. Let *ROLES* be the lattice based on 2^{PERMS} in which roles with support equal to 0 have been eliminated, except for the meet and join. Such set has a very simple property: *every candidate role set is contained within*, since it provides all user-assignable permission combinations [Colantonio *et al.* (2008c)]. Beyond eliminating roles having support equal to 0, this section shows that *it is also possible to remove roles presenting equivalence with other roles*, as they do not belong to any "reasonable" candidate role set.

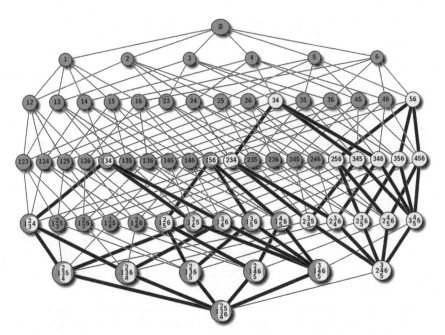

Fig. 5.7: Hasse diagram of permission powerset derived from Table 5.2

Table 5.2 shows an example of *UP* presenting equivalence relationships. By observing the data, it can be noted that all users simultaneously possessing permissions 3 and 4 also always have permissions 2, 5 and 6. Figure 5.7 shows the role lattice built on the given set *UP* with junior roles above and senior roles below. Despite this being a directed graph, direction indicators are absent (from top to bottom) to avoid complicating the figure. Thicker lines represent hierarchical relationships with confidence equal to 1, namely equivalence relationships (see Lemma 5.4). Colantonio *et al.* (2008c) demonstrated that *the combination of permissions of equivalent roles represents an equivalent role.* For example, $\{3,4\} \equiv \{2,3,4\}$, $\{3,4\} \equiv \{3,4,5\}$ and $\{3,4\} \equiv \{3,4,6\}$ implies $\{3,4\} \equiv \{2,3,4,5,6\}$. Moreover, the set of equivalent seniors forms a sublattice. In particular:

Theorem 5.5. *Given a role pair $r_1, r_2 \in ROLES$ such that $r_2 \succeq r_1$ and $r_1 \equiv r_2$, then all roles on the interval $[r_1, r_2]$ are equivalent to each other:*

$$\forall r, r_1, r_2 \in ROLES : r_2 \succeq r \succeq r_1 \wedge r_1 \equiv r_2 \quad \Rightarrow \quad r \equiv r_1 \equiv r_2.$$

Theorem 5.6. *A role $r \in ROLES$ is equivalent to the role represented by the union of permissions assigned to any set of its equivalent seniors:*

$$\forall r \in ROLES, \ \forall R \subseteq \uparrow r, \ \forall r' \in R : r' \equiv r \ \Rightarrow$$
$$\Rightarrow \ \exists s \in ROLES : r \equiv s \ \wedge \ \text{ass\_perms}(s) = \bigcup_{r' \in R} \text{ass\_perms}(r').$$

Theorem 5.7. *Given $r \in ROLES$, the role $\bar{r}$ represented by the union of permissions of its immediate equivalent seniors, that is*

$$\text{ass\_perms}(\bar{r}) = \bigcup_{r' \in ROLES \ | \ r' \gtrdot r \ \wedge \ r' \equiv r} \text{ass\_perms}(r'),$$

is a maximal role, namely it has the highest degree:

$$\forall r' \in ROLES : r' \equiv r \ \wedge \ r' \neq \bar{r} \ \Rightarrow \ \text{degree}(r') < \text{degree}(\bar{r}).$$

Theorem 5.8. *Given $r, s \in ROLES : s \succeq r$, the interval $[r, s]$ is a sublattice of ROLES.*

Definition 5.17. Given a role $r \in ROLES$, we define the *equivalent sublattice* of r, indicated by $\varepsilon(r)$, the interval $[r, \bar{r}]$, that is $\varepsilon(r) \triangleq [r, \bar{r}]$.

Based on the earlier observations, *all these replicas can be eliminated from the set of candidate roles except for maximum equivalent roles.* In fact, a maximum role can be considered a "representative" of all sublattices to which it belongs. Removing equivalent sublattices prunes the candidate role set solution space. Since $\varepsilon(r)$ contains roles that are equivalent to r, all the roles in $\varepsilon(r)$ but $\bar{r}$ can be removed. Colantonio *et al.* (2008c) also described an efficient algorithm to use in conjunction with Apriori (see Chap. 6) to remove such equivalences. In this case, since $\bar{r}$ is a maximal role, such algorithm is equivalent to a frequent closed itemset miner [Yahia *et al.* (2006)].

5.5   Final Remarks

This chapter posed the basis to build a formal theory about role mining. In particular, it showed how a role mining problem can be expressed in both terms of graph- or matrix-related problems. The main benefit of providing this concept mapping is the possibility to leverage existing methodologies and results existing in the current literature about graphs and binary matrices.

As for binary matrices, this chapter also introduced a new concept specifically thought for role mining, namely pseudo-roles. In the subsequent chapters we will see several applications of this powerful tool.

PART 2

Pattern Identification in Users' Entitlements

In this part we survey the state-of-the-art about *pattern identification* in users' entitlements. In particular, we show the relationship between roles and frequent itemset mining, clustering, subset enumeration, and other well-know data mining strategies. Besides "classical" data mining, we also describe how to efficiently enumerate interesting patterns via specific algorithms for role mining. Further, we report on several approaches to obtain a *minimal set of roles*, by also showing how to estimate the minimum number of roles required to cover all user-permission relationships. We demonstrate that the minimum number of roles is sharply concentrated around its expected value—this result can be applied, for example, to decide whether it is advisable to undertake the efforts to renew an RBAC state. In turn, we generalize the role-finding problem by offering a *cost-based approach* that seeks to minimize the overall administration complexity of RBAC systems.

Chapter 6

Enumerating Candidate Roles

In this chapter we introduce the problem of automatically eliciting roles by analyzing user-to-permission assignments in existing access control systems. To this aim, we leverage a mapping between the role-finding problem and well-known data mining problems. We mention some of the most used techniques and algorithms to find recurring patterns within analyzed access data in order to propose candidate roles.

After having shown how to apply data mining techniques to enumerate candidate roles, the chapter focuses on those techniques that strive for minimizing the number of roles needed to cover all the existing user-permission assignments. We also show a probabilistic method to estimate the cardinality of such a minimal set of roles.

6.1 Eliciting Patterns From Access Data

The term "role mining" and the application of well established data mining technology to role engineering have been shown for the first time by Kuhlmann *et al.* (2003). In their work, the authors presented a process for detecting patterns in a database of access rights and deriving enterprise roles from these patterns. As a matter of fact, role mining has the potential to accelerate the role engineering process, which is the costliest part of migrating to an RBAC system (see Sec. 2.4.1). For this reason, since the paper of Kuhlmann *et al.* there has been an increasing interest in role mining. Section 3.2.2 already introduced a brief survey of existing role mining techniques. The work of Molloy *et al.* (2009) also introduced a comprehensive framework for evaluating them. In particular, they categorize role mining approaches in the literature into two main classes:

- *Algorithms that produce prioritized roles.* These algorithms output a
  sorted list of candidate roles, ordered by their "priority". They generally
  envision a *role generation phase,* followed by a *role prioritization phase.*
  The generation phase identifies roles from user-permission relationships.
  It usually outputs a large number of candidate roles. The prioritization
  phase assigns a priority value to each candidate role; roles with a larger
  priority value are likely to be more important and interesting.
- *Algorithms that produce RBAC states.* These algorithms yield complete
  RBAC states, usually minimizing some cost measure, such as minimizing
  the number of roles or the number of user-assignments and permission-
  assignments.

In the rest of this section, we focus on the first class of algorithms,
pointing out the rational behind most of the role mining techniques. We
believe that outputting a list of candidate roles can be more useful in practice than generating a complete RBAC state. It is dubious that automated
techniques can completely overcome and replace the cognitive capacity of
humans [Colantonio *et al.* (2011b)]. A typical role engineering process cannot be completely automatic, because the input data often contains several
exceptions that need reviewing from domain experts. Hence, it is unlikely
that an organization will adopt a complete RBAC state outputted by a
role mining program. By providing a sequence of candidate roles to administrators, we allow them to examine the roles one-by-one and determine
whether these roles should be used or not. Nevertheless, the next Sec. 6.2
will discuss the problem of generating complete RBAC states by facing the
problem of minimizing the number of roles. Indeed, knowing the minimum
number of roles might be helpful when analyzing the complexity of the role
mining problem. Please refer to Chap. 7 for other optimization objectives,
as well as measures to prioritize roles and to evaluate the quality of roles
and RBAC states.

6.1.1   *Clustering Techniques* ⋆

The first kind of data mining algorithms that can be applied to role engineering is represented by *clustering.* Generally speaking, we refer to clustering as the process of grouping the data into *classes* or *clusters,* so that
objects within a cluster have high *similarity* in comparison to one another
but are very dissimilar to objects in other clusters [Han and Kamber (2006)].
A cluster of data objects can be treated collectively as one group, hence

representing a form of data compression. Often, *distance* measures are used to identify similar objects. Clustering is also called *data segmentation* in some applications because clustering partitions large data sets into groups according to their similarity.

Cluster analysis has been widely used in numerous applications, including market research, pattern recognition, data analysis, and image processing. In a business context, clustering can help marketers discover distinct groups in their customer bases and characterize customer groups based on purchasing patterns. As for access control data, a RBAC role actually represent a cluster, insofar as each role identifies a group of users that are "similar" due to the set of permissions they share.

Cluster analysis can also be used as a stand-alone tool to gain insight into the distribution of data. Alternatively, it may serve as a preprocessing step for other algorithms, such as subset selection. In other words, analysts can partition the set of data into groups based on data similarity. Chapter 10 offers a possible application of partitioning as a preprocessing phase in access control.

In the reminder of this section we survey some of the existing clustering techniques that can be applied in a role mining context. As a branch of statistics, cluster analysis has been extensively studied for many years, focusing mainly on distance-based cluster analysis. In machine learning, clustering is an example of *unsupervised learning*. Indeed, unlike classification, clustering do not rely on predefined classes and class-labeled training examples. For this reason, clustering is a form of *learning by observation*, rather than *learning by examples*.

6.1.1.1 *Categorization of Clustering Methods*⋆

Many clustering algorithms exist in the literature. The most important can be found in [Han and Kamber (2006); Tan *et al.* (2006); Cios *et al.* (2007)]. Very often, existing methods are classified according to (at least) the following categories:

Partitioning methods Given a database of n objects, partitioning means constructing $k \leq n$ subsets of the data, where each subset represents a cluster. Specifically, a partitioning method classifies the data into k groups, which together satisfy the following requirements: (1) each group must contain at least one object, and (2) each object must belong to exactly one group (see Fig. 6.1a). Notice that the second requirement can

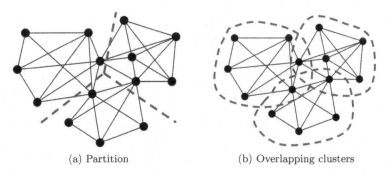

(a) Partition   (b) Overlapping clusters

Fig. 6.1: Different approaches to clustering

be relaxed in some fuzzy partitioning techniques (see Fig. 6.1b). Given
the number of partitions to construct k, a partitioning method creates
an initial partitioning. In turn, it typically uses an iterative relocation
technique that attempts to improve the partitioning by moving objects
from one group to another. The general criterion of a good partitioning
is that objects in the same cluster are "close" or related to each other,
whereas objects of different clusters are "far apart" or very different.

Hierarchical methods A hierarchical method creates a hierarchical decomposition of the given set of data objects. It can be classified as being
either *agglomerative* or *divisive*, based on how the hierarchical decomposition is formed. The agglomerative (or bottom-up) approach starts with
each object forming a separate group. It successively merges the objects
or groups that are close to one another, until all of the groups are merged
into one (the topmost level of the hierarchy), or until a termination condition holds. The divisive (or top-down) approach starts with all of the
objects in the same cluster. In each successive iteration, a cluster is split
up into smaller clusters, until eventually each object is in one cluster,
or until a termination condition holds. Hierarchical methods suffer from
the fact that once a step (merge or split) is done, it can never be undone.
This rigidity is useful in that it leads to smaller computation costs.

Density-based methods Most partitioning methods aggregate objects
based on the distance between objects. Such methods can find only
spherical-shaped clusters and encounter difficulty at discovering clusters
of arbitrary shapes. Alternative clustering methods have been developed
based on the notion of *density*. Their general idea is to continue growing
the given cluster as long as the number of objects in the "neighborhood"

(i.e., the density) exceeds some threshold; that is, for each data point within a given cluster, the neighborhood of a given radius has to contain at least a minimum number of points. Such a method can be used to filter out noise (outliers) and discover clusters of arbitrary shape.

Model-based methods These methods hypothesize a model for each cluster and find the best fit of the data to the given model. A model-based algorithm may locate clusters by constructing a density function that reflects the spatial distribution of the data points. It also leads to a way of automatically determining the number of clusters based on standard statistics.

The choice of clustering algorithm depends both on the type of data available and on the particular purpose of the application. To date, it is still not clear what is the best approach for role mining. If cluster analysis is used as a descriptive or exploratory tool, it is possible to try several algorithms on the same data to see what the data may disclose. As an example, the following section offers an application of the hierarchical approach to role mining.

6.1.1.2   *ORCA: A Hierarchical Clustering for Role Mining*⋆

We now present one possible application of clustering algorithms to a role engineering problem, namely we introduce the role mining tool called ORCA [Schlegelmilch and Steffens (2005)]. The algorithm performs a cluster analysis on permission assignments to build a hierarchy of permission clusters and presents the results to the user in graphical form. It is based on a *single-linkage* variant of a classical hierarchical clustering method, which works by grouping data objects into a tree of clusters [Han and Kamber (2006)]. In particular, ORCA can be classified as an *agglomerative hierarchical clustering*: it starts by placing each permission in its own cluster and then merges these atomic clusters (i.e., roles) into larger and larger clusters. Notice that most hierarchical clustering methods are agglomerative, differing only in their definition of intercluster similarity. A tree structure called a *dendrogram* is commonly used to represent the process of hierarchical clustering. It shows how objects are grouped together step by step. In [Schlegelmilch and Steffens (2005)] the authors also adopt this kind of visual representation of clusters.

The algorithm ORCA is summarized in Fig. 6.2. Given the set *USERS* and the pertaining permissions identified by *perms*($\cdot$), the aim is identifying

Require: *PERMS* = {permissions}, *users*(·) = {perm-to-user mapping}
Ensure: $\mathcal{C}$ = {all found clusters}, $\mathcal{H}$ = {cluster hierarchy}

1: *{initialize the variables}*
2: $\mathcal{C} \leftarrow \emptyset, \quad \mathcal{H} \leftarrow \emptyset$
3: *{for all single permissions, define a cluster}*
4: **for all** $p \in PERMS$ **do**
5:     $\mathcal{C} \leftarrow \mathcal{C} \cup \{\langle p, users(p)\rangle\}$
6: **end for**

7: **loop**
8:     *{identify clusters not yet in hierarchy}*
9:     $\mathcal{C}' \leftarrow \{c \in \mathcal{C} \mid \nexists d \in \mathcal{C}, \langle c, d\rangle \in \mathcal{H}\}$
10:     *{find pairs of clusters with a maximal overlap}*
11:     $m \leftarrow max_{\langle c,d\rangle \in \mathcal{C}' \times \mathcal{C}'}\{|\mathit{ass\_users}(c) \cap \mathit{ass\_users}(d)|\}$
12:     $\mathcal{M} \leftarrow \{\langle c,d\rangle \in \mathcal{C}' \times \mathcal{C}' \mid m = |\mathit{ass\_users}(c) \cap \mathit{ass\_users}(d)|\}$
13:     $n \leftarrow max_{\langle c,d\rangle \in \mathcal{M}}\{|\mathit{ass\_perms}(c) \cup \mathit{ass\_perms}(d)|\}$
14:     $\mathcal{N} \leftarrow \{\langle c,d\rangle \in \mathcal{M} \mid n = |\mathit{ass\_perms}(c) \cup \mathit{ass\_perms}(d)|\}$
15:     *{check if C is "stable"}*
16:     **if** $\mathcal{N} = \emptyset$ **then**
17:         **return** $\langle \mathcal{C}, \mathcal{H}\rangle$
18:     **end if**
19:     *{create a new cluster}*
20:     $\langle c, d\rangle \leftarrow$ pick one pair at random from $\mathcal{N}$
21:     $e \leftarrow \langle \mathit{ass\_perms}(c) \cup \mathit{ass\_perms}(d), \mathit{ass\_users}(c) \cap \mathit{ass\_users}(d)\rangle$
22:     $\mathcal{C} \leftarrow \mathcal{C} \cup \{e\}$
23:     $\mathcal{H} \leftarrow \mathcal{H} \cup \{\langle c, e\rangle, \langle d, e\rangle\}$
24: **end loop**

Fig. 6.2: The algorithm ORCA

the set $\mathcal{C}$ of all clusters, and the set $\mathcal{H} \subseteq \mathcal{C} \times \mathcal{C}$ that represents a partial order on clusters of $\mathcal{C}$. Figure 6.2 will not be further discussed here. More details can be found in [Schlegelmilch and Steffens (2005)].

Finally, note that the quality of ORCA (as a pure hierarchical clustering method) suffers from its inability to perform adjustment once a merge decision has been executed. That is, if a particular merge operation between two clusters later turns out to have been a poor choice, the method cannot backtrack and correct it. Moreover, notice that ORCA only proposes non-overlapping clusters, apart from the provided hierarchy of clusters. This might not reflect the actual requirements of a typical RBAC policy.

6.1.2 *Frequent Itemsets* ⋆

In the data mining literature, we usually refer to *frequent patterns* as recurring data (such as "itemsets", "subsequences", or "substructures") that appear in the analyzed data frequently [Tan *et al.* (2006); Cios *et al.* (2007); Han and Kamber (2006)]. *Frequent pattern mining* searches for recurring relationships in a given data set. For example, given a set of items such as milk and bread, if they appear frequently together among transactions, it is a frequent itemset. Since finding frequent patterns helps in several data mining tasks, frequent pattern mining has become an important topic in data mining research. The discovery of interesting correlations among huge amounts of business transactions can help in many business decision-making processes, such as catalog design, cross-marketing, and customer behavior analysis.

In the following we introduce the basic concepts of frequent pattern mining that can be used for the discovery of interesting correlations between permissions and users in access control databases. In an access control scenario, mining *frequent permission-sets* means to discover associations and correlations among permissions possessed by a large set of users. In fact, role mining can be seen as a reworking of the well-known *market basket analysis*. This process analyzes customer buying habits by finding associations between the different items that customers place in their "shopping baskets." The discovery of such associations can help retailers develop marketing strategies by gaining insight into which items are frequently purchased together by customers. Analogously, role mining aims at identifying a certain set of users that share the same set of permissions. Moreover, given a user and a certain set of granted permissions, we want to know how likely other permissions are granted to the same users as well.

If we think of the universe as the set of permissions managed through the given access control system, then each permission has a Boolean variable representing the presence or absence of that permission. Each user can then be represented by a Boolean vector of values assigned to these variables. The Boolean vectors can be analyzed for granting patterns that reflect permissions that are frequently granted together. These patterns can be represented in the form of *association rules*. For example, the information that users who have access to the privileged section of company's intranet also are entitled to make purchase order requests at the same time is represented in the association rule below:

access intranet privileged section $\implies$ *make purchase order requests*
[support $= 2\%$, confidence $= 60\%$]

Support and *confidence* are two measures of rule interestingness. They respectively reflect the usefulness and certainty of discovered rules. A support of 2% for the previous association rule means that 2% of all the users under analysis show that "access intranet privileged section" and "make purchase order requests" are granted together. A confidence of 60% means that 60% of the users who are entitled to access the intranet privileged section also make purchase order requests. Typically, association rules are considered interesting if they satisfy both a minimum support threshold and a minimum confidence threshold. Such thresholds can be set by analysts or domain experts.

6.1.2.1 *Definitions*⋆

Let $I = \{i_1, i_2, \ldots, i_m\}$ be a set of items. Let D be a set of database transactions where each transaction T is a set of items such that $T \subseteq I$. Each transaction is associated with an identifier, called *TID*. Let A be a set of items. A transaction T is said to contain A if and only if $A \subseteq T$. An association rule is an implication of the form $A \implies B$, where $A \subset I$, $B \subset I$, and $A \cap B = \emptyset$. The rule $A \implies B$ holds in the transaction set D with *support* '*s*,' where s is the percentage of transactions in D that contain $A \cup B$. This is taken to be the probability, $\Pr(A \cup B)$. The rule $A \implies B$ has *confidence* '*c*' in the transaction set D, where c is the percentage of transactions in D containing A that also contain B. This is taken to be the conditional probability, $\Pr(B \mid A)$. That is [Han and Kamber (2006)]:

$$support(A \implies B) = \Pr(A \cup B), \tag{6.1}$$

$$confidence(A \implies B) = \Pr(B \mid A). \tag{6.2}$$

Rules that satisfy both a minimum support threshold (MINSUPP) and a minimum confidence threshold (MINCONF) are called *strong*. By convention, we write support and confidence values so as to occur between 0% and 100%, rather than 0 to 1.

A set of items is referred to as an *itemset*. An itemset that contains k items is a k-*itemset*. The *occurrence frequency* of an itemset is the number of transactions that contain the itemset. This is also known, simply, as the *frequency*, *support count*, or *count of an itemset* of the itemset. Note that the itemset support defined in Eq. (6.1) is sometimes referred to as *relative support*, whereas the occurrence frequency is called the *absolute support*.

Table 6.1: Examples of frequent itemsets, MINSUPP $= 50\%$

(a) Transactions   (b) Result

TID	Items
100	$\{A, B, C\}$
200	$\{A, C\}$
300	$\{A, D\}$
400	$\{B, E, F\}$

Frequent Itemset	Support
$\{A, C\}$	50%
$\{A\}$	75%
$\{C\}$	50%
$\{B\}$	50%

The set of frequent k-itemsets is commonly denoted by L_k. Table 6.1 shows an example of frequent itemsets.

In general, association rule mining can be viewed as a two-step process: (1) find all frequent itemsets, (2) generate strong association rules from the frequent itemsets. A major challenge in mining frequent itemsets from a large data set is the fact that such mining often generates a huge number of itemsets satisfying the minimum support (MINSUPP) threshold, especially when MINSUPP is set low. This is because if an itemset is frequent, each of its subsets is frequent as well. A long itemset will contain a combinatorial number of shorter, frequent sub-itemsets. For example, a frequent itemset of length 100, the total number of frequent itemsets that it contains is $2^{100} - 1 \approx 1.27 \times 10^{30}$. Figure 6.3 depicts this property. This often leads to a too huge number of itemsets to compute or store. To overcome this difficulty, we introduce the concepts of *closed* frequent itemset in Sec. 6.1.2.4.

6.1.2.2 The Algorithm Apriori⋆

As an example of frequent itemset mining algorithm that can also be applied in a role engineering context, we now illustrate Apriori. It is the basic algorithm for finding frequent itemsets [Han and Kamber (2006)]. Apriori is a seminal algorithm proposed by Agrawal and Srikant (1994) for mining frequent itemsets for Boolean association rules. The name of the algorithm is based on the fact that the algorithm uses prior knowledge of frequent itemset properties, as we shall see following. Apriori employs an iterative approach known as a *level-wise search*, where k-itemsets are used to explore $(k + 1)$-itemsets. First, the set of frequent 1-itemsets is found by scanning the database to accumulate the count for each item, and collecting those items that satisfy minimum support. The resulting set is denoted L_1. Next,

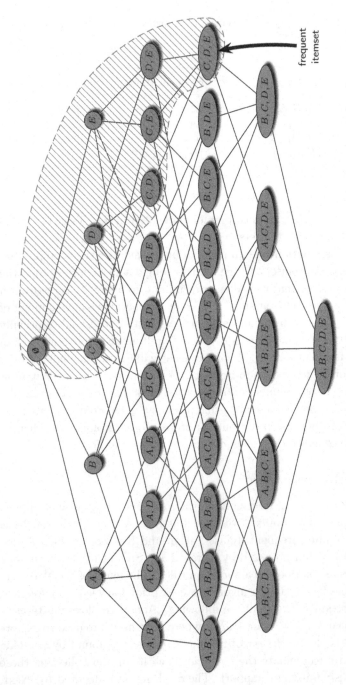

Fig. 6.3: An example of frequent itemsets. The figure depicts the Hasse diagram [Davey and Priestley (2002)] of all possible itemsets that can be derived from five items $\{A, B, C, D, E\}$. The figure points out that if $\{C, D, E\}$ is frequent, then all its proper subsets are frequent as well

L_1 is used to find L_2, the set of frequent 2-itemsets, which is used to find L_3, and so on, until no more frequent k-itemsets can be found.

To improve the efficiency of the level-wise generation of frequent itemsets, an important property, presented below, is used to reduce the search space [Agrawal and Srikant (1994)]:

Theorem 6.1 (Apriori Property). *All non-empty subsets of a frequent itemset must also be frequent.*

The Apriori property is based on the following observation. By definition, if an itemset I does not satisfy the minimum support threshold, MINSUPP, then I is not frequent; that is, $\Pr(I) <$ MINSUPP. If an item A is added to the itemset I, then the resulting itemset (i.e., $I \cup A$) cannot occur more frequently than I. Therefore, $I \cup A$ is not frequent either. Figure 6.4 depicts this property.

This property belongs to a special category of properties called *antimonotone* in the sense that if a set cannot pass a test, all of its supersets will fail the same test as well. To understand how the Apriori property is used in the algorithm, let us look at how L_{k-1} is used to find L_k for $k \geq 2$. A two-step process is followed, consisting of join and prune actions (see Fig. 6.5 and Fig. 6.6):

(1) *Join step*: To find L_k, a set of candidate k-itemsets is generated by joining pairs of $(k-1)$-itemsets from L_{k-1}. This set of candidates is denoted C_k.

(2) *Prune step*: C_k is a superset of L_k, that is, its members may or may not be frequent, but all of the frequent k-itemsets are included in C_k. A scan of the database to determine the count of each candidate in C_k would result in the determination of L_k.

Figure 6.5 and Fig. 6.6 describes Apriori with pseudo-code, while Fig. 6.7 shows a concrete example of Apriori.

6.1.2.3 *Generating Association Rules*

Once the frequent itemsets (i.e., frequent permission-sets) from transactions (i.e., users) in a database D have been found, it is straightforward to generate strong association rules from them. This can be done using the following equation [Han and Kamber (2006)]:

$$\text{confidence}(A \implies B) = \Pr(A \mid B) = \frac{\text{support\_count}(A \cup B)}{\text{support\_count}(A)}. \qquad (6.3)$$

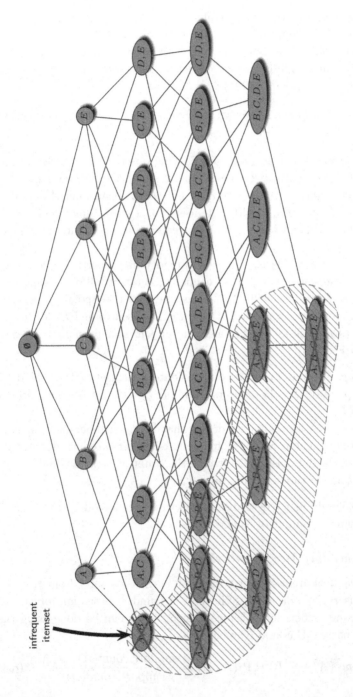

Fig. 6.4: An example of infrequent itemsets. The figure points out that if $\{A, B\}$ is infrequent, then all its proper supersets are infrequent as well

Require: $D = \{$all transactions$\}$, MINSUPP $=$ minimum support
Ensure: $L = \{$frequent itemsets in $D\}$

1: *{Identify large 1-itemsets}*
2: $L_1 \leftarrow \{$large 1-itemset in $D\}$
3: *{Identify large k-itemsets for $k > 1$}*
4: $k \leftarrow 2$
5: **while** $L_{k-1} \neq \emptyset$ **do**
6:      *{Generate k-itemsets from $(k-1)$-itemsets}*
7:      $C_k \leftarrow$ APRIORI-GEN(L_{k-1})
8:      *{Compute support}*
9:      **for all** $t \in T$ **do**
10:         $C_t \leftarrow$ subset(C_k, t)
11:         **for all** $c \in C_t$ **do**
12:            c.count $\leftarrow c$.count $+ 1$
13:         **end for**
14:      **end for**
15:      *{Only large itemsets}*
16:      $L_k \leftarrow \{c \in C_k \mid c.\text{count} \geq \text{MINSUPP}\}$
17:      $k \leftarrow k + 1$
18: **end while**
19: *{Union of itemsets generated at each iteration}*
20: **return** $\bigcup_k L_k$

Fig. 6.5: The algorithm Apriori

The conditional probability is expressed in terms of itemset support count, where *support_count*$(A \cup B)$ is the number of transactions containing the itemsets $A \cup B$, and *support_count*(A) is the number of transactions containing the itemset A. Based on this equation, association rules can be generated as follows:

- For each frequent itemset ℓ, generate all non-empty subsets of ℓ.
- For every non-empty subset s of ℓ, output the rule "$s \implies (\ell - s)$" if *support_count*$(\ell) \geq$ MINCONF, where MINCONF is the minimum confidence threshold.

Because the rules are generated from frequent itemsets, each one automatically satisfies minimum support.

```
1: procedure APRIORI-GEN(L_{k-1})
2:     {Join step}
3:        insert into C_k
4:            select p[1], p[2], ..., p[k − 1], q[k − 1]
5:            from L_{k-1} as p, L_{k-1} as q
6:            where p[1] = q[1]
7:                ∧ p[2] = q[2]
8:                ⋮
9:                ∧ p[k − 2] = q[k − 2]
10:               ∧ p[k − 1] < q[k − 1]

11:    {Prune step}
12:    for all c ∈ C_k do
13:        for all s ⊂ c : |s| = k − 1 do
14:            if s ∉ L_{k-1} then
15:                C_k ← C_k \ c
16:            end if
17:        end for
18:    end for
19: end procedure
```

Fig. 6.6: Line 7 of Fig. 6.5

6.1.2.4   *Closed Itemset Mining★*

In Sec. 6.1.2.1 we saw how frequent itemset mining may generate a huge number of frequent itemsets, especially when the MINSUPP threshold is set low or when there exist long patterns in the data set. To overcome this disadvantage, concise representations has been proposed in the literature to drastically reduce the number of elicited patterns [Kryszkiewicz (2002); Hamrouni *et al.* (2008)]. Among all condensed representations, *frequent closed itemsets* (FCIs) [Pasquier *et al.* (1999)] grasped particular attention within the data mining community. A frequent itemset is "closed" when there exists no proper superset of items supported by the same set of transactions. Formally, an itemset X is closed in a dataset S if there exists no proper super-itemset Y such that Y has the same support count as X in S. An itemset X is a closed frequent itemset in set S if X is both closed and frequent in S. FCIs are said to be *lossless*, *sound*, and *informative* representation of all frequent itemsets (FIs) [Kryszkiewicz (2002)], namely they exactly represent the same knowledge of FIs—it is trivial to generate

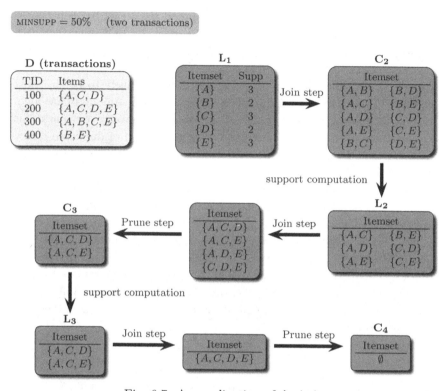

Fig. 6.7: An application of Apriori

all FIs along with their supports. Put another way, let $\mathcal{C}$ be the set of closed frequent itemsets for a data set S satisfying a minimum support threshold, MINSUPP; $\mathcal{C}$ and its count information can be used to derive the whole set of frequent itemsets. Thus we say that $\mathcal{C}$ contains complete information regarding its corresponding frequent itemsets. When a dataset is dense, namely when each transaction contains a large percentage of items, mined FCIs can be orders of magnitude fewer than corresponding FIs, since they implicitly benefit from data correlations.

How can we mine closed frequent itemsets? A naïve approach would be to first mine the complete set of frequent itemsets and then remove every frequent itemset that is a proper subset of, and carries the same support as, an existing frequent itemset. However, this is quite costly. A recommended methodology is to search for closed frequent itemsets directly during the mining process. This requires to prune the search space as soon as we can identify closed itemsets during the mining process. In recent years, a large number of algorithms have been proposed to extract frequent closed itemsets due to their importance. Several surveys on FCI show that each algorithm based on its applied strategy has some advantages and disadvantages for mining in dense and sparse datasets [Yahia *et al.* (2006)]. To date, the algorithm called DCI [Lucchese *et al.* (2006)] is likely to be the most effective in terms of computational resources required. Among FCIM algorithms, DCI has higher performance due to various innovative optimizations in closure calculations of items, preventing generation of duplicate closed itemsets, and no extra closure operations [Lucchese *et al.* (2006); Yahia *et al.* (2006); Shekofteh (2010)].

As for role mining, it is possible to note that *closed permissions-sets* (that is, sets of permissions such that no additional permission is granted to the same set of users that possess them) satisfies the properties enumerated in Sec. 5.4.3. Moreover, it is easy to see that any solution to the role minimization problem (see Sec. 6.2) is a subset of all closed permission-sets that can be found in *UP*, or any role in the solution can be replaced with a closed permission-set without increasing the number of roles [Molloy *et al.* (2010)]. Thus, enumerating frequent closed permission-sets is interesting for role engineers.

6.1.2.5 *CompleteMiner: Enumeration of Closed Permission-Sets*★

As a possible application of the previous concepts in role-finding, this section briefly illustrates an algorithm that is able to enumerate closed permission-sets. It is called CompleteMiner and it has been introduced by Vaidya *et al.* (2006) to solve the role mining problem. Even though CompleteMiner is inefficient when compared to other algorithm such as DCI [Lucchese *et al.* (2006)], we decided to illustrate it mainly because it is easy to explain. Moreover, it is one of the first algorithms explicitly devised for role mining.

The algorithm CompleteMiner consists of three phases, described below and detailed with pseudo-code in Fig. 6.8:

(1) *Identification of the initial set of roles.* In this phase, we group all users who have the exact same set of permissions. Each set of permissions identified in this way forms an initial role. The initial set of roles is denoted by 'InitRoles.'

(2) *Subset enumeration.* In this phase, we determine potentially interesting roles by computing "intersection sets" between pairs of roles created in the initial phase. Let this set be 'GenRoles.' In particular, given a

Require: Dataset *UP*
Require: perms(u) permissions granted to u
Require: role(X) role made up of permissions X and users $\{u \in USERS \mid \exists p \in X, \langle u, p \rangle \in UP\}$
Require: count[r] number of users associated to the role r
1: {*Identify roles made up of permissions possessed by each user*}
2: InitRoles $\leftarrow \emptyset$
3: **for all** $u \in USERS$ **do**
4:     $r \leftarrow$ role(perms(u))
5:     **if** $r \notin$ InitRoles **then**
6:         orig_count[r] $\leftarrow 1$
7:         InitRoles $\leftarrow$ InitRoles $\cup \{r\}$
8:     **else**
9:         orig_count[r] $\leftarrow$ orig_count[r] $+ 1$
10:     **end if**
11: **end for**
12: {*Enumerate candidate roles*}
13: GenRoles $\leftarrow \emptyset$
14: **for all** $r \in$ InitRoles **do**
15:     InitRoles $\leftarrow$ InitRoles $\setminus \{r\}$
16:     **for all** $s \in$ InitRoles **do**
17:         GenRoles $\leftarrow$ GenRoles $\cup (r \cap s)$
18:     **end for**
19:     **for all** $s \in$ GenRoles **do**
20:         GenRoles $\leftarrow$ GenRoles $\cup (r \cap s)$
21:     **end for**
22: **end for**
23: {*Count the number of users associated to each candidate role*}
24: **for all** $r \in$ GenRoles **do**
25:     **for all** $s \in$ InitRoles **do**
26:         **if** $r \subset s$ **then**
27:             count[r] $\leftarrow$ count[r] $+$ orig_count[s]
28:         **end if**
29:     **end for**
30: **end for**

Fig. 6.8: The algorithm CompleteMiner

Table 6.2: A toy example for subset enumeration

(a) Dataset				

User	p_1	p_2	p_3	p_4
u_1	0	0	0	0
u_2	1	1	0	1
u_3	0	1	1	0
u_4	1	1	0	1
u_5	1	1	0	1
u_6	0	1	1	1
u_7	0	1	1	1
u_8	0	1	1	0
u_9	0	1	1	0
u_{10}	0	0	0	1
u_{11}	0	0	0	1
u_{12}	0	0	0	0
u_{13}	1	1	0	1
u_{14}	1	1	0	1
u_{15}	0	1	1	1

(b) Result

Subset	Original Count	Generated Count
p_1, p_2, p_4	5	0
p_2, p_3, p_4	3	0
p_2, p_3	3	3
p_2, p_4	0	8
p_2	0	11
p_4	2	8

pair of roles, we intersect their sets of permissions while contextually computing the union of their users. Only the unique set of intersections is maintained. In order to reduce the memory footprint required, as well as to speed up intersections, a compression schema such as [Colantonio and Di Pietro (2010)] can be adopted.

(3) *User count computation.* In this phase, for each generated role in 'Gen-Roles,' we count the number of users who have the permissions associated with that role. We actually maintain two sets of counts: (i) the 'orig_count(r),' the original number of users who have exactly the set of permissions corresponding to role r and nothing else, and (ii) 'count(r),' an updated count of users whose permissions are a superset of the permissions associated with this role r.

The following toy example demonstrates how the algorithm works. Assume a hypothetical organization with 15 users and 4 permissions. Table 6.2a shows one sample database with the assignment of permissions to users. Since there are 4 permissions, and a role is defined as a collection of permissions, the number of possible different roles is $2^4 - 1 = 15$. Figure 6.9 depicts those roles. Empty sets can be always discarded, so they are not considered in this example. Table 6.2b shows the result of

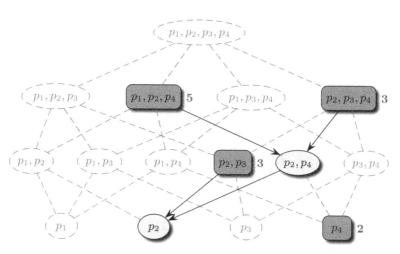

Fig. 6.9: Result of subset enumeration. Rectangles identify sets of permissions in initial roles, while oval nodes are generated through intersections. The number on the right of each rectangle is the value of 'orig_count'

the algorithm. In the first phase, the set 'InitRoles' gets initialized to $\{\{p_1, p_2, p_4\}, \{p_2, p_3, p_4\}, \{p_2, p_3\}, \{p_4\}\}$. These roles along with their corresponding counts are rectangled in Fig. 6.9. In the second phase, we enumerate all possible unique intersection sets of the initial roles found in the first phase. These result in two additional roles, $\{\{p_2, p_4\}, \{p_2\}\}$, which are ovaled in the figure. Since $\{p_2, p_3\}$ and $\{p_4\}$ are also the result of some intersections, at the end of the second phase, 'GenRoles' gets set to the roles $\{\{p_2, p_3\}, \{p_2, p_4\}, \{p_2\}, \{p_4\}\}$. In the third phase, the generated roles are matched to the corresponding counts which are 6, 8, 11, 10, and 2, as shown in Table 6.2b.

Finally, since CompleteMiner typically identifies lots of potential roles, these need to be prioritized/ordered in some way. Without the use of semantics, there is very little that we can do. One possibility is to simply order the roles according to the number of users having that role. However, instead of simply using the final Count, we use the following predicate to sort: $(\text{orig\_count}[r] \times \text{priority} + \text{count}[r])$. Here, 'priority' is simply the multiplication factor used to bias the results towards the roles found in the initial phase (i.e., do not report a generated set as a role unless it is really interesting).

6.2   Minimizing the Number of Roles ⋆

We now introduce the main results in the literature to solve the *role minimization problem*, namely the process of finding a smallest collection of roles that can be used to implement a pre-existing user-to-permission relation. Specifically, we will describe the results obtained by Ene *et al.* (2008) and Lu *et al.* (2008). We provide a brief explanation of each proposed solution, pointing out the main characteristics. For a detailed description of the algorithms, or further details in general, please refer to the above papers.

6.2.1   *A Graph Reduction for Role Minimization* ⋆

One of the most important approach to role minimization is probably the one presented by Ene *et al.* (2008). They introduced fast graph reductions that allowed recovery of the optimum solution from the solution to a problem on a graph smaller than the original input. For several realistic problems for which the authors tried their methodology, these reductions completely solved the problem. On the remaining problems, they reduced the problem enough that they could find the exact solution with an exponential (in the worst case) method.

First, the authors pointed out that there are a variety of equivalent ways to view the role minimization problem. One possibility is the factorization of a $\{0, 1\}$ matrix as a boolean product (as shown by [Siewert (2000)] and advocated later by [Streich *et al.* (2009); Lu *et al.* (2008)]), tiling of a database (as shown by [Geerts *et al.* (2004)] and also used by [Vaidya *et al.* (2007, 2010, 2008)]), or the representation of a given bipartite graph as the transitive closure of a tripartite graph in which the set of roles is a newly introduced subset of vertices (also used by [Colantonio *et al.* (2009c,a,b, 2010d)]). In particular, minimizing roles equals to solving the minimum biclique cover problem, that is finding a minimum cardinality collection of bicliques that covers the edges of a bipartite graph. Further details are provided in Sec. 5.2.

Then, the authors provided a practical and exact (but exponential in the worst case) algorithm that leverages the previous mapping to graph theory. The algorithm can be summarized as follows:

(1) Construct a undirected graph G' according to the Eq. (5.3).
(2) Find a minimum clique partition of that graph via graph reduction:

    (i) Remove vertices and their incident edges from the graph according to the strategy below, until no further removal is possible.

(ii) Form the complement of the resulting reduced graph, the "irreducible kernel."

(iii) Use a branch-and-bound backtracking method to color this graph.

(iv) Each color class is a clique in a clique partition of the irreducible kernel.

(v) Include the removed vertices in the reverse of the order they were removed, recovering a clique partition of G'.

(3) Each clique in G' is a set of edges of the bipartite graph representing user-to-permission relationships. Create one role corresponding to these edges. The set of roles thus created solves the role minimization problem.

Although the proposed algorithm can be used to solve large, real-world problems, this technique has limits. As a practical matter, there are datasets for which finding a minimum biclique cover is not feasible in a reasonable amount of time. Therefore, in [Ene *et al.* (2008)] can also be found a fast (polynomial), accurate approximation algorithm. They proposed a greedy algorithm that builds a biclique cover by identifying and including one biclique at a time in the cover until all edges are covered.

6.2.2 *Optimal Boolean Matrix Decomposition* ⋆

Another solution to the role minimization problem was proposed by Lu *et al.* (2008). They leveraged the matrix representation described in Sec. 5.3.1. A decomposition of a binary matrix into two matrices gives a set of basis vectors and their appropriate combination to form the original matrix. While a binary matrix can be decomposed in several ways, however, certain decompositions better characterize the semantics associated with the original matrix in a succinct but comprehensive way. Indeed, one can find different decompositions optimizing different criteria matching various semantics. In [Lu *et al.* (2008)], the authors presented a number of variants to the optimal Boolean matrix decomposition problem. They presented a unified framework for modeling the optimal binary matrix decomposition and its variants using binary integer programming. Such modeling allowed them to directly adopt existing heuristic solutions and tools developed for binary integer programming.

According to the notation introduced in Sec. 5.3.1, and for a given Boolean user-permission matrix $A \in \{0,1\}^{n \times m}$, the role minimization problem asks us to find two boolean matrices, the user-role assignment $B \in \{0,1\}^{n \times k}$ and the role-permission mapping $C \in \{0,1\}^{k \times m}$ with the fewest possible roles, i.e., such that k is minimized. Thus, the role minimization problem can be succinctly put as an optimization problem as follows:

$$\text{Minimize } |ROLES| \ s.t. \ A = B \otimes C.$$

The above statement is simply a high level representation of the optimization problem. To make it usable, we need to give the concrete constraints and the actual objective function. Let A_i denote the permission set that user i has. Since there are m total permissions, the total number of possible roles is 2^m. Clearly, enumerating an exponential number of roles is not feasible. Therefore, suppose there are k candidate roles $\{R_1, R_2, \ldots, R_k\}$ such that c_{ij} of the matrix C is 1 if R_i includes permission j. Thus, every user's permission set can be represented as a union of some roles from the candidate role set. This can be phrased as the following constraint:

$$A_i = \bigcup_{j=1}^{k} b_{ij} R_j,$$

where $b_{ij} = 1$ indicates that the user i has the role j, 0 otherwise. Now, we can restate the role minimization problem as follows:

$$\text{Minimize } |ROLES| \ s.t. \ A_i = \bigcup_{j=1}^{k} b_{ij} R_j, \quad 1 \leq i \leq k.$$

The previous constraint says that if some user has a particular permission, at least one role having that permission has to be assigned to that user. In turn, if that user does not have some permission, none of the roles having that permission can be assigned to it. Accordingly, the number of roles assigned the constraint $A_i = \bigcup_{j=1}^{k} b_{ij} R_j$ can be transformed following set of equalities and inequalities:

$$\begin{cases} \sum_{j=1}^{k} b_{ij} r_{jt} \geq 1, & a_{it} = 1; \\ \sum_{j=1}^{k} b_{ij} r_{jt} = 0, & a_{it} = 0. \end{cases}$$

Next, we consider the objective function $|ROLES|$. In order to count the number of roles required, we need some way to know which roles are present. Therefore, we define a new set of indicator variables $\{d_1, \ldots, d_i, \ldots, d_k\}$, where $d_i = 1$ indicates role i is present, otherwise not. Then $|ROLES| = \sum_{i=1}^{k} d_i$. Since d_i indicates the presence of a role, d_i should only be 1 when at least one user is assigned role i. Thus, $d_i = 1$ when at least one of $\{b_{1i}, \ldots, b_{ni}\}$ is 1. We can formulate this by adding in the constraints

$$d_j \geq b_{ij}, \quad 1 \leq i \leq n.$$

Putting every thing together, the role minimization problem can be modeled as follows:

$$\min \sum_{i=1}^{k} d_i$$

$$\begin{cases} \sum_{j=1}^{k} b_{ij} r_{jt} \geq 1, & a_{it} = 1, 1 \leq i \leq n, 1 \leq t \leq m; \\ \sum_{j=1}^{k} b_{ij} r_{jt} = 0, & a_{it} = 0, 1 \leq i \leq n, 1 \leq t \leq m; \\ d_j \geq b_{ij}, & 1 \leq i \leq n, 1 \leq j \leq k; \\ d_j \in \{0,1\}, & 1 \leq j \leq k; \\ b_{ij} \in \{0,1\}, & 1 \leq i \leq n, 1 \leq j \leq k. \end{cases}$$

Lu *et al.* (2008) also proposed a greedy algorithm to solve the above binary integer programming problem. Indeed, binary integer programming is the most difficult problem in operations research, because most of them are $\mathcal{NP}$-complete problems. The traditional simplex and interior-point methods are not suitable for it, because its feasible solution field is not continuous. Thus the common methods dealing with it are cutting-plane and branch-and-bound methods. However, when there are more than a hundred users and a hundred candidate roles, it is already beyond the computing power of ordinary computers. Thus a good heuristic algorithm is necessary, although it is at the cost of approximating or missing the optimal solution. Please refer to [Lu *et al.* (2008)] for further details about the algorithm proposed.

6.3   Estimating the Minimum Number of Roles ⋆

In this section we provide a probabilistic method to estimate the cardinality of the minimal set of roles needed to cover all the existing user-permission assignments [Colantonio *et al.* (2009c)]. The method leverages a known reduction of the role number minimization problem to the chromatic number of a graph. We prove that the optimal role number is sharply concentrated around its expected value. We also show how this result can be used as a *stop condition* when striving to find an approximation of the optimum for any role mining algorithm. The corresponding rational is that if a result is close to the optimum, and the effort required to discover a better result is high, it might be appropriate to accept the current result. The methodology can also be used to decide whether it is advisable to undertake the efforts to renew a RBAC state.

6.3.1 *Martingales and Azuma-Hoeffding Inequality*★

We shall now present some definitions and theorems that provide the mathematical basis we will further discuss later on in this chapter. In particular, we introduce: martingales, Doob martingales, and the Azuma-Hoeffding inequality. These are well known tools for the analysis of randomized algorithms [Mitzenmacher and Upfal (2005); Williams (1991)].

Definition 6.1 (Martingale). *A   sequence   of   random   variables* $Z_0, Z_1, \ldots, Z_n$ *is a martingale with respect to the sequence* $X_0, X_1, \ldots, X_n$ *if for all $n \geq 0$, the following conditions hold:*

- Z_n *is function of* $X_0, X_1, \ldots, X_n$,
- $\mathbb{E}[|Z_n|] \leq \infty$,
- $\mathbb{E}[Z_{n+1} \mid X_0, \ldots, X_n] = Z_n$,

where the operator $\mathbb{E}[\cdot]$ indicates the expected value of a random variable. A sequence of random variables $Z_0, Z_1, \ldots$ is called martingale *when it is a martingale with respect to himself. That is $\mathbb{E}[|Z_n|] \leq \infty$ and $\mathbb{E}[Z_{n+1} \mid Z_0, \ldots, Z_n] = Z_n$.*

Definition 6.2 (Doob Martingale). *A Doob martingale refers to a martingale constructed using the following general approach.   Let $X_0, X_1, \ldots, X_n$ be a sequence of random variables, and let Y be a random variable with $\mathbb{E}[|Y|] < \infty$. (Generally Y, will depend on $X_0, X_1, \ldots, X_n$.) Then*

$$Z_i = \mathbb{E}[Y \mid X_0, \ldots, X_i], \quad i = 0, 1, \ldots, n,$$

gives a martingale with respect to $X_0, X_1, \ldots, X_n$.

The previous construction assures that the resulting sequence $Z_0, Z_1, \ldots, Z_n$ is always a martingale.

A useful property of the martingales that we will use in this chapter is the Azuma-Hoeffding inequality [Mitzenmacher and Upfal (2005)]:

Theorem 6.2 (Azuma-Hoeffding inequality). *Let* $X_0, \ldots, X_n$ *be a martingale s.t.*

$$B_k \leq X_k - X_{k-1} \leq B_k + d_k,$$

for some constants d_k *and for some random variables* B_k *that may be functions of* $X_0, X_1, \ldots, X_{k-1}$. *Then, for all* $t \geq 0$ *and any* $\lambda > 0$,

$$\Pr(|X_t - X_0| \geq \lambda) \leq 2 \exp\left(\frac{-2\lambda^2}{\sum_{k=1}^t d_k^2}\right). \tag{6.4}$$

The Azuma-Hoeffding inequality applied to the Doob martingale gives the so called *Method of Bounded Differences* (MOBD) [McDiarmid (1989)].

6.3.2 A Concentration Result for Number of Roles ⋆

Using the model described in the previous section, we will prove that the cost of an optimal candidate role-set ψ for a given system configuration φ is tightly concentrated around its expected value. We will use the concept of martingales and the Azuma-Hoeffding inequality to obtain a concentration result for the chromatic number of a graph G [McDiarmid (1989); Mitzenmacher and Upfal (2005)]. Since finding the chromatic number is equivalent to both minimum biclique cover and minimum clique partition problems (see Sec. 5.2.2), we can conclude that the minimum number of roles required to cover the user-permission relationships in a given configuration is tightly concentrated around its expected value.

Let G be an undirected unipartite graph (defined according to Eq. (5.3) at page 68), and $\chi(G)$ its chromatic number. The following holds [Colantonio *et al.* (2009c)]:

Theorem 6.3. *Given a graph* G *with* n *vertices, the following equation holds:*

$$\Pr(|\chi(G) - \mathbb{E}[\chi(G)]| \geq \lambda) \leq 2 \exp\left(\frac{-2\lambda^2}{n}\right) \tag{6.5}$$

Note that this result holds even without knowing $\mathbb{E}[\chi(G)]$. Informally, Theorem 6.3 states that the chromatic number of a graph G is sharply concentrated around its expected value. Translating these concepts in terms of RBAC entities, this means that the cost of an optimal candidate role-set of any configuration φ with $|UP| = n$ is sharply concentrated around its expected value according to Eq. (6.5), where $\chi(G)$ is equal to the minimum number of required roles.

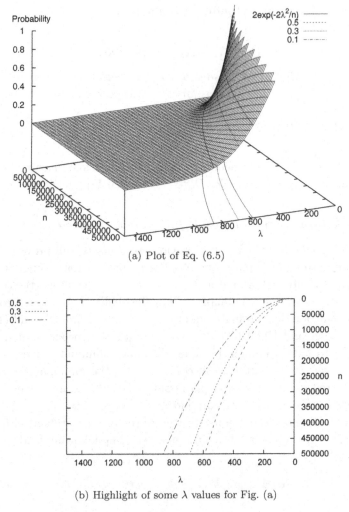

(a) Plot of Eq. (6.5)

(b) Highlight of some λ values for Fig. (a)

Fig. 6.10: Relationship between λ, n, and resulting probability

Fig. 6.10a shows the plot of the Eq. (6.5) for n varying between 1 and 500,000, and λ less than 1,500. It is possible to see that for $n = 500,000$ it is sufficient to choose $\lambda = 900$ to assure that $\Pr(|\chi(G) - \mathbb{E}[\chi(G)]| \geq \lambda) \leq 0.1$. In the same way, choosing $\lambda = 600$, then $\Pr(|\chi(G) - \mathbb{E}[\chi(G)]| \geq \lambda)$ is less than 0.5. Figure 6.10b shows the values for λ and n to have the left part of the inequality in Eq. (6.5) to hold with probability less than 0.5, 0.3, and 0.1 respectively.

Setting $\lambda = \sqrt{n \log n}$, Eq. (6.5) can be expressed as:

$$\Pr(|\chi(G) - \mathbb{E}[\chi(G)]| \geq \sqrt{n \log n}) \leq \frac{2}{n^2} \qquad (6.6)$$

That is, the probability that our approach differ from the optimum more than $\sqrt{n \log n}$ is less than $2/n^2$. This probability becomes quickly negligible as n increases. To support the viability of the result, note that in a large organization there are usually thousands user-permission assignments.

6.3.3   *Applications of the Bound*★

Assuming that we can estimate an approximation $\tilde{\mathbb{E}}[\chi(G)]$ for $\mathbb{E}[\chi(G)]$ such that $|\tilde{\mathbb{E}}[\chi(G)] - \mathbb{E}[\chi(G)]| \leq \varepsilon$ for any $\varepsilon > 0$, Theorem 6.3 can be used as a *stop condition* when striving to find an approximation of the optimum for any role mining algorithm. Indeed, suppose that we have a probabilistic algorithm that provides an approximation of $\chi(G)$, and suppose that its output is $\tilde{\chi}(G)$. Since we know $\tilde{\mathbb{E}}[\chi(G)]$, we can use this value to evaluate whether the output is acceptable and therefore decide to stop the iterations procedure. Indeed, we have that:

$$\Pr(|\chi(G) - \tilde{\mathbb{E}}(\chi(G))| \geq \lambda + \varepsilon) \leq 2 \exp\left(\frac{-2\lambda^2}{n}\right).$$

This is because

$$\Pr(|\chi(G) - \tilde{\mathbb{E}}(\chi(G))| \geq \lambda + \varepsilon) \leq \Pr(|\chi(G) - \mathbb{E}(\chi(G))| \geq \lambda)$$

and, because of Theorem 6.3, this probability is $\leq 2 \exp\left(-2\lambda^2/n\right)$. Thus, if $|\tilde{\chi}(G) - \tilde{\mathbb{E}}[\chi(G)]| \leq \lambda + \varepsilon$ holds, then we can stop the iteration, otherwise we have to reiterate the algorithm until it outputs an acceptable value.

For a direct application of this result, we can consider a system configuration with $|UP| = x$. If $\lambda = y$, the probability that $|\chi(G) - \mathbb{E}[\chi(G)]| \leq y$ is greater than $2 \exp\left(-2y^2/x\right)$. We do not know $\mathbb{E}[\chi(G)]$, but since we have that $|\tilde{\mathbb{E}}[\chi(G)] - \mathbb{E}[\chi(G)]| \leq \varepsilon$ we can conclude that $|\chi(G) - \tilde{\mathbb{E}}[\chi(G)]| < y + \varepsilon$ with probability at least $2 \exp\left(-2y^2/x\right)$. For instance, we have considered the real case of a large size company, with 500,000 user-permissions assignments. With $\lambda = 1,200$ and $\varepsilon = 100$, the probability that $|\chi(G) - \tilde{\mathbb{E}}[\chi(G)]| < \lambda + \varepsilon$ is at least 99.36%. This means that, if $\tilde{\mathbb{E}}[\chi(G)] = 24,000$, with the above probability the optimum is between 22,700 and 25,300. If a probabilistic role mining algorithm outputs a value $\tilde{\chi}(G)$ that is estimated quite from this range, then it is appropriate to reiterate the process in order to find a better result. Conversely, let us assume that the algorithm outputs a value within the given range. We know that the identified solution differs, from the optimum, by at most $2(\lambda + \varepsilon)$, with probability at least 99.36%. Thus, one can assess whether it is appropriate to continue investing resources in the effort to find a better solution, or to simply accept the provided solution. This choice can depend on many factors, such as the computational cost of the algorithm, the economic cost due to a new analysis, and the error that we are prone to accept, to name a few.

There is also another possible application for this bound. Assume that a company is assessing whether to renew its RBAC state, just because it is several years old [Vaidya *et al.* (2008)]. By means of the proposed bound, the company can establish whether it is the case to invest money and resources in this process. Indeed, if the cost of the RBAC state in use is between $\tilde{\mathbb{E}}[\chi(G)] - \lambda - \varepsilon$ and $\tilde{\mathbb{E}}[\chi(G)] + \lambda + \varepsilon$, the best option would be not to renew it because the possible improvement is likely to be marginal. Moreover, changing the RBAC state requires a huge effort for the administrators, since they need to get used to the new configuration. In our proposal it is quite easy to assess if a renewal is needed. This indication can lead to important time and money saving.

Note that in our hypothesis, we assume that the value of $\tilde{\mathbb{E}}[\chi(G)]$ is known. Currently, not many researchers have addressed this specific issue in reference to a generic graph, whereas plenty of results have been provided for Random Graphs. In particular, it has been proven [Łuczak (1991); Bollobás (1988)] that for $G \in G_{n,p}$:

$$\mathbb{E}[\chi(G)] \sim \frac{n}{2 \log_{\frac{1}{1-p}} n}.$$

6.4   Final Remarks

In this chapter we introduced the problem of automatically eliciting roles by analyzing user-to-permission assignments in existing access control systems. In particular, we provided a link to well-known data mining problems. We discussed some of the most used techniques and algorithms to find recurring patterns within analyzed access data in order to propose candidate roles.

Further, we also summarized the main results in the literature to elicit a minimal set of roles, i.e, finding one of the smallest sets of roles that cover a given set of existing user-permission assignments. We also showed that the optimal administration cost for RBAC, when striving to minimize the number of roles, is sharply concentrated around its expected value. The result is achieved by adopting a model reduction and advanced probabilistic tools. Further, we showed how to apply this result to deal with practical issues in administering RBAC; that is, how it can be used as a stop condition in the quest for the optimum.

Chapter 7

Minimizing the Effort of Administering RBAC

The objective of this chapter is to fill a gap existing in several role engineering methods, which lack a metric for measuring the "quality" of candidate roles produced. To this aim, we propose an approach guided by a *cost-based metric*, where "cost" represents the effort to administer the resulting RBAC configuration. Further, we propose RBAM (*Role-Based Association-rule Mining*), an algorithm that leverages the cost metric to find candidate role-sets with the lowest possible administration cost.

7.1 A Cost-Driven Approach to Role Engineering

According to Sec. 3.2, there are two general approaches to define the roles that make up a RBAC-based system: top-down and bottom-up. In the top-down approach, people perform a detailed analysis of organization's security requirements and processes, deriving roles from such an analysis. Instead, bottom-up approaches are mainly based on performing data mining algorithms (role mining algorithms, in particular) and can potentially accelerate the deployment of RBAC-based systems. One might argue that a top-down approach would produce higher-quality results, hence making it more desirable despite the higher effort involved. However, this is not always the case, insofar as manually designed roles conceal several inefficiencies. For instance, some configurations might be unnecessarily complicated due to redundancies, so that roles can be removed without affecting the privileges of anyone. In other cases, due to the complexity pertaining a top-down approach, there might be the temptation to use one-to-one correspondence between roles and permissions; in this case, the company can hardly enjoy the advantages of RBAC [Molloy *et al.* (2010)]. Therefore, it is advisable that effective role mining tools provide valuable help to analysts, thus complementing top-down approaches to role engineering.

A common problem of many existing role mining algorithms is that they only rely on user-permission assignment information, as they typically derive from classical approaches to data mining (see Chap. 6). As a matter of fact, the set of users, the set of permissions, and the binary relationships between them are the minimal set of data required to perform a mining activity [Colantonio et al. (2009a)]. However, since user- and permission-names are often considered just "labels" without a meaning, this limits analyst's ability to identify meaningful roles. In some cases, role engineering can also take advantage of having other useful information, such as user attributes (e.g., job title, department, and location) or permission parameters (e.g., application, domain, and supported task). All those pieces of information could be used to evaluate whether a given RBAC state: i) optimizes some *complexity measure*, that is, it actually maximizes the benefits related to adopting RBAC; ii) contains roles with *good semantic meanings*, that is, roles that correspond to real-world concept units [Colantonio et al. (2008b); Molloy et al. (2010); Takabi and Joshi (2010); Frank et al. (2010)].

Notice that given the same access control configuration, many RBAC states are consistent with it (see Chap. 5). Therefore, role engineers should adopt some metrics to evaluate how good an RBAC state is in order to select among them. For instance, Vaidya et al. (2007) proposed to count the number of roles, while Zhang et al. (2007) adopted a measure that considered the total number of edges when a RBAC state is visualized as a graph. In both cases, the intuition is that a major advantage of using RBAC is to simplify management. In fact, given n users and m permissions, directly assigning permissions to users requires $m \times n$ relationships to manage. However, using RBAC, the number of relationships that we need to maintain is reduced to $m + n$, which is always advantageous when $m, n > 2$ [Colantonio et al. (2008b)].

Overall, it is possible to define a general measure of the effort required to administer an RBAC system referred to as *cost function* [Colantonio et al. (2008b)], also known as *weighted structural complexity* [Molloy et al. (2010); Frank et al. (2010)]. Intuitively, the main objective of a cost function is to help analyst identify a RBAC state that leads to the least administration effort. Another aspect that the cost function should consider is the meaning of roles. Indeed, an issue that has not been adequately addressed in the current literature is how to discover roles with semantic meanings or other objectives (see also Chap. 8). Roles that are discovered by existing role mining approaches are no more than a set of permissions and it is unclear whether such roles correspond to any real-world concepts such as job functions or departments [Colantonio *et al.* (2009a)]. Without a clear meanings for the organization, roles may be hard to use and maintain in practice. Therefore, it is advisable that the cost function is also capable to evaluate the business meaning of roles.

Another important observation is that role mining can be used in combination with a top-down role engineering effort, to achieve a hybrid method for role engineering. Role engineers may have already performed an incomplete role engineering activity to produce a minimal set of predefined roles. Role mining techniques can then be used to complete this preliminary work. However, most of them do not consider existing roles and try to define everything from scratch, which is not acceptable for organizations that already have an RBAC system in place [Takabi and Joshi (2010); Molloy *et al.* (2010)]. As a consequence, an additional goal of the cost function should be measuring how far a candidate role-set is from existing roles. Hence, leading to a role mining approach that preserves the permissions that already defined roles have, by merging and/or splitting roles, finding more efficient ways of assigning permissions to roles, or removing redundant hierarchical relationships.

In the following section we formalize the cost function concept introduced before.

7.2   Problem Formalization ★

To measure the complexity of an RBAC state as well as the meaning of its roles, in the previous section we introduced the cost function concept. A cost function is a combination of several *cost elements*, each of them considering a particular business- or IT-related aspect. Among the data available to the organization, it is possible to find information that might either directly influence the required system administration effort (e.g., number of roles, number of role-user relationships to be administered, etc.) or information that might help role engineers assign business meaning to roles (e.g., business processes, organization structure, etc.). Once an organization has identified the relevant data for access control purposes, this data should be "translated" into cost elements and then combined into a cost function. This makes it possible to identify the *optimal* candidate roles which best describes the actual needs of the organization. More specifically, minimizing the cost function can simultaneously optimize the administration effort as well as the business meaning related to the elicited roles. Hence allowing for a hybrid approach to role engineering.

Formally, the proposed approach is founded on the following definitions:

Definition 7.1 (Cost Function). *Let Φ, Ψ be respectively the set of all possible system configurations and RBAC states. We define the* cost *function as*

$$\text{cost}: \Phi \times \Psi \to \mathbb{R}^+$$

where $\mathbb{R}^+$ indicates positive real numbers including 0. It represents an administration cost estimate for the state ψ used to obtain the configuration φ.

Leveraging the cost metric enables to find candidate role-sets (see Definition 5.3 at page 62) with the lowest effort to administer them:

Definition 7.2 (Optimal Candidate Role-Set). *Given a configuration φ, an* optimal candidate role-set *is the corresponding configuration ψ that simultaneously represents a candidate role-set for φ and minimized the cost function $\text{cost}(\varphi, \psi)$.*

In order to find the optimal candidate role-set, different kinds of cost functions could be proposed. Selecting a cost function that better fits the needs of an organization is further discussed in Chap. 8. For the sake of simplicity, we just consider a "flat" RBAC model, in which permission inheritance between roles does not exist. In this case, $auth\_perms(r) = ass\_perms(r)$, while $auth\_users(r) \supseteq ass\_users(r)$. Given this hypothesis, a reasonable cost function could be:

$$f = \alpha |UA| + \beta |PA| + \gamma |ROLES| + \delta \sum_{r \in ROLES} c(r) \qquad (7.1)$$

where $\alpha, \beta, \gamma, \delta \geq 0$. A linear combination of the cost factors is only one of many possibilities, even if the simplest. Indeed, finding the optimal candidate role-set can be seen as a *multi-objective optimization problem* [Deb (2001)]. An optimization problem is multi-objective when there are a number of objective functions that are to be minimized or maximized. In our case, objectives are minimizing $|ROLES|$ or minimizing $|PA|$. Since trade-off for conflicting criteria can be defined in several ways, there exist multiple approaches to define what an optimum is. The simplest one is that of computing a *weighted sum*: multiple objectives are transformed into an aggregated scalar objective function by multiplying each objective by a weighted factor and summing up all contributors.

The function $c: ROLES \rightarrow \mathbb{R}$ expresses an additional cost related to other business information different from $|ROLES|$, $|UA|$ and $|PA|$. For example, the cost function can be used in a bottom-up approach to discard roles which increment the administration cost of the candidate role-set. In this case, when a complete or partial role design is available from a top-down engineering process, we can avoid deletion of all pre-defined roles representing them with $c(r) \rightarrow -\infty$. Thus, creating a hybrid role engineering method. Similarly, we could think about a "blacklist" in which all roles have $c(r) \rightarrow +\infty$. This could be useful in implementing separation of duties rules, assigning an infinite cost to combinations of permissions which allow incompatible activities. Another important aspect to be taken into account via $c(r)$ relates to user attributes. For example, a role exclusively used within a given organizational unit may have a higher cost than a role used across multiple organizational units, as it requires the co-ordination of various user managers (see Chap. 8). The actual utilization of permissions, derivable from system log analysis, can also influence the administration cost. Furthermore, permission validity is often time limited [Bertino *et al.* (1998)]. Permanently and temporarily assigned permission could be distinguished during the role mining process by $c(r) \rightarrow +\infty$ for those roles containing permissions with a set expiration time for some user. Alternatively, a lesser value of $c(r)$ could be given to roles with assigned profiles of longer duration. Finally, when hierarchical RBAC is adopted, $c(r)$ could take into account the number of hierarchical associations.

The following section describes how to identify possible complete candidate role-sets starting from the set *UP*, analyzing how the cost changes as soon as roles are deleted.

7.3 Finding Optimal Role-Sets ⋆

Given a cost function that grasps the main security and business requirements of an organization, this section describes how such a cost function can be used to identify an optimal role-set. It is important to note that finding the best solution is an $\mathcal{NP}$-hard problem [Molloy *et al.* (2010)]. Therefore, this section only discusses how to identify an optimal solution from a theoretical point of view. The following Sec. 7.4 will introduce an heuristic to practically identify a sub-optimal solution for the role mining problem.

7.3.1   *Discarding Candidate Roles* ⋆

Suppose we define a role for each possible permission combination, that is, a candidate role-set based on the *lattice* derived from the powerset of *PERMS* (see Sec. 5.4). Such a set is interesting in that it is a superset of every possible candidate role-set. The administration cost of the role-set built upon the *PERMS* lattice is neither a maximum nor a minimum of the cost function. In fact, it is possible to increase the cost by increasing the number of role-user relationships. For example, let $PERMS = \{1, 2, 3\}$ so that $ROLES = \{\,\{1\}, \{2\}, \{3\}, \{1, 2\}, \{1, 3\}, \{2, 3\}, \{1, 2, 3\}\,\}$. If the role $\{1, 2, 3\}$ is removed from *ROLES*, a combination of the remaining candidate roles must be used to cover its permissions, such as $\{1, 2\}$ and $\{1, 3\}$. This doubles the number of relationships in *UA*. Depending on α, β, γ, δ, $c(r)$ of Eq. (7.1) and the number of users assigned to $\{1, 2, 3\}$, this could increase the cost even if *ROLES* and *PA* are smaller. Moreover, the cost is greater than the optimal. In fact, if we delete all roles representing combinations of permissions not possessed by any user, the cardinality of *ROLES* and *PA* diminishes while *UA* remains the same. If $c(r) \geq 0$, the cost diminishes as well.

Therefore, the objective is to analyze which combinations should be removed from the lattice in order to converge toward the optimal candidate role-set. Suppose that we want to delete a role r whose permissions can be obtained from the union of permissions assigned to a subset of *ROLES*. Removing r does not alter the completeness property of the role-set, but could lead to positive or negative fluctuation of the cost function value. In particular, the new administration cost would be changed by:

$$-\alpha u_r + \alpha \mu_r u_r - \beta p_r - \gamma - \delta c(r) \tag{7.2}$$

in that:

- $-\gamma$ indicates a role is removed from *ROLES*;
- $-\beta p_r$ indicates that p_r relationships are removed from *PA*, where $p_r = |auth\_perms(r)|$;
- $-\alpha u_r$ indicates that u_r relationships are removed from *UA*, where $u_r = |ass\_users(r)|$;
- $+\alpha \mu_r u_r$ indicates that role r must be replaced with different μ_r roles, so that each user having a relationship with role r would now have new relationships with μ_r different roles;
- $-\delta c(r)$ indicates that the cost related to other business information about r is no longer needed.

In order to reduce the administration cost, Eq. (7.2) must thus be negative, that is:

$$(\mu_r - 1)u_r \leq \sigma p_r + \tau + vc(r) \tag{7.3}$$

where $\sigma = \beta/\alpha$, $\tau = \gamma/\alpha$ and $v = \delta/\alpha$. According to Eq. (7.3), deleting a role from the candidate role-set is advantageous when the role is not supported by a sufficient number of users. The deletion becomes more advantageous as the role's degree increases or as the number of roles needed to replace it decreases. It should be noted that:

- when $\tau = 0$ (that is $\gamma = 0$) no weight is given to the number of roles;
- when $\sigma = 0$ (that is $\beta = 0$) no weight is given to the management of role-permission assignment;
- when $\sigma, \tau, v \to \infty$ (that is $\alpha \to 0$) no weight is given to the management of role-user assignment. Since Eq. (7.3) is always true, deleting roles not affecting the completeness property is always worthwhile.

The choice of parameters σ, τ, and v is clearly dependent on the company we analyze, while $c(r)$ fluctuates based on its specific definition. However, p_r is constant respecting the role, while u_r and μ_r vary according to deletion of other roles, as follows:

u_r **analysis** Given two roles $r_1, r_2 \in ROLES$ such that $auth\_perms(r_1) \supset auth\_perms(r_2)$, it is more advantageous that all users possessing all the permissions of r_1 be assigned to r_1 and not to r_2. In fact, in the latter case further user-role assignments would be necessary. If r_1 is deleted, users assigned to r_1 would probably be assigned to r_2, resulting in an increase in the variable u_{r_2}. Only roles whose permissions are proper supersets of the deleted role are affected. In the case in which role r_1 has one or more 1:1 or 1:n equivalent supersets, no user will be assigned to role r_1, thus we will have $u_{r_1} = 0$. This implies that all candidate roles having equivalent roles that are also supersets in terms of permissions can always be deleted since Eq. (7.3) is always true.

μ_r **analysis** The roles which may replace r have to be exclusively sought among proper subsets in terms of permissions. Deleting a role whose permissions are a subset of the current one can result in growth of μ_r if, for instance, instead of such a subset we choose roles with lower degrees. In other cases, deletion of a role whose permissions are subset of the current one may prevent the deletion of role r.

7.3.2   *Finding the Optimum* ⋆

In the previous section we detailed how the administration cost can vary after the deletion of a candidate role. The optimal set is certainly to be a subset of the *PERMS* lattice. The aim is thus to identify which combinations must be deleted from the *PERMS* lattice to obtain the minimum cost while maintaining the completeness property.

The order in which the deletions take place is relevant when testing Eq. (7.3). In particular, deleting a role exclusively affects the cost of direct parents and children. However, deleting a parent or child role can affect the deletion of other roles. Thus, the problem of identifying the correct set of roles to delete is not trivial. One possible solution is to scan the whole solutions space in search of a set that minimizes administration cost. Although such an algorithm leads to the optimal set, it is unfeasible as it has exponential complexity. In fact, finding the best solution is an $\mathcal{NP}$-hard problem [Molloy *et al.* (2010)]. This can also be proven by setting $\alpha, \gamma = 1$, and $\beta, \delta = 0$ in Eq. (7.1), as the identification of the optimal set becomes equivalent to the *Role Mining Problem* (RMP) described in [Vaidya *et al.* (2007)], which has proved to be $\mathcal{NP}$-complete.

Next section introduces an algorithm that allows us to approximate the optimal solution.

7.4   Finding Sub-Optimal Role-Sets ⋆

In this section we present an algorithm, called **RBAM** (*Role-Based Association-rule Mining*), that offers a sub-optimal solution for the problem of identifying the optimal candidate role-set. The heuristic introduced by RBAM are discussed throughout the section, highlighting how these do not invalidate the quality of the obtained output. Supporting examples will be given at the end of this section.

Other possible algorithms to minimize the cost function have been proposed by Molloy *et al.* (2010) and Takabi and Joshi (2010), but not detailed in this book.

7.4.1   *Lattice Generation* ⋆

The generation of the candidate role-set based on the *PERMS* lattice is derived from the **Apriori** algorithm introduces in Chap. 6. **Apriori** can be seen as an algorithm for the generation of a partial lattice. The solutions space is obtained by pruning the combinations whose support is lower than a pre-established and constant minimum. We now provide the following definition:

Definition 7.3. Among all users possessing the permissions assigned to role r, only a subset will likely be assigned to r. Therefore, we define *actual support*, as $actual\_support(r) = |ass\_users(r)|/|USERS|$.

Eq. (7.3) shows that the gain introduced by a role is related to the number of users assigned to such a role. Since $u_r = |ass\_users(r)|$ then $actual\_support(r) = u_r/|USERS|$, so that Eq. (7.3) becomes:

$$(\mu_r - 1)\, actual\_support(r) \leq \bar{\sigma} p_r + \bar{\tau} + \bar{\upsilon} c(r) \tag{7.4}$$

where $\bar{\sigma}$, $\bar{\tau}$ and $\bar{\upsilon}$ are obtained from σ, τ and υ dividing them by $|USERS|$. Equation (7.4) presents the advantage of being normalized by the number of users, thus $\bar{\sigma}$, $\bar{\tau}$ and $\bar{\upsilon}$ may be specified as parameters independent from the set UP to be analyzed.

Eq. (7.4) may be used to implement an Apriori version with *variable minimum support*. Only roles not increasing the administration cost of previously calculated roles will be generated. The proposed RBAM algorithm is consequently composed of the following steps:

Step 1 An initial analysis of the set UP provides the set R_1 containing candidate roles of degree 1 with a support greater than the minimum.

Step k When $k \geq 2$ set R_k is generated merging all possible role pairs in R_{k-1} (*join step*). In order not to generate roles with the same permission set, a lexicographical order for the permission is given. Thus, only role pairs differing in the greater permission are considered. Combinations not meeting minimum support constraints are rejected (*prune step*). Hierarchical association set H_k is also identified, relating roles in R_k whose assigned permissions are a superset of permissions assigned to roles in R_{k-1}.

Stop The algorithm completes when $R_k = \emptyset$, returning $ROLES$ as the union of all calculated R_i and RH as the union of all calculated H_i.

Compared to the Apriori algorithm, the produced set RH is equivalent to "association-rules" between itemsets. Since we supposed a non hierarchical RBAC model, RH is not intended for inheritance of role-permission or role-user assignments. Nevertheless, identifying hierarchical relationships is still worthwhile, since it provides a means to "navigate" the candidate roles.

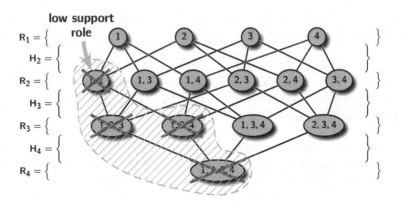

Fig. 7.1: An instance of Theorem 7.1

The first difference from Apriori is represented by the pruning operation. The minimum support constraint used in the prune step is a particular case of Eq. (7.4). In fact:

- During the step k, level-$(k + 1)$ roles are not yet generated. Thus, we have that $support(r) = actual\_support(r)$ for each $r \in R_k$.
- The join step combines role pairs calculated in the previous step which differ by only one permission. Then, all roles in R_k have degree k. This means that $p_r = k$ for each $r \in R_k$.
- Each role in R_k is established by merging a pair of roles in R_{k-1}, therefore it is always $\mu_r = 2$.

Starting from Eq. (7.4), we can define the following pruning condition:

$$support(r) > \bar{\sigma}k + \bar{\tau} + \bar{\upsilon}c(r). \qquad (7.5)$$

In order to preserve all the properties of the Apriori algorithm, the correctness of the prune step must be ensured through the following theorem:

Theorem 7.1. *Given* $r_1, r_2 \in ROLES$ *such that* $r_1 \succeq r_2$ *and* $c(r_1) \geq c(r_2)$, *if a role does not satisfy Eq. (7.5), then none of its child roles will be generated.*

On the basis of Theorem 7.1, if a role r is rejected because of minimal support, then all its child roles will certainly not be generated (see Fig. 7.1). This is coherent with the Apriori approach, but it does not always lead to the optimal administration cost. In fact, a role r with degree $k + 1$, by construction of the algorithm, should be generated at step $k + 1$. The generation of r could result in the deletion of level-k roles as it decreases users assigned to parents. However, Eq. (7.5) does not take into account that generation of a role may result in the deletion of other roles.

Another important observation is that applying Eq. (7.5) when $k = 1$ implies that all permissions whose support is too low are rejected. This means that the candidate role-set *is not always complete*. Rejected permissions must be individually managed through the creation of an *ad hoc* role for each permission. The number of users with such permissions is low, hence the approximation is usually acceptable.

Notice that when children of r are generated in step $k + 1$, the value of u_r will decrease. This means that immediately after the generation of level-$(k + 1)$, Eq. (7.4) must be checked again for all level-k roles. At the end of level k the RBAM-purge procedure performs such an operation. This represents the other main difference from Apriori. RBAM-purge is described in the following section.

7.4.2 *Removing Costly Roles★*

Since the generation of level-k roles influences the variable u_r of level-$(k-1)$ roles, further deletion of generated roles may thus be necessary. Figure 7.2 details the RBAM-purge procedure used to do so. The algorithm performs operations upon the following data structures:

- The set *ROLES*. It represents the union of all the sets R_k. For each $r \in ROLES$ are identified:

  (a) r.supp: role r support;
  (b) r.act_supp: role r actual support;
  (c) r.degree: the number of permissions assigned to r.

- The set *RH* that hierarchically links candidate roles to one another. It represents the union of all sets H_k. This means that *only direct relationships are determined*. For each $h \in RH$ are identified:

  (a) h.prnt and h.child: parent and child roles hierarchically related;
  (b) h.conf: confidence value between roles.

- The set *PA*. This set merely correlates candidate roles with their assigned permissions.
- The set *UA*. It contains the *proposed role-user assignments*. At the end of step k, relationships between users and permissions assigned to the level-k roles are added to the set.

```
 1: procedure RBAM-PURGE($R_{k-1}, H_k, H_{k-1}, PA, UA, \bar{\sigma}, \bar{\tau}, \bar{v}$)
 2:     {Remove from parents the users also assigned to children}
 3:     $UA \leftarrow \{\langle u, r \rangle \in UA \mid u \notin \bigcup_{h \in H_k : h.\text{prnt}=r} ass\_users(h.\text{child})\}$
 4:     for all $r \in R_{k-1}$ do
 5:         $r.\text{act\_supp} \leftarrow |\{\langle u, r' \rangle \in UA \mid r' = r\}|/|USERS|$
 6:     end for

 7:     {Identify removable roles with low support}
 8:     $\Delta \leftarrow \{r \in R_{k-1} \mid r.\text{act\_supp} = 0 \vee (r.\text{act\_supp} \leq \bar{\sigma}(k-1)+\bar{\tau}+\bar{v}c(r) \wedge$
 9:                 $r.\text{supp} \cdot |USERS| = |\bigcup_{h \in H_{k-1} : h.\text{child}=r} ass\_users(h.\text{prnt})|)\}$

10:     {Remove roles with low support}
11:     for all $r \in \Delta$ do
12:         {Transfer only direct hierarchies}
13:         for all $h_p \in H_{k-1}, h_c \in H_k : h_p.\text{child} = h_c.\text{prnt} = r$ do
14:             if $\nexists h' \in H_k : h'.\text{child} = h_c.\text{child} \wedge h'.\text{prnt} \notin \Delta \wedge$
15:                         $\wedge ass\_perms(h'.\text{prnt}) \supseteq ass\_perms(h_p.\text{prnt})$ then
16:                 $h.\text{prnt} \leftarrow h_p.\text{prnt}$
17:                 $h.\text{child} \leftarrow h_c.\text{child}$
18:                 $h.\text{conf} \leftarrow h_p.\text{conf} \cdot h_c.\text{conf}$
19:                 $H_k \leftarrow H_k \cup \{h\}$
20:             end if
21:         end for

22:         {Transfer users to parents, then remove r}
23:         $UA \leftarrow \{\langle u, r' \rangle \mid \exists h \in RH, u \in USERS :$
24:                         $h.\text{prnt} = r' \wedge h.\text{child} = r \wedge \langle u, r \rangle \in UA\}$
25:         for all $r' \in \{h.\text{prnt} \mid h \in RH \wedge h.\text{child} = r\}$ do
26:             $r'.\text{act\_supp} \leftarrow |\{\langle u, r'' \rangle \in UA \mid r'' = r'\}|/|USERS|$
27:         end for
28:         $R_{k-1} \leftarrow R_{k-1} \setminus \{r\}$
29:         $H_{k-1} \leftarrow \{h \in H_{k-1} \mid h.\text{child} \neq r\}$
30:         $H_k \leftarrow \{h \in H_k \mid h.\text{prnt} \neq r\}$
31:         $PA \leftarrow \{\langle p, r' \rangle \in PA \mid r' \neq r\}$
32:         $UA \leftarrow \{\langle u, r' \rangle \in UA \mid r' \neq r\}$
33:     end for
34:
35:     return $\langle R_k, R_{k-1}, H_k, H_{k-1}, PA, UA \rangle$
36: end procedure
```

Fig. 7.2: RBAM-purge procedure, used to implement RBAM as a customized version of Apriori

Figure 7.2 provides the following steps:

- *Lines 3–6*: Among the users assigned to level-$(k-1)$ roles, those assigned to level k children are removed from UA, thus updating the actual support.
- *Lines 8–9*: All level-$(k-1)$ roles that meet Eq. (7.5) are identified after level-k role generation. Such roles can be deleted only if they preserve the completeness property, that is $u_r = 0$ (there is a 1:1 or 1:n equivalence with their children) or there are suitable sets of parent roles to replace them.
- *Lines 11–33*: Users assigned to roles being deleted are transferred to their parents. Hierarchies are transferred to children, ensuring that indirect hierarchy relationships are not generated. Then roles are deleted.

The algorithm introduces some approximations. Indeed, if a level-k role is deleted, the value of u_r relating to a level-$(k-1)$ role r could grow, so that Eq. (7.4) is not likely to be satisfied. However, before step k is performed, Eq. (7.4) could have been satisfied for role r. Thus it could have been deleted. If this is the case, the algorithm does not undelete r. Another approximation is represented by lines 8–9. Variable μ_r does not explicitly appear as it is presumed to always be equal to 2. This gets rid of the need to calculate the actual value of μ_r, but it can result in a higher number of deletions with respect to the optimal solution. Another simplification is introduced in lines 23–24, which "transfer" the users assigned to deleted roles to *all* their parents, without identifying a minimum set of parent roles to replace deleted roles. In this way, it is likely to have proposed more role-user assignments than actually needed, leaving to the administrator the burden of selecting the best subset among all proposed roles. This cannot be avoided without providing further elements defining role semantics.

Regarding hierarchical relationships, when a role is deleted all the relationships with the parents must be "transferred" to the child roles. When a path between the child role and the inherited parent already exists, this operation can create indirect hierarchical relationships. Analyzing the set PA helps us determine if a hierarchical relationship must (or must not) be inherited. Given $r_1, r_2 \in ROLES$ such that $r_1 \to r_2$, where r_2 is the role being deleted, r_1 inherits $p \in ROLES$ such that of $r_2 \to p$ if and only if: $\nexists p' \in ROLES : r_1 \to p' \land ass\_perms(p') \supseteq ass\_perms(p)$. This is reflected in lines 14–15. In this way, we guarantee that RH only contains direct relationships. According to Lemma 5.2, the confidence of a new relationship is calculated as the product of confidences along the hierarchical path.

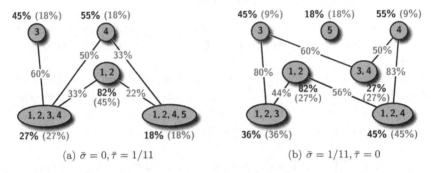

(a) $\bar{\sigma} = 0, \bar{\tau} = 1/11$ (b) $\bar{\sigma} = 1/11, \bar{\tau} = 0$

User	Permissions	Roles (a)	Roles (b)
A	3	{3}	{3}
B	4	{4}	{4}
C	1, 2	{1, 2}	{1, 2}
D	1, 2	{1, 2}	{1, 2}
E	1, 2	{1, 2}	{1, 2}
F	1, 2, 3	{1, 2} + {3}	{1, 2, 3}
G	1, 2, 3, 4	{1, 2, 3, 4}	{1, 2, 3} + {1, 2, 4} + {3, 4}
H	1, 2, 3, 4	{1, 2, 3, 4}	{1, 2, 3} + {1, 2, 4} + {3, 4}
I	1, 2, 3, 4, 5	{1, 2, 3, 4} + {1, 2, 4, 5}	{1, 2, 3} + {1, 2, 4} + {3, 4} + {5}
J	1, 2, 4	{1, 2} + {4}	{1, 2, 4}
K	1, 2, 4, 5	{1, 2, 4, 5}	{1, 2, 4} + {5}

(c) Input user-permission assignment and proposed role-user assignment for examples (a) and (b)

Fig. 7.3: Application of RBAM to toy examples

7.4.3 Examples ★

Two instances of the RBAM algorithm are provided below and summarized in Fig. 7.3. Edges in the represented graph show confidence values, while values next to nodes show *support()* in bold and *actual_support()* between brackets.

Fig. 7.3a shows the application of the algorithm to the data in Fig. 7.3c, given $\tau = 1/11$ and $\sigma, v = 0$. The cost of this model is:

$$|UA| + \sigma|PA| + \tau|ROLES| = 14 + 0 \times 12 + 1 \times 5 = 19$$

where the obtained value is divided by the parameter α. Since $\tau \neq 0$, the algorithm produces a low number of roles and attempts to minimize the number of user-role relationships. In fact, each user is assigned to a single role except for F, I, and J who are assigned to two roles. To understand the minimality of the result, it should be noted that the set $ROLES = \{\{1\}, \{2\}, \{3\}, \{4\}, \{5\}\}$ also consists of five roles. In this case, the number of user-role assignments would be higher as each user should be assigned to a number of roles equal to the permissions held, that is $|PA| = 31$.

Fig. 7.3b details the case in which $\tau, v = 0$ and $\sigma = 1/11$. The cost of the obtained model divided by α is:

$$|UA| + \sigma|PA| + \tau|ROLES| = 19 + 1 \times 13 + 0 \times 7 = 32.$$

Since $\sigma \neq 0$, the algorithm generates roles with lower degree than the previous example. However, due to the approximations introduced by the algorithm, three roles are proposed for G, H, and I, even if only two are strictly necessary. Indeed, for these users it is sufficient to assign only one couple among $\{\,\{1,2,3\}, \{3,4\}\,\}$, $\{\,\{1,2,4\}, \{3,4\}\,\}$ and $\{\,\{1,2,3\}, \{1,2,4\}\,\}$. The final decision can only be made by an administrator who knows the actual meaning of the permissions grouping. By deleting the redundant role $\{1,3\}$, the administration cost would become $16 + 1 \times 11 + 0 \times 6 = 27$.

The cost advantage obtained through the RBAM algorithm can be seen in comparison to the administration cost of an access control system which does not rely on the RBAC model. We can think about an RBAC model consisting of roles having only one permission, simulating a situation in which the permissions are directly assigned to users. The administration cost of role-permission relationships can be overlooked (that is $\sigma = 0$) as it could be easily automated. Given $\tau = 1/11$ the cost without RBAC would be:

$$|UA| + \tau|ROLES| = 31 + 1 \times 5 = 36.$$

Using RBAM the cost is almost half compared to the result provided in Fig. 7.3a.

7.4.4 *Testing With Real Data*★

To assess the efficiency of the RBAM algorithm, many tests have been conducted using real data. In order to highlight the properties of the algorithm, consider analysis results of data from an application presenting a heterogeneous distribution of permissions among users. Thus, the resulting authorization situation was virtually unanalyzable using standard role mining tools. In total, 4743 users possessing 2907 permissions were analyzed. By applying the RBAM algorithm with $\bar{\tau} = 200/4743 = 4.2\%$ and $\bar{\sigma} = 0$, the total of 42 roles were generated. The related cost is:

$$|UA| + \sigma|PA| + \tau|ROLES| = 6547 + 0 \times 100 + 200 \times 42 = 14947.$$

Not all the 2907 permissions were analyzed by RBAM, since only 23 permissions were held by at least 200 users (that is $\bar{\tau} = 4.2\%$). In particular, 4161 users (88%) were possessing these permissions. Without RBAC, the administration cost of the aforementioned 23 permissions would be:

$$|UA| + \sigma|PA| + \tau|ROLES| = 31557 + 0 \times 23 + 200 \times 23 = 36157$$

reducing the cost by 59%. Of course, the result can drastically improve if more complex cost functions are used.

The remaining $2907 - 23 = 2884$ permissions were scattered over 4654 users through 32182 user-permission associations. Consequently, permissions must be individually managed. Alternatively, the value of τ should be decreased so that more permissions can be considered. Otherwise, the analysis can be restricted to only those permission belonging to a single application module.

Finally, we consider computational complexity. It could be showed that in the worst case scenario RBAM is $\mathcal{NP}$-hard, as it derives from Apriori [Yang (2006)]. However, performing tests on real data sets has shown the algorithm to be quite efficient when using suitable values for parameters $\bar{\sigma}$ and $\bar{\tau}$ despite the tens of thousands of users and thousands of permissions. For example, if the value of $\bar{\tau}$ is high (i.e. we find only permission sets belonging to a large number of users) most of the permission lattice is pruned, thus reducing the combinations being analyzed.

7.5   Final Remarks

In this chapter we described a formal model to derive optimal role-users assignment. This model is driven by a cost-based function, where the cost is expressed in terms of the administration effort in managing the resulting RBAC model. Further, we proposed the RBAM algorithm, that approximates the optimal solution for this cost-based model. For specific parameter settings, the proposed algorithm even emulates other known algorithms.

PART 3

Devising Meaningful Roles

This part copes with the problem of assigning a *business meaning* to roles. To this aim, different approaches are proposed. First, we introduce a metric to assess how "good" are roles from a business perspective. The key observation is that a role is likely to be meaningful from a business perspective when it involves activities within the same business process or organizational units within the same branch. Second, a novel approach referred to as *visual role mining* is also delineated. The key idea is that of adopting a visual representation of existing user-permission assignments, hence allowing for a quick analysis and elicitation of meaningful roles. We propose a few algorithms that seek to best represent user-permission relationships.

Chapter 8

Measuring the Meaning of Roles

As stated in Chap. 3, a key problem that has not yet been adequately addressed by existing role mining approaches is how to propose roles that have *business meaning*. To this aim, this chapter provides a formal framework that leverages business information—such as business processes and organization structure—to implement role mining algorithms. Our key observation is that a role is likely to be meaningful from a business perspective when it involves activities within the same business process or organizational units within the same branch. To measure the "spreading" of a role among business processes or organization structure, we resort to centrality indices. Such indices are used in our cost-driven approach described in Chap. 7 during the role mining process. Finally, we illustrate the application of the framework through a few examples.

8.1 Meaningful Roles

According to Chap. 2, the most important benefit of adopting RBAC is that *it minimizes system administration effort* due to the reduced number of relationships required to relate users to permissions. RBAC offers benefits to business users as well. A role represents a job function or a title established for a set of users within an organization. Thus, the adoption of RBAC makes it easier to define security policies by business users who have no knowledge of IT systems. For this reason, *business alignment* is always required during the security policies definition and, in particular, to establish the rational for roles.

To capture the needs and functions of the company, and thus maximizing the advantages offered by roles, the model must be customized through a proper role engineering process. Role mining can drastically reduce the burden of role engineers. However, a key problem that affect existing role mining approaches is how to propose roles that have business meaning. Roles discovered by analyzing existing access permissions through role mining algorithms are often no more than a set of permissions with no connection to the business practice. Indeed, the main objective of most of the role mining approaches is only to reduce the number of roles or to simplify the access control administration from a system perspective. But organizations are unwilling to deploy roles they cannot understand, even though such roles are limited in number.

In the remainder of this chapter we provide a formal framework for role engineering that also enjoys practical relevance. The framework allows for the implementation of a concrete hybrid role engineering approach through the combination of existing role mining algorithms (bottom-up approach) and business analysis (top-down approach). In particular, we describe how business processes and organization structure can be modeled in order to define a *metric* for evaluating the business meaning of candidate role-sets. This metric is used during the role mining algorithm execution to establish which roles should be included in the candidate role-set. The key insight is that a role is likely to be meaningful from a business perspective when: it involves activities within the same business process; or, it involves users belonging to the same organization structure branch. To measure the spreading of a role among business processes or organization units we resort to *centrality*, a well-known concept in graph theory. In particular, we define two different centrality indices, namely the *activity-spread* and the *organization-unit-spread*. Leveraging our cost-driven approach (see Chap. 7) makes it feasible to take into account the proposed indices during the role mining process.

8.2 Modeling Business

In this section we shall provide some models to formally describe business information. These models will be later used to formalize the main contribution of this chapter.

8.2.1 *Business Activities*

Activities (or *tasks*) are a natural way to think about user actions and their contexts [Colantonio *et al.* (2009a)]. Activities usually arise from the decomposition of the *business processes* of an organization. A business process is a collection of inter-related activities that accomplish a specific goal. From an access control point of view, an activity induces a set of permissions necessary to perform an elementary part of a more complex job. Activities are typically assigned to users on the basis of their job positions [Oh and Park (2003)].

Since the activity and the role concepts are similar in that they both group permissions, one might think that there is no difference between them. However, they have completely different meanings and characteristics. A role focuses on "actors" and places emphasis on *how* the business should be organized, while an activity focuses on "actions" and emphasizes *what* should be done. For example, a typical workflow management system requires that each actor should complete certain tasks. In this case, each task may be performed by several actors with different business roles. It would be ineffective to assign an RBAC role to each task. Neither should an activity be considered a "sub-role": role-permission relationships are identified with different rationales from activity-permission relationship identification.

It is important to highlight that defining and maintaining the activity model up to date can increase the workload of business users within the company. However, a good understanding of the organization is a mandatory requirement when implementing an access control management framework. Therefore, the activity model is already available within an organization.

In the following we formally describe the activity concept.

Activity Tree ★ Decomposing the business processes of an organization usually results in an activity tree structure. For the sake of simplicity, we do not make a formal distinction between business processes and activities. In particular [Colantonio *et al.* (2009a)]:

- The set $ACTVT$ contains all activities.
- The set $ACTVT\text{-}H \subseteq ACTVT \times ACTVT \times \mathbb{R}$ defines a partial order on the hierarchy tree. The pair $\langle a_p, a_c, w \rangle \in ACTVT\text{-}H$ indicates that the activity a_p is the parent of the activity a_c, whereas w is the *weight* of the connection between a_p and a_c (see below). The existence of the tuple $\langle a_p, a_c, w \rangle$ in $ACTVT\text{-}H$ may alternatively be indicated as $a_c \xrightarrow{w} a_p$. The simplified notation $a_c \rightarrow a_p$ can also be used when w is always 1.
- $\forall a \in ACTVT$, the activity a has only one direct parent, namely $\forall a_p, a_c \in$

$$ACTVT: a_c \to a_p \implies \nexists a_p' \in ACTVT: a_p' \neq a_p, a_c \to a_p'.$$

- The activity tree has only one root.

Given a pair $a_p, a_c \in ACTVT$, the ordering operator $a_c \succeq a_p$ indicates the existence of a hierarchical pathway of "$\to$" from a_c to a_p. Note that, without loss of generality, it is always possible to identify a unique root for a set of activities; for example, a virtual activity that "collects" all the high level activities of the organization can always be defined.

Given an activity $a \in ACTVT$, the following sets can be defined out of convenience:

- $\uparrow a = \{a' \in ACTVT \mid a \succeq a'\}$ represents all possible parents of a. Since each activity has only one direct parent in the tree, $\uparrow a$ contains the path from a to the root of $ACTVT$-H. Note that $|\uparrow a|$ is the length of this path. Given a pair $a_1, a_2 \in ACTVT$, the value of $|\uparrow a_1 \cap \uparrow a_2|$ represents the length of the path from the root to the "nearest" common parent of both a_1, a_2.
- $\downarrow a = \{a' \in ACTVT \mid a' \succeq a\}$ represents all possible children of a.

Each activity is supported by sets of permissions which allow the activity to be performed. To execute a given activity, a user must have *all* the permissions associated to it. This concept can be formalized as follows:

- The set $ACTVT$-$A \subseteq ACTVT \times PERMS$ expresses the origin of a permission in a given activity.
- The function $actvt\_perms\colon ACTVT \to 2^{PERMS}$ provides the set of permissions associated to an activity. Given $a \in ACTVT$, it can be formalized as: $actvt\_perms(a) = \{p \in PERMS \mid \exists \langle a, p \rangle \in ACTVT\text{-}A\}$.
- The function $actvt\_perms^*\colon ACTVT \to 2^{PERMS}$ provides all the permissions assigned to a and its children, namely it takes into account the activity breakdown structure. Given $a \in ACTVT$, it can be formalized as: $actvt\_perms^*(a) = \{p \in PERMS \mid \exists a' \in \downarrow a : \langle a', p \rangle \in ACTVT\text{-}A\}$.

A permission can belong to multiple activities. Moreover, given the activity pair $a_1, a_2 \in ACTVT$ such that $a_1 \succeq a_2$ and $p \in PERMS$, if $\langle p, a_1 \rangle \in ACTVT$-$A$ then we require that $\langle p, a_2 \rangle \notin ACTVT$-$A$ since a_2 inherits p from its child.

Connection Weights ⋆   Assigning a weight to connections between activities is a flexible way to model the business process break-down structure [Colantonio *et al.* (2009a)]. In particular, weights indicate if there is a

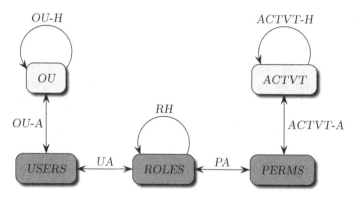

Fig. 8.1: Relationships among activities, organization units, and RBAC entities

strong or a weak decomposition. For example, there is likely to be a large weight value between the root activity and activities such as "Human Resources Management" or "Inventory Management." Conversely, the weight between the parent activity "Customer Data Management" and its child "Customer Data Update" is likely to be weak. How weights are derived depends on the given organization, however this topic is not further analyzed in this chapter.

The given weight definition can easily be extended to the partial order as the sum of weights along the path between activities. Given $a_c, a_p \in ACTVT : a_c \succeq a_p$, the weight of the path between them is:

$$w_{\text{actvt}}(a_c \succeq a_p) = \sum_{\omega \in \Omega} \omega, \ \Omega = \{\omega \in \mathbb{R} \mid \forall a, a' \in ACTVT,$$
$$\exists \langle a, a', \omega \rangle \in ACTVT\text{-}H : a_c \succeq a', \ a \succeq a_p\}. \quad (8.1)$$

Fig. 8.1 gives a graphical representation of the aforementioned entities and the interaction with the RBAC entities. It also depicts other elements described in next section.

8.2.2 Organization Units

An *organization unit* (OU) is a group of employees which collaborate to perform certain business tasks [Colantonio *et al.* (2009a)]. The organizational structure is designed by the top management and defines the lines of authority and the division of work. A typical organization is organized as a tree structure, represented by an organization chart. From an access control point of view, it is likely that users of the same OU have the same access permissions. For this reason, users usually have roles located within the organization units [Perwaiz and Sommerville (2001)].

There are many examples of benefits related to the introduction of the organization structures into the access control model. For instance, OUs are used in various frameworks as a means to identify user pools [Oh *et al.* (2006); Perwaiz and Sommerville (2001)]. In some of these works, roles can be assigned directly with OUs instead of individually with users. In this chapter, we prefer to directly assign users to roles, thus allowing a complete delegation of organization unit maintenance to HR.

The following is a formal description of the organization unit structure, that reflects the notation used in Sec. 8.2.1.

Organization Unit Tree ⋆   Organization units can usually be represented in a tree structure. In particular [Colantonio *et al.* (2009a)]:

- The set OU contains all organization units.
- The set $OU\text{-}H \subseteq OU \times OU \times \mathbb{R}$ defines a partial order on the hierarchy tree. The pair $\langle o_p, o_c, w \rangle \in OU\text{-}H$ indicates that the organization unit o_p is the parent of the organization unit o_c, whereas w is the *weight* of the connection between o_p and o_c (see below). The existence of the tuple $\langle o_p, o_c, w \rangle$ in $OU\text{-}H$ may alternatively be indicated as $o_c \xrightarrow{w} o_p$. The simplified notation $o_c \rightarrow o_p$ can also be used when w is always 1.
- $\forall a \in OU$, the organization unit a has only one direct parent, namely $\forall o_p, o_c \in OU : o_c \rightarrow o_p \implies \nexists a'_p \in OU : a'_p \neq o_p, o_c \rightarrow a'_p$.
- The organization unit tree has only one root.

Given a pair $o_p, o_c \in OU$, the ordering operator $o_c \succeq o_p$ indicates the existence of a hierarchical pathway of "$\rightarrow$" from o_c to o_p. Note that, without loss of generality, it is always possible to identify a unique root for the organization units—namely, a unit representing the entire organization. Given an organization unit $o \in OU$, we define:

- $\uparrow o = \{o' \in OU \mid o \succeq o'\}$ represents all possible parents of o. It contains the path from o to the root of $OU\text{-}H$, thus $|\uparrow o|$ is the length of this path. Given $o_1, o_2 \in OU$, $|\uparrow o_1 \cap \uparrow o_2|$ is the length of the path from the root to the "nearest" common parent of both o_1, o_2.
- $\downarrow o = \{o' \in OU \mid o' \succeq o\}$ is the set of all children of o.

Each organization unit contains a sets of users. This concept can be formalized as follows:

- The set $OU\text{-}A \subseteq OU \times USERS$ expresses the origin of a user in a given organization unit.
- The function $ou\_users \colon OU \to 2^{USERS}$ provides the set of users belonging to an organization unit. Given an organization unit $o \in OU$, it can be formalized as: $ou\_users(o) = \{u \in USERS \mid \exists \langle o, u \rangle \in OU\text{-}A\}$.
- The function $ou\_users^* \colon OU \to 2^{USERS}$ provides all the users belonging to o and its children, namely it takes into account the organization unit breakdown structure. Given $o \in OU$, it can be formalized as: $ou\_users^*(o) = \{u \in USERS \mid \exists o' \in \downarrow o : \langle o', u \rangle \in OU\text{-}A\}$.

Usually, each user belongs to only one organization unit. Hence, given $o_1, o_2 \in OU$ and $u \in USERS$, if $\langle u, o_1 \rangle \in OU\text{-}A$, then $\langle u, o_2 \rangle \notin OU\text{-}A$.

Connection Weights $\star$ Weighting connections between OUs is a new concept when compared to the existing framework related to OUs [Colantonio *et al.* (2009a)]. It is a more flexible way to model the organization break-down structure. For example, user sets can be divided into various *administrative domains* represented by organization unit branches [Oh *et al.* (2006)]. It is assumed that each domain is independently administered. In such a case, weights may indicate whether domains are loosely or tightly coupled. Another case is when OUs are decomposed into a set of branches to model geographic areas; this often represents a weak partitioning since there are no big differences among users across different geographic areas. Decomposing a project in various working teams is another example of weak partitioning, since all users work for the same objectives. Conversely, domains represented by business units are more important as they usually identify users assigned with completely different jobs. Therefore, this is an example of strong OU partitioning.

The weight concept can be easily extended to the partial order as the sum of all weights between units along the shortest path between them. Given $o_c, o_p \in OU : o_c \succeq o_p$, the weight of the path between them is:

$$\mathrm{w_{ou}}(o_c \succeq o_p) = \sum_{\omega \in \Omega} \omega, \ \Omega = \{\omega \in \mathbb{R} \mid \forall o, o' \in OU,$$
$$\exists \langle o, o', \omega \rangle \in OU\text{-}H : o_c \succeq o', \ o \succeq o_p\}. \quad (8.2)$$

Fig. 8.1 gives a representation of the aforementioned entities and the interaction with standard RBAC entities.

8.3 Measuring the Meaning of Roles

In this section we demonstrate how the business processes model and the organization structure model can be leveraged to evaluate the business meaning of roles elicited by role mining algorithms. We define a *metric* for evaluating the business meaning of candidate role-sets. This metric is used during the role mining algorithm execution to establish which roles should be included in the candidate role-set. The key insight is that a role is likely to be meaningful from a business perspective when: it involves activities within the same business process; or, it involves users belonging to the same organization structure branch. To measure the "spreading" of a role among business processes or organization units we resort to *centrality*, a well-known concept in graph theory. In particular, we define two different centrality indices, namely the *activity-spread* and the *organization-unit-spread*. Leveraging a cost-driven approach (see Chap. 7) makes it feasible to take into account the proposed indices during the role mining process. Finally, we demonstrate the effectiveness of our proposal through a few examples and applications to real data. To measure the business meaning of roles, we introduce the following indices:

- *activity-spread* (detailed in Sec. 8.3.2) that measures the "dispersion" of business activities that are enabled by permissions assigned to a role;
- *organization-unit-spread* (detailed in Sec. 8.3.3) that measures the "dispersion" of organization units that users assigned to roles belong to.

The reason why we resort to business processes and organization structure is quite simple. Given $r \in ROLES$, it identifies both a set of permissions (i.e., $auth\_perms(r)$) and a set of users (i.e., $auth\_users(r)$). Hence, both these sets should be analyzed in order to evaluate the "quality" of the candidate role. Regarding the user set, the structure of the organization is probably the most significant business-related information that is always available in every medium to large sized organization. As a matter of fact, it is usually found within the HR-related IT systems. Similarly, business activities represent the main justification for the adoption of IT applications within a company. Indeed, each application is usually introduced to support business activities. Usually, the business activity tree can be provided by business staff.

Once activity-spread and organization-unit-spread indices are defined, we propose to adopt our cost-driven approach to take them into account during the role mining process. In particular, leveraging the cost function concept makes it possible to combine such indices with other "cost" elements in a single metric (function) to be used for the evaluation of elicited roles during the role mining process. Minimizing such a function means eliciting those roles that contextually minimize the overall administration effort and fit the needs of an organization from a business perspective. This approach is particularly suitable for role mining algorithms since it makes it possible to introduce business elements within the analyzed data, thus leading to a hybrid role engineering approach. Note though that identifying cost elements and then combining them in a cost function is something that can be done in several ways. This, however, is a completely separate subject of research and it is only marginally addressed here. Instead, we mainly focus on the formal description of business elements that can contribute in defining a suitable cost function.

8.3.1 *Farness* ⋆

We first introduce a tool that is particularly useful in topology and related areas in mathematics. This tool will be adapted to our analysis in order to consider business information during the role mining process. Given a graph, we usually refer to a sequence of vertices connected by edges as a *walk*. We also refer to a walk with no repeated vertices as a *path*, while the shortest path between two vertices is referred to as a *geodesic*. These concepts make it possible to introduce the *farness* index [Colantonio *et al.* (2009a)], namely a quantity related to the lengths of the geodesics from one vertex to every other vertex in the graph. Vertices that "tend" to have long geodesic distances to other vertices within the graph have higher farness. In the literature it is more common to find another index in place of farness, that is the *closeness* index. Closeness is the inverse of farness, so they can be considered perfectly equivalent. Both farness and closeness are examples of *centrality* measures [Wasserman and Faust (1994)].

The farness index that is used in this chapter can be defined in every metric space where a notion of distance between elements is defined. Given a vertex v_j, its farness f is:

$$f = \frac{\sum_{i=1}^{n} d(i,j)}{n-1}, \tag{8.3}$$

where $d(i,j)$ is the distance between the vertices v_i and v_j.

Other centrality measures such as *betweenness*, *degree*, and *eigenvector* centrality [Wasserman and Faust (1994)] might be applicable to our analysis. Since farness is the most suitable and simple one for our analysis, we omit discussions of the others.

8.3.2   *Activity-Spread*

We now describe an index intended to evaluate business meaning. It is based on the analysis of business processes and their decomposition into activities. For this purpose, we observe that a typical organization is unlikely to have users that perform activities derived from different business processes. For example, given the processes "Human Resources Management" and "Inventory Management", it is very difficult that the organization needs a role that simultaneously allows activities within both these processes. This observation might also be applicable to the decomposition of a business process into simpler activities. It is difficult to have the same users involved in "Training and development" and "Recruitment" of employees, even though they are both activities of "Human Resources Management." However, this constraint becomes weaker as we compare simpler activities; for example, "Screening" and "Selection" might be two possible activities of "Recruitment", but it now becomes possible for a single user to perform both of them.

In general, given a role and the activities involved with it, the basic idea is that a role is likely to have a business meaning when such activities are "close" to one another within the process break-down structure. According to this, "Screening" and "Selection" are close since they are both children activities of "Recruitment"; instead, "Screening" is far from any other activity below "Inventory Management."

To measure the spreading of a role within the activity tree we resort to the farness concept introduced in Sec. 8.3.1. Given a role, farness may be used to evaluate the distances among activities granted by the role. After having calculated the farness index for each involved activity, averaging such indices offers a metric to capture the "degree of spread" of the role among its activities. We refer to such an index as *activity-spread* of a role [Colantonio *et al.* (2009a)]. The higher the activity-spread is, the less business meaning the role has.

Distance Function $\star$ Before describing the activity-spread index in a formal way, we need to introduce the *distance* among two activities $a, a' \in$

ACTVT as:

$$d_{\text{actvt}}(a, a') = w_{\text{actvt}}(a \succeq \bar{a}) + w_{\text{actvt}}(a' \succeq \bar{a}),$$

$$\bar{a} = \{\alpha \in (\uparrow a \cap \uparrow a') \mid \forall \alpha' \in (\uparrow a \cap \uparrow a') : \alpha \succeq \alpha'\}, \quad (8.4)$$

whereas $\bar{a}$ is the nearest common parent of a, a'. If weights between activities are always equal to 1, the following alternative distance definition can be given:

$$d_{\text{actvt}}(a, a') = |\uparrow a| + |\uparrow a'| - 2 |\uparrow a \cap \uparrow a'|. \quad (8.5)$$

Since activities are organized as a tree with a unique root, Eq. (8.5) represents the number of edges between a and a'. Indeed, the distance between two vertices is the number of edges in the geodesic connecting them. Furthermore, it can be easily shown that the activity set is a metric space, since the provided function d_{actvt} is a metric; that is, given activities $a, a', a'' \in ACTVT$ the following properties holds:

- Distance is positive between two different activities, and precisely zero from an activity to itself, namely: $d_{\text{actvt}}(a, a') \geq 0$, and $d_{\text{actvt}}(a, a') = 0 \iff a = a'$.
- The distance between two activities is the same in either directions, namely: $d_{\text{actvt}}(a, a') = d_{\text{actvt}}(a', a)$.
- The distance between two activities is the shortest one along any path, namely: $d_{\text{actvt}}(a, a'') \leq d_{\text{actvt}}(a, a') + d_{\text{actvt}}(a', a'')$ *(triangle inequality)*.

Activity-Spread Formalization ★ Given a role $r \in ROLES$, we identify the set of activities allowed by the role r as

$$\mathcal{A}_r = \{a \in ACTVT \mid \nexists a' \in (\downarrow a) \setminus \{a\}, \text{auth\_perms}(r) \supseteq \text{actvt\_perms}^*(a),$$

$$\text{auth\_perms}(r) \supseteq \text{actvt\_perms}^*(a')\}. \quad (8.6)$$

Eq. (8.6) requires that *all* the permissions needed to execute the activities of $\mathcal{A}_r$ must be assigned to the role r. Thus, $\mathcal{A}_r$ contains only those activities that are allowed by assigning a user just to the role r. Further, given $a \in \mathcal{A}_r$ none of the parents of a are contained in $\mathcal{A}_r$, that is $\mathcal{A}_r$ contains only activities that are farther from the root.

We therefore define the *activity farness* for $a \in \mathcal{A}_r$ as:

$$d_{\mathcal{A}_r}(a) = \frac{1}{|\mathcal{A}_r| - 1} \sum_{a' \in \mathcal{A}_r} d_{\text{actvt}}(a, a'). \quad (8.7)$$

Eq. (8.7) directly derives from Eq. (8.3) (see Sec. 8.3.1) by adopting the distance function d_{actvt}. The greater $d_{\mathcal{A}_r}(a)$ is, the farther a is from all other activities allowed by permissions assigned to r.

Now we define a metric that takes into consideration the farness generated among *all* activities in $\mathcal{A}_r$. To this aim, the *variance* concept is likely to be the most intuitive and suitable to use. Given the arithmetic mean of all the farness indices calculated over $\mathcal{A}_r$, namely

$$\bar{d}_{\mathcal{A}_r} = \frac{1}{|\mathcal{A}_r|} \sum_{a \in \mathcal{A}_r} d_{\mathcal{A}_r}(a) = \frac{1}{|\mathcal{A}_r|(|\mathcal{A}_r| - 1)} \sum_{a,a' \in \mathcal{A}_r} d_{\text{actvt}}(a, a'), \qquad (8.8)$$

we define the *activity-spread* of a role $r \in ROLES$ as the farness variance among all the activities in $\mathcal{A}_r$, that is:

$$actvt\_spread(r) = \left(\frac{1}{|\mathcal{A}_r|} \sum_{a \in \mathcal{A}_r} d_{\mathcal{A}_r}^2(a) \right) - \bar{d}_{\mathcal{A}_r}^2. \qquad (8.9)$$

Note that the value of $actvt\_spread(r)$ should be adjusted in order to assign a higher value to those roles associated with permissions that do not allow the execution of any activity. This way, it is possible to "dissuade" a role engineering process from eliciting roles where the corresponding permissions are not associated to any activities. Indeed, when a role contains permissions that are not related to any activities, it becomes harder to identify a business meaning for it. The number of permissions not related to activities are:

$$\left| auth\_perms(r) \setminus \bigcup\nolimits_{a \in \mathcal{A}_r} actvt\_perms(a) \right|. \qquad (8.10)$$

If Eq. (8.10) is equal to 0, there is no need to adjust $actvt\_spread(r)$. Otherwise, $actvt\_spread(r)$ may be multiplied by a coefficient that is proportional to Eq. (8.10).

8.3.3   *Organization-Unit-Spread*

We now describe an index to evaluate business meaning of roles by analyzing the organization unit structure. With this aim in mind, note that users located into different OUs are likely to perform different tasks. Moreover, a role used across multiple organization units may require the co-ordination of various administrators; thus, requiring a higher administration effort than one for roles used exclusively within a single organizational unit. Hence, the idea is that the more distant the involved organization units are from each other, the less business meaning the role has. The ideal situation is when a role is almost exclusively assigned with users belonging to the "most central" OUs. Similar to the previous section, we calculate a farness index for each OU involved by a role—namely those OUs which contain the users assigned to this role. After having calculated the farness index for each involved OU, averaging such indices offers a metric to capture the "degree of spread" of the role among OUs. We refer to such an index as *organization-unit-spread* of a role [Colantonio *et al.* (2009a)]. The higher the organization-unit-spread is, the less business meaning the role has.

Distance Function ★ Before formally describing the organization-unit-spread index, we need to introduce the *distance* among two organization units $o, o' \in OU$ as:

$$d_{ou}(o, o') = w_{ou}(o \succeq \bar{o}) + w_{ou}(o' \succeq \bar{o}), \quad \bar{o} = \{\omega \in (\uparrow o \cap \uparrow o') \mid$$
$$\forall \omega' \in (\uparrow o \cap \uparrow o') : \omega \succeq \omega'\}, \quad (8.11)$$

whereas $\bar{o}$ is the nearest common parent of o, o'. If weights between organization units are always equal to 1, the following alternative distance definition can be given:

$$d_{ou}(o, o') = |\uparrow o| + |\uparrow o'| - 2 |\uparrow o \cap \uparrow o'|. \quad (8.12)$$

Since organizational units are organized as a tree with a unique root, Eq. (8.12) represents the number of edges between o and o'. Furthermore, given $o, o', o'' \in OU$, for both distance definitions it can be demonstrated that:

- The distance is positive between two different organization units, and precisely zero from an organization unit to itself: $d_{ou}(o, o') \geq 0$, and $d_{ou}(o, o') = 0 \iff o = o'$.
- The distance between two organization units is the same in either direction: $d_{ou}(o, o') = d_{ou}(o', o)$.
- The distance between two organization units is the shortest one along any path: $d_{ou}(o, o'') \leq d_{ou}(o, o') + d_{ou}(o', o'')$ *(triangle inequality)*.

Organization-Unit-Spread Formalization ★ Note that the number of users supporting each organization unit can influence the administration cost of roles. Indeed, bigger OUs require more effort from a single administrator or perhaps require multiple administrators. For this reason, the spreading index must be influenced both by the organization structure and by the percentage of users assigned to a given role and contextually belonging to the same organization unit.

Given a role $r \in ROLES$, we define the following sets:

- The set $\mathcal{O}_r = \{o \in OU \mid \nexists o' \in (\downarrow o) \setminus \{o\}, auth\_users(r) \supseteq ou\_users^*(o),$ $auth\_users(r) \supseteq ou\_users^*(o')\}$, namely the set of organization units being involved with the role r.

- The set $\mathcal{U}_r = auth\_users(r)$, namely the set of users assigned to r.
- Given $o \in \mathcal{O}_r$, then $\mathcal{U}_o = ou\_users^*(o)$ is the set of users assigned to an organization unit o.

Given $o \in \mathcal{O}_r$ none of the parents of o is contained in $\mathcal{O}_r$, that is $\mathcal{O}_r$ contains only OUs that are farther from the root. We therefore define the *OU farness* index for $o \in \mathcal{O}_r$ as:

$$d_{\mathcal{O}_r}(o) = \frac{1}{|\mathcal{U}_r|} \sum_{o' \in \mathcal{O}_r} |\mathcal{U}_{o'} \cap \mathcal{U}_r| \, d_{ou}(o, o'). \tag{8.13}$$

We assume that $(1/|\mathcal{U}_r|) \sum_{o \in \mathcal{O}_r} |\mathcal{U}_o \cap \mathcal{U}_r| = 1$, namely organization units in $\mathcal{O}_r$ contain all the users assigned to r and no user simultaneously belongs to more than one OU. The greater $d_{\mathcal{O}_r}(o)$ is, the farther o is from OUs containing the majority of users assigned to r. For example, if there is one particular OU containing most of the users of the role, then $d_{\mathcal{O}_r}(o)$ is close to the distance between o and such an OU.

Now we define the *variance* of all farness indices related to organization units in $\mathcal{O}_r$. Given the weighted arithmetic mean of all the farness indices calculated upon $\mathcal{O}_r$, namely

$$\bar{d}_{\mathcal{O}_r} = \frac{1}{|\mathcal{U}_r|} \sum_{o \in \mathcal{O}_r} |\mathcal{U}_o \cap \mathcal{U}_r| \, d_{\mathcal{O}_r}(o) = \frac{1}{|\mathcal{U}_r|^2} \sum_{o, o' \in \mathcal{O}_r} |\mathcal{U}_o \cap \mathcal{U}_r| \, |\mathcal{U}_{o'} \cap \mathcal{U}_r| \, d_{ou}(o, o'),$$
$$\tag{8.14}$$

the *organization-unit-spread* is defined as

$$ou\_spread(r) = \left(\frac{1}{|\mathcal{U}_r|} \sum_{o \in \mathcal{O}_r} |\mathcal{U}_o \cap \mathcal{U}_r| \, d^2_{\mathcal{O}_r}(o) \right) - \bar{d}^2_{\mathcal{O}_r}. \tag{8.15}$$

Note that the value of $ou\_spread(r)$ grows when: OUs contain many users—identified through $|\mathcal{U}_o \cap \mathcal{U}_r|$; or, OUs are far from each other—according to $d^2_{\mathcal{O}_r}(o)$.

8.3.4　*Revising the Cost Function* ⋆

In this section we briefly explain how cost elements can be combined in a global cost function, leveraging our cost-driven approach. In general, finding the optimal candidate role-set can be seen as a *multi-objective optimization problem* [Deb (2001)]. An optimization problem is multi-objective when there are a number of objective functions that are to be minimized or maximized. Multi-objective optimization often means to trade-off conflicting goals. In a role engineering context, possible objectives are:

- Minimize the number of roles;
- Minimize the number of role possessed by each user;
- Maximize the business meaning of roles, that corresponds to minimizing the activity-spread and/or the organization-unit-spread indices of all elicited roles.

The previous statements can be formalized as:

- $\min\{|ROLES|\}$;
- $\min\left\{\sum_{r\in ROLES} ass\_users(r)\right\} = \min\{|UA|\}$;
- $\min\left\{\sum_{r\in ROLES} actvt\_spread(r)\right\}$;
- $\min\left\{\sum_{r\in ROLES} ou\_spread(r)\right\}$.

The constraint of this optimization problem is that elicited roles must "cover" all possible combinations of permissions, namely they represent a candidate role-set.

The dependencies among these objectives are quite complex. For example, if on one side $|ROLES|$ decreases, there is a strong chance that more roles will be required to cover all the permissions possessed by users, causing $|UA|$ to increase. Since each role has a high number of assigned users, it is likely that the number of involved organization units is high, thus increasing the value of the ou_spread function. On the other hand, if we want to reduce the average number of roles per user, we will need more *ad-personam* roles, then $|ROLES|$ will likely increases.

Hence, there is little use in the quest for a global maximum or a global minimum. Since trade-off for conflicting criteria can be defined in many ways, there exist multiple approaches to define what an optimum is. The simplest approach is that of computing a *weighted sum* [Deb (2001)]: multiple objectives are transformed into an aggregated scalar objective function by multiplying each objective by a weighted factor and summing up all contributors. As for role engineering, we can combine all the proposed objectives as follows:

$$\min\Big\{w_r|ROLES| + w_u|UA| +$$
$$w_a \sum_{r\in ROLES} actvt\_spread(r) + w_o \sum_{r\in ROLES} ou\_spread(r)\Big\}. \quad (8.16)$$

where w_i indicates the importance of the ith objective in the overall optimization problem. Sec. 8.4.2 will show a real application of Eq. (8.16) to a role mining algorithm.

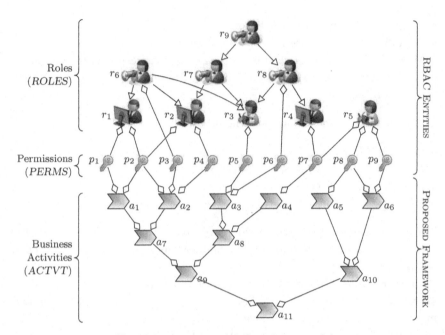

Fig. 8.2: An example of activity model

8.4   Spread Indices in Action

In this section we will analyze the distinguishing features of the proposed
framework through some practical examples. We first show a use case of
the activity-spread index via a simple example. Then, we demonstrate the
effectiveness of the organization-unit-spread index through the RBAM role
mining algorithm (see Chap. 7) applied to an existing company. Due to
space limitation, we do not provide examples of the combined usage of
both indices.

8.4.1   *Example of Activity-Spread*⋆

Figure 8.2 depicts a possible candidate role set and an activity tree. At the
top there are representations of RBAC entities, namely roles and permissions. Example of roles are $ass\_perms(r_1) = \{p_1, p_2\}$, $ass\_perms(r_6) = \{p_3\}$,
while we have that $auth\_perms(r_6) = \{p_1, p_2, p_3, p_4\}$ since $r_1 \succeq r_6$ and
$r_2 \succeq r_6$. At the bottom of the figure, there are activities organized in a
tree structure. For instance, a_{11} is the root of the tree, while $a_9 \rightarrow a_{11}$
and $a_7 \succeq a_{11}$ holds. To ease exposition, weights of connections between

activities are not represented in Fig. 8.2, and they are all assumed to be equal to 1. Further, $\downarrow a_8 = \{a_3, a_4, a_8\}$ and $\uparrow a_1 = \{a_1, a_7, a_9, a_{11}\}$. Activity a_7 is performed when a user possesses the permissions p_1, p_2 (that allows for the child activity a_1) and p_2, p_3, p_4 (that are related to the child activity a_2).

As for the business meaning estimation, let us calculate the activity-spread of role r_6. By looking at Fig. 8.2 it is easy to verify that role r_6 allows for the execution of the activities $\mathcal{A}_{r_6} = \{a_1, a_2\}$. In line with Eq. (8.7), the farness index for each activity in $\mathcal{A}_{r_6}$ is:

$$d_{\mathcal{A}_{r_6}}(a_1) = \frac{d_{\mathrm{actvt}}(a_1, a_1) + d_{\mathrm{actvt}}(a_1, a_2)}{2 - 1} = \frac{0+2}{2-1} = 2,$$

$$d_{\mathcal{A}_{r_6}}(a_2) = \frac{d_{\mathrm{actvt}}(a_2, a_1) + d_{\mathrm{actvt}}(a_2, a_2)}{2 - 1} = \frac{2+0}{2-1} = 2.$$

For such indices we have $\bar{d}_{\mathcal{A}_{r_6}} = \frac{2+2}{2} = 2$ and thus:

$$\mathrm{actvt\_spread}(r_6) = \frac{2^2 + 2^2}{2} - 2^2 = 0.$$

The activity spread is 0 since the activities associated to r_6 are somewhat "balanced" within the tree. Thus, r_6 is probably a good role; indeed, it allows the execution of activities a_1, a_2, and consequently the execution of a_7.

A different result is obtained by analyzing role r_5. In this case, $\mathcal{A}_{r_5} = \{a_4, a_5, a_6\}$. Then:

$$d_{\mathcal{A}_{r_5}}(a_4) = \frac{d_{\mathrm{actvt}}(a_4, a_4) + d_{\mathrm{actvt}}(a_4, a_5) + d_{\mathrm{actvt}}(a_4, a_6)}{4 - 1} = \frac{0+5+5}{3-1} = 5,$$

$$d_{\mathcal{A}_{r_5}}(a_5) = \frac{d_{\mathrm{actvt}}(a_5, a_4) + d_{\mathrm{actvt}}(a_5, a_5) + d_{\mathrm{actvt}}(a_5, a_6)}{4 - 1} = \frac{5+0+2}{3-1} = \frac{7}{2},$$

$$d_{\mathcal{A}_{r_5}}(a_6) = \frac{d_{\mathrm{actvt}}(a_6, a_4) + d_{\mathrm{actvt}}(a_6, a_5) + d_{\mathrm{actvt}}(a_6, a_6)}{4 - 1} = \frac{5+2+0}{3-1} = \frac{7}{2}.$$

Notice that a_4 has the largest farness, hence it is far from other activities. These observations can also be graphically justified by observing Fig. 8.1. The arithmetic mean of such indices is $\bar{d}_{\mathcal{A}_{r_5}} = \frac{5+7/2+7/2}{3} = 4$ and thus:

$$\mathrm{actvt\_spread}(r_5) = \frac{(5)^2 + (7/2)^2 + (7/2)^2}{3} - 4^2 = 0.5.$$

This means that r_5 has less business meaning than r_6, since r_5 is more spread out among its activities.

Finally, it is worth noticing that both the farness index and the activity-spread make up useful information that could also be visualized in a role engineering tool for each activity that is involved within a given role. Having access to this information could help users validate roles from a business perspective.

Organization Unit Tree	Users			
	$w_o = 0$	$w_o = 1$		
	Role107	Role107	Role752	Role293
ORGANIZATION				
EMPLOYEES				
CORPORATE				
ADMINISTRATION PLANNING & CONTROL				
FISCAL ADMINISTRATION	2		2	
PLANNING CONTROL SERVICES & STAFF				
PC/SERVICE AREA & STAFF-ICT				
PC/SERVICE AREA	2			2
INTERCOMPANY SERVICES AND OTHER ACTIVITIES				
SERVICES AND REAL ESTATE				
NORTH WEST AREA				
PLANNING AND GENERAL SERVICES	1	1		
TOTAL USERS	5	1	2	2

Fig. 8.3: An example of elicited roles with different values for w_o

8.4.2 *Organization-Unit-Spread on Real Data*⋆

To highlight the framework viability in real applications, we examined a large private company. In particular, we analyzed permissions related to an ERP application. The system configuration was made up of 1,139 permissions that were used by 1,034 users within 231 organization units, resulting in 10,975 user-permission assignments.

To test the effectiveness of our approach, we used an improved version of the RBAM algorithm (see Chap. 7 for further details), seeking to elicit roles which minimize the function

$$c = w_r|ROLES| + w_u|UA| + w_o \sum_{r \in ROLES} ou\_spread(r). \qquad (8.17)$$

The algorithm was set to discard permission combinations possessed by less than 4 users. Moreover, we assigned a weight 1 to all direct hierarchical relationships between organization units. Then, we compared the algorithm output obtained in two distinct settings: in the first one (from now on indicated as "Experiment 1"), we did not considered the contribution of the organization-unit-spread index, by using $w_o = 0$ and $w_r = 10$, $w_u = 1$; in the second one (from now on indicated as "Experiment 2"), we considered all the cost elements provided by Eq. (8.17), using $w_o = 1$ and the same values for the other weights, namely $w_r = 10$, $w_u = 1$.

The first thing that we can observe from Experiment 2 is that the number of elicited roles is greater than the number of elicited roles in

Experiment 1. In particular, we have 157 roles in the first case (that cover 7,857 user-permission assignments with 2,191 role-user relationships) and 171 roles in the second (that cover 7,857 user-permission assignments with 2,196 role-user relationships). The justification for this behavior is that when using $w_o \neq 0$ (namely, taking into account the organization-unit-spread) in some cases it is necessary to reduce the number of users assigned to a role by introducing additional roles to be assigned with a subset of such users. The greater the number of users assigned to a role are, the more organization units are likely to be involved. Hence, according to Eq. (8.15), the value of the function ou_spread is likely to be higher.

Fig. 8.3 shows an interesting example. In Experiment 1 ($w_o = 0$), we noticed that 2 out of 1,139 permissions were possessed by 22 users, and these users were granted these permissions by assigning them to only one of the two roles which the algorithm automatically called role107 and role594. Moreover, role594 $\succeq$ role107, while $|auth\_perms(\text{role107})| = 2$ and $|auth\_perms(\text{role594})| = 15$. Further, we have that $|ass\_users(\text{role107})| = 5$ and users were belonging to 3 different organization units, namely 'FISCAL ADMINISTRATION', 'PC/SERVICE AREA' and 'PLANNING AND GENERAL SERVICES'. Because of the spreading of users among these OUs, $ou\_spread(\text{role107}) = 12.243$. Figure 8.3 also offers a partial view of the entire organization structure, showing the already cited organization units with a bold font. Conversely, in Experiment 2 (where $w_o = 1$) the same 2 permissions were completely covered by 4 roles that the algorithm automatically called role107, role752, role293, role594. Roles with the same name between the two experiments contain the same permission set, but are assigned with different user sets. Indeed, by observing Fig. 8.3 it is possible to verify that the same 5 users from the other experiment now spread among 3 roles, having $|ass\_users(\text{role107})| = 1$, $|ass\_users(\text{role752})| = 2$, and $|ass\_users(\text{role293})| = 2$. In this case, each of these roles have assigned users who belong to only one organization unit. Moreover, role752 $\succeq$ role107 and role293 $\succeq$ role107. One role has $|auth\_perms(\text{role752})| = 13$ and the other one has $|auth\_perms(\text{role293})| = 8$. Their organization-unit-spread equal 0, thus demonstrating that taking the organization-unit-spread into account may help identify roles with higher business meaning.

Another interesting behavior of the RBAM algorithm, if used with the cost function described in Eq. (8.17), is that increasing the value of w_o causes the decrease of the average organization-unit-spread. Indeed, when $w_o = 0$ we have an average value of $\left(\sum_{r \in ROLES} ou\_spread(r) \right) / |ROLES| = 5.96$. Instead, when $w_o = 1$ the average spread drops down to 4.86, and

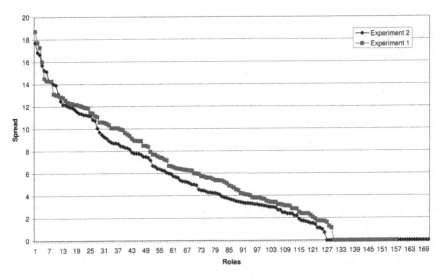

Fig. 8.4: Roles obtained via different values of w_o and sorted by spread

$w_o = 10$ causes an average spread of 2.87. This means that a high value of w_o allows to elicit roles with a more relevant business meaning on average. In such a case, the price to pay to obtain more meaningful roles is in terms of the cardinality of *ROLES*. By analyzing Fig. 8.4, it could also be noted that even though Experiment 2 has more roles, the percentage of roles with spread equal to 0 is increased in comparison with Experiment 1.

8.5   Final Remarks

This chapter provided a formal framework for the role engineering problem that allows to implement a concrete hybrid approach through the combination of existing role mining algorithms (bottom-up) and business analysis (top-down). Once the business processes of an organization have been correctly modeled, we then analyze roles in order to evaluate their business meaning. In particular, a role is likely to be meaningful when it involves activities within the same business process. Thus, we measure the spreading of a role among business processes by introducing the spread index. Leveraging the cost-driven approach of Chap. 7 makes it possible to take into account the spread during the role engineering process. The proposed framework has been implemented on a real case, and the results support the its viability.

Chapter 9

Visual Role Mining

This chapter devises a new approach, referred to as *visual role mining*. Abstract user-permission patterns (i.e., RBAC roles) are managed as *visual patterns* that are able to show at glance what it would take a lot of data to expound. We offer a graphical way to effectively *navigate* the result of *any* existing role mining algorithm, showing at glance what it would take a lot of data to expound. Moreover, we allow to *visually identify meaningful roles* within access control data without resorting to traditional role mining tools. Visualization of the user-permission assignments is performed in such a way to isolate the *noise*, allowing role engineers to focus on relevant patterns, leveraging their cognition capabilities. Further, *correlations* among roles are shown as overlapping patterns, hence providing an intuitive way to discover and utilize these relations.

9.1 Role Visualization Problem

We refer to *visual role mining* as the problem of visually representing user-permission assignments to simplify the role engineering process [Colantonio *et al.* (2011b)]. Indeed, we assert that a proper representation of user-permission assignments allows role designers to gain insight, draw conclusions, and design meaningful roles from both IT and business perspectives. Visual role mining can be considered a *complement* for all the existing role engineering methodologies and tools since it allows for an effective, viable, and intuitive way to evaluate and select roles generated by other approaches. The rationale behind our approach is that visual representations of roles can actually amplify cognition, leading to optimal analysis results [Fekete *et al.* (2008); Keim *et al.* (2008)]. Even though visual approaches sometimes raise some skepticism, they are generally considered to be highly beneficial when used to gain an overview of the underlying dataset.

The main objective of visual role mining can be summarized ad follows: given a set of *already* discovered roles of interest, identify the best graphical representation for them. In particular, we want the representation for user-permission assignments that allows for both an intuitive role validation and a visual identification of the relationships among roles. We will show that roles are easier to recognize than describe via a binary matrix representation. The proposed representation can answer questions that classical statistical or mining approaches cannot (easily) provide. Represented roles can be the outcome of any role engineering process, as well as roles already in place in a RBAC system. Hence, making such a tool an ideal companion for any existing role mining algorithm.

9.1.1 *Binary Matrix Representation*

The role mining objective is to analyze access control data in order to elicit a set of *meaningful* roles that *simplify* RBAC management [Colantonio *et al.* (2008b, 2009a); Frank *et al.* (2009)]. To this aim, various business information can be analyzed [Colantonio *et al.* (2008b, 2009a)], but user-permission assignments are the minimal data-set required. A natural representation for this information is the *binary matrix*, where rows and columns correspond to users and permissions, and each cell is "on" when a certain user has a certain permission granted.

Figure 9.1a shows a possible set of user-permission assignments. It is quite clear that it is impossible to analyze such a set without resorting to a more intuitive representation. By reading data in the same order as presented in Fig. 9.1a we obtain the matrix depicted in Fig. 9.1b. Though this representation is still confusing, it is now possible to observe some patterns. For example, all users possess the permission p_1. Hence, p_1 is likely involved in "base" authorizations to be granted, for example, to new users which join the organization. Practically, we have looked for and found out consecutive cells that are "on." These patterns are usually referred to as *tiles* [Geerts *et al.* (2004)] or *biclusters* [Santamaria *et al.* (2008)]. Figure 9.1c demonstrates that it could be easier to find more patterns if *users and permissions were reordered*. Given the roles listed in Fig. 9.1d, they can be identified more easily in Figure 9.1c than in Fig. 9.1b. In particular, Fig. 9.1e highlights these roles.

Several considerations can be made from the previous example. First,

User-permission Assignments
$\{\langle u_0, p_1\rangle, \langle u_0, p_3\rangle, \langle u_0, p_8\rangle, \langle u_0, p_9\rangle, \langle u_1, p_1\rangle, \langle u_1, p_2\rangle, \langle u_1, p_3\rangle, \langle u_1, p_4\rangle,$ $\langle u_1, p_6\rangle, \langle u_1, p_8\rangle, \langle u_1, p_9\rangle, \langle u_2, p_1\rangle, \langle u_2, p_2\rangle, \langle u_2, p_4\rangle, \langle u_2, p_6\rangle, \langle u_2, p_9\rangle,$ $\langle u_3, p_1\rangle, \langle u_3, p_3\rangle, \langle u_3, p_8\rangle, \langle u_3, p_9\rangle, \langle u_4, p_1\rangle, \langle u_4, p_3\rangle, \langle u_4, p_8\rangle, \langle u_4, p_9\rangle,$ $\langle u_5, p_1\rangle, \langle u_5, p_2\rangle, \langle u_5, p_4\rangle, \langle u_5, p_5\rangle, \langle u_5, p_6\rangle, \langle u_5, p_9\rangle, \langle u_6, p_1\rangle, \langle u_6, p_2\rangle,$ $\langle u_6, p_4\rangle, \langle u_6, p_6\rangle, \langle u_6, p_9\rangle, \langle u_7, p_0\rangle, \langle u_7, p_1\rangle, \langle u_7, p_7\rangle, \langle u_8, p_0\rangle, \langle u_8, p_1\rangle,$ $\langle u_8, p_7\rangle, \langle u_9, p_1\rangle, \langle u_9, p_2\rangle, \langle u_9, p_4\rangle, \langle u_9, p_6\rangle, \langle u_9, p_9\rangle\}$

(a) Input data

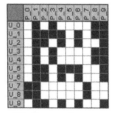 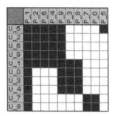

(b) Unsorted matrix   (c) Sorted matrix

Role	Permissions	Users
r_1	$\{p_1\}$	$\{u_0, u_1, u_2, u_3, u_4, u_5, u_6, u_7, u_8, u_9\}$
r_2	$\{p_2, p_4, p_6, p_9\}$	$\{u_1, u_2, u_5, u_6, u_9\}$
r_3	$\{p_3, p_8, p_9\}$	$\{u_0, u_1, u_3, u_4\}$
r_4	$\{p_0, p_7\}$	$\{u_7, u_8\}$
r_5	$\{p_5\}$	$\{u_5\}$

(d) Candidate roles

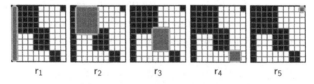

r_1 r_2 r_3 r_4 r_5

(e) Visual representation of roles

Fig. 9.1: Visualization examples

we can easily deduce all the roles listed in Fig. 9.1d by only inspecting Fig. 9.1c, namely *without resorting to any role mining algorithm*. Figure 9.1c is definitely more communicative: for instance, it is evident that p_1 may be assigned to roles r_2, r_3, r_4, thus making r_1 no longer necessary. Alternatively, if p_1 represents a permission that should *always* be granted to all users, keeping r_1 may be more advantageous. This kind of considerations require additional knowledge that might be hard to translate into structured data. Putting humans in the loop allows for a better correlation of business requirements with IT-related access control data.

Second, a *visual representation can highlight potential exceptions within data in an effective manner.* For example, the user u_5 is the only one that has permission p_5 granted. This finding warns about a potentially wrong assignment due to causes such as privilege accumulation or illicit authorization. One could observe that this kind of analysis can be performed even without graphically representing user-permission assignments by adopting approximate mining algorithms [Gupta *et al.* (2008)]. However, most algorithms can lead to several false-positive exceptions, degrading the output quality of the automatic analysis.

Third, a textual role representation (Fig. 9.1d) reports on information about role-user and role-permission relationships in a less communicative fashion than a graphical representation (Fig. 9.1e). For instance, Fig. 9.1e clearly shows that r_2 and r_3 partially overlap, without the need for any additional textual or graphical report. Notice that these representations are not mutually exclusive, but they can coexist in the same role engineering tool. The tool can also enrich the matrix by providing interactive functionalities such as: drill-down capabilities, highlighting multiple roles, tooltips over cells, etc.. Interactions on the matrix can be turned into intelligence to tune underlying analytical process.

Finally, note that it could be difficult to produce a graphical representation for huge datasets. Yet, scalability is a major problem in both automatic and visual analysis [Chen (2005)]. In fact, a large number of user-permission assignments to analyze usually leads existing role mining algorithms to elicit a large number of roles, thus making hard any kind of data analysis. A viable solution is restricting the analysis to smaller subsets of data that are "homogeneous" with respect to some business-related information (e.g., partitioning users by department, job title, cost center, etc., see Chap. 10).

9.1.2 *Problem Formalization* ⋆

In the previous section we intuitively demonstrated that reordering rows and columns of a user-permission matrix can ease the pattern-finding task. We now formalize this problem, offering a tool for the identification of the best representation for a given set of roles. In addition to RBAC concepts (see Chap. 2), we also require the following definitions:

Definition 9.1. A *matrix permutation* $\sigma_{UP} = \langle \sigma_U, \sigma_P \rangle$ is a pair of bijective functions defined as $\sigma_U \colon USERS \to \{1, \ldots, |USERS|\}$ and $\sigma_P \colon PERMS \to$

$\{1, \dots, |PERMS|\}$.

Matrix permutation is introduced just to provide an ordering for users and permissions by "labeling" them with a number. Note that a matrix permutation uniquely identifies a matrix representation—we will thus use the terms "permutation" and "representation" as synonyms.

Definition 9.2. Given a matrix permutation $\sigma_{\mathrm{UP}} = \langle \sigma_{\mathrm{U}}, \sigma_{\mathrm{P}} \rangle$ and a role $r \in ROLES$, the functions $\omega_{\mathrm{U}} \colon ROLES \to \mathbb{N}$ and $\omega_{\mathrm{P}} \colon ROLES \to \mathbb{N}$ identify the *height* and *width*, respectively, of r in the given permutation. That is:

$$\omega_{\mathrm{U}}(r) = \max_{u \in ass\_users(r)} \sigma_{\mathrm{U}}(u) - \min_{u \in ass\_users(r)} \sigma_{\mathrm{U}}(u) + 1, \tag{9.1}$$

$$\omega_{\mathrm{P}}(r) = \max_{p \in ass\_perms(r)} \sigma_{\mathrm{P}}(p) - \min_{p \in ass\_perms(r)} \sigma_{\mathrm{P}}(p) + 1. \tag{9.2}$$

In other words, $\omega_{\mathrm{U}}(r)$ (or $\omega_{\mathrm{P}}(r)$) represents the distance between the first and the last user (or permission) of r in the given matrix representation.

Definition 9.3. Given a matrix permutation $\sigma_{\mathrm{UP}} = \langle \sigma_{\mathrm{U}}, \sigma_{\mathrm{P}} \rangle$ and a role $r \in ROLES$, the functions $\pi_{\mathrm{U}} \colon ROLES \to \mathbb{N}$ and $\pi_{\mathrm{P}} \colon ROLES \to \mathbb{N}$ identify the *number of user and permission fragments* in the given permutation, that is

$$\pi_{\mathrm{U}}(r) = \sum_{u \in ass\_users(r)} \left[\min_{\substack{u' \in ass\_users(r): \\ \sigma_{\mathrm{U}}(u') > \sigma_{\mathrm{U}}(u)}} \sigma_{\mathrm{U}}(u') - \sigma_{\mathrm{U}}(u) \neq 1 \right] + 1, \tag{9.3}$$

$$\pi_{\mathrm{P}}(r) = \sum_{p \in ass\_perms(r)} \left[\min_{\substack{p' \in ass\_perms(r): \\ \sigma_{\mathrm{P}}(p') > \sigma_{\mathrm{P}}(p)}} \sigma_{\mathrm{P}}(p') - \sigma_{\mathrm{P}}(p) \neq 1 \right] + 1, \tag{9.4}$$

where $[b]$ equals 1 when the predicate b is true, and 0 otherwise.

When $\pi_{\mathrm{U}}(r) = 1$ (or $\pi_{\mathrm{P}}(r) = 1$) all the users (or permissions) assigned to the role r are contiguous in the matrix representation. Otherwise, the corresponding rows (or columns) are partitioned into a certain number $\pi_{\mathrm{U}}(r)$ (or $\pi_{\mathrm{P}}(r)$) of subsets of contiguous rows (or columns).

Definition 9.4. Given a matrix permutation $\sigma_{\mathrm{UP}} = \langle \sigma_{\mathrm{U}}, \sigma_{\mathrm{P}} \rangle$ and a role $r \in ROLES$, the *Role Visualization-Cost* $\nu_{\sigma_{\mathrm{UP}}} \colon ROLES \to \mathbb{N}$ is:

$$\nu_{\sigma_{\mathrm{UP}}}(r) = \left(\pi_{\mathrm{U}}(r) \times \pi_{\mathrm{P}}(r) \right) \times$$
$$\left(\omega_{\mathrm{U}}(r) \times \omega_{\mathrm{P}}(r) - |ass\_users(r)| \times |ass\_perms(r)| \right). \tag{9.5}$$

The previous definition is a measure of the visual *fragmentation* of a role. It depends on the number of role fragments (i.e., sub-matrices made up of contiguous "on" cells), represented by the quantity $\pi_U(r) \times \pi_P(r)$, weighted by the number of cells "wasted" to represent the role with respect to its compact representation, that is $\omega_U(r) \times \omega_P(r) - |ass\_users(r)| \times |ass\_perms(r)|$. Notice that when all the cells of a role are contiguous, the corresponding cost is zero.

We would like to point out that an alternative visualization-cost that we could have used is the *half-perimeter* [Jin *et al.* (2008)], defined as:

$$\nu'_{\sigma_{UP}}(r) = \omega_U(r) + \omega_P(r), \qquad (9.6)$$

namely the sum of the height and width of roles in the given matrix representation. In our opinion, Eq. (9.5) is more straightforward because a high role fragmentation greatly hinders the readability of the matrix, an aspect that Eq. (9.6) does not catch. In Sec. 9.5 we will support this statement by comparing the two measures in several real scenarios.

Having introduced a visualization cost function makes it possible to define the following problem:

Definition 9.5. Given a set of roles $ROLES$, let $\sigma^*_{UP} = \langle \sigma^*_U, \sigma^*_P \rangle$ be a matrix permutation, and let $\nu_{\sigma^*_{UP}}$ be the corresponding role visualization-cost. We say that σ^*_{UP} is *optimal* when it minimizes the following:

$$\underset{\sigma_{UP}}{\arg\min} \sum_{r \in ROLES} \nu_{\sigma_{UP}}(r). \qquad (9.7)$$

We refer to the search for the optimal permutation as the *Optimal Matrix-Permutation* (OMP) *optimization problem*. An important property of OMP is [Colantonio *et al.* (2011b)]:

Theorem 9.1. *The OMP optimization problem is $\mathcal{NP}$-hard.*

The previous theorem entails no polynomial-time solution for OMP. Hence, the following section describes a fast heuristic algorithm that is able to find an acceptable solution for the problem in many practical scenarios.

9.2   Matrix Sorting Algorithm ⋆

By leveraging on the observations made in the previous section, we now describe a viable, fast heuristic algorithm called **ADVISER** (*Access Data*

VISualizER). Given a set of roles, this algorithm is able to provide a compact representation of them. In particular, it reorders rows and columns of the user-permission matrix to minimize the fragmentation of each role. Despite being relatively simple, it provides a good—though not necessarily optimal—and fast solution to the otherwise intractable OMP problem. In particular, its running time is $\mathcal{O}\left(n \times (|ROLES| + \log n)\right)$ where $n = max\{|USERS|, |PERMS|\}$.

9.2.1 *Algorithm Description* ⋆

As a heuristic, ADVISER is based on some intuitions, summarized in the following:

- Introducing a "gap" in the visualization of "large" roles (namely, those roles that involve many users and permissions) increases Eq. (9.7) more than introducing gaps on smaller roles. Hence, larger roles should be better represented.
- The more fragments in the visualization of a role, the higher the role visualization-cost.
- Reordering users but not permissions only affects the number of gaps between columns, and so do permissions.

As for the first point, one can argue that small roles can be more important from a business perspective since they likely represent administrative tasks. To focus on exceptions, large roles can be removed after their identification as shown in Sec. 9.4. Notice that searching for large-area tiles is also the choice of many other mining techniques [Geerts *et al.* (2004); Vaidya *et al.* (2007); Colantonio *et al.* (2008c); Vaidya *et al.* (2006)].

The algorithms described in Fig. 9.2 implements our approach. A detailed description follows:

1. Rows and columns are sorted independently. ADVISER decomposes the optimal matrix-permutation problem into two sub-problems, that is users (Line 2) and permissions (Line 3) are sorted independently. Due to this symmetry, from now on we generically refer to rows and columns as *items*.

2. If some items are assigned to the same set of roles, they are put together. For this reason, the algorithm sorts groups of items, called *itemsets*, instead of individual items. In Fig. 9.2 the function *roles*: $IA \to 2^{ROLES}$ identifies all roles associated with an item, namely $roles(i) = \{r \in ROLES \mid$

```
 1: procedure ADVISER(USERS, PERMS, ROLES, UA, PA)
 2:     σ_U ← SORTSET(USERS, UA, ROLES)
 3:     σ_P ← SORTSET(PERMS, PA, ROLES)
 4:     return σ_U, σ_P
 5: end procedure

 6: procedure SORTSET(ITEMS, IA, ROLES)
 7:     ITEMS ← {I ⊆ ITEMS | ∀i, i' ∈ I, roles(i) = roles(i')}
 8:     σ ← ∅
 9:     for all I ∈ ITEMS sorted by descending areas of roles(I) do
10:         if |σ| < 2 then
11:             σ.append(I)
12:         else
13:             if Jacc(I, σ.first) > Jacc(I, σ.last) then
14:                 p ← 1,          j ← Jacc(I, σ.first)
15:             else
16:                 p ← |σ| + 1,    j ← Jacc(I, σ.last)
17:             end if
18:             for i = 2 ... |σ| do
19:                 j_prec ← Jacc(I, σ[i − 1]),   j_succ ← Jacc(I, σ[i])
20:                 j_curr ← Jacc(σ[i − 1], σ[i])
21:                 if max{j_prec, j_succ} > j ∧ min{j_prec, j_succ} ≥ j_curr then
22:                     p ← i,   j ← max{j_prec, j_succ}
23:                 end if
24:             end for
25:             σ.insert(p, I) {between the (p − 1)^{th} and the p^{th} elements}
26:         end if
27:     end for
28:     return σ.expand
29: end procedure
```

Fig. 9.2: The ADVISER algorithm

$\langle i, r \rangle \in IA\}$. Figure 7 identifies items assigned to the same roles. Given an itemset $I \in \overline{ITEMS}$, with abuse of notation in the following we refer to $roles(I)$ as the set of roles $roles(i)$ for any $i \in I$.

3. Itemset positions are decided one-by-one. In order to facilitate a better representation of large roles, itemsets involving roles with larger areas are analyzed first. Line 9 implements this behavior. In particular, let

$I, I' \in \overline{ITEMS}$ be two itemsets. Then, I is considered before I' only if

$$\max_{r \in roles(I) \setminus roles(I')} |ass\_users(r) \times ass\_perms(r)| >$$
$$\max_{r' \in roles(I') \setminus roles(I)} |ass\_users(r') \times ass\_perms(r')|.$$

When $roles(I) \setminus roles(I') = \emptyset$ or $roles(I') \setminus roles(I) = \emptyset$ we assume that $\max = 0$.

4. The algorithm tries to avoid large gaps by putting itemsets close to each other when they share large roles. First of all, we introduce a metric to rank the similarity of items in terms of shared large-area roles. To do this we resort to a widely used set-similarity measure, namely the *Jaccard coefficient* [Chierichetti et al. (2010)]. Given two sets X and Y, $J(X, Y) = |X \cap Y| / |X \cup Y|$. A natural generalization is to consider n-dimensional non-negative vectors X, Y and define $J(X, Y) = \sum_{i=1}^{n} \min\{X_i, Y_i\} / \sum_{i=1}^{n} \max\{X_i, Y_i\}$. In our context, we measure the similarity of two items $i, i' \in ITEMS$ in terms of their assigned roles, weighted by the "depth" of possible gaps in roles. This is done via the following variation of the Jaccard coefficient:

$$\mathsf{Jacc}(i, i') = \frac{\sum_{r \in roles(i) \cap roles(i')} |m(r)|}{\sum_{r \in roles(i) \cup roles(i')} |m(r)|} \quad , \tag{9.8}$$

where $m(\cdot)$ is the membership function $ass\_users(\cdot)$ when we sort permissions, or the function $ass\_perms(\cdot)$ when we sort users. Summarizing, we try to put closer those users (permissions) that share roles with lots of permissions (users). This allows to reduce the number of cells between fragments of large roles. Given $I, I' \in \overline{ITEMS}$, with abuse of notation we refer to $\mathsf{Jacc}(I, I')$ as the value of $\mathsf{Jacc}(i, i')$ for any $i \in I$ and $i' \in I'$.

5. Each itemset is preferentially positioned at the beginning or at the end of already sorted itemsets. The idea is to avoid to "worsen" already found, high similarities. Having defined the previous similarity metric between items, lines 10–26 implement the itemset-sorting strategy by deciding a position p for the itemset I in an itemset permutation σ. The first two itemsets are just inserted in the first two positions (lines 10–11). Then, subsequent itemsets are inserted among already-sorted itemsets only when this operation actually improves the existing sorting. In particular, an itemset I is put but between two consecutive itemsets $\sigma[i-1], \sigma[i]$ (i.e., the two already-sorted items at positions $i-1$ and i) only when both the similarities between I and $\sigma[i-1]$ and between I and $\sigma[i]$ are below the similarity between $\sigma[i-1]$ and $\sigma[i]$ (lines 19–23). Among all possible positions, the

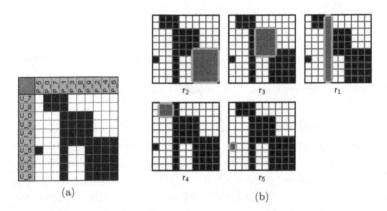

Fig. 9.3: Application of ADVISER on two role sets

algorithm seeks the one that provides the highest similarity: this is done by updating the variables "j" (maximum similarity value found) and "p" (position where the maximum similarity has been found). If inserting the itemset between already sorted itemsets is not advantageous, the itemset will be inserted at the beginning (lines 13–14) or at the end (lines 15–16) of the permutation σ.

6. Itemset sorting is converted to item sorting. This is the inverse of previous point 2. When all itemsets in $\overline{ITEMS}$ have been sorted, they are "expanded" (see Line 28) to return the ordering of each single item in *ITEMS*—instead of providing an ordering for group of items that share the same roles.

We now demonstrate that the computational complexity of AD-VISER as depicted in Fig. 9.2 is $\mathcal{O}\left(n \times \left(|ROLES| + \log n\right)\right)$ where $n = max\{|USERS|, |PERMS|\}$. To prove this, we first show that SORTSET has a running time $\mathcal{O}\left(|ITEMS|\left(|ROLES| + \log|ITEMS|\right)\right)$. Indeed, Line 7 requires a running time $\mathcal{O}(|ITEMS||ROLES|)$ because we have to scan all items and, for each item, check the corresponding roles. The set $\overline{ITEMS}$, such that $|\overline{ITEMS}| \leq |ITEMS|$, can be sorted at Line 9 in $\mathcal{O}(|ITEMS|\log|ITEMS|)$. All the statements of the loop from Line 9 to Line 27 can be executed in a constant time, except for the computation of Jacc($\cdot$, $\cdot$) that requires a running rime $\mathcal{O}(|ROLES|)$. Consequently, the total computation cost is $\mathcal{O}\left(|ITEMS|\left(|ROLES| + \log|ITEMS|\right)\right)$. The complexity of ADVISER immediately follows.

9.2.2 Example ⋆

A simple example can help to better understand the behavior of the algorithm ADVISER. Starting from the user-permission relationships introduced in Fig. 9.1, Fig. 9.3a is obtained by applying ADVISER over the roles depicted in Fig. 9.3b, sorted by descending area. We only describe the sorting of users, since similar considerations can be made for permissions.

- First, the algorithm groups users assigned to the same roles and sort them by descending role areas. In our example, sorted user-sets are: $\{u_1\}$ (assigned to roles r_2, r_3, r_1), $\{u_5\}$ (assigned to roles r_2, r_1, r_5), $\{u_2, u_6, u_9\}$ (assigned to roles r_2, r_1), $\{u_0, u_3, u_4\}$ (assigned to roles r_3, r_1), and $\{u_7, u_8\}$ (assigned to roles r_1, r_4).
- Then, the first two user-set are just put together, namely $\sigma = \{\{u_1\}, \{u_5\}\}$.
- In turn, we seek a position for $\{u_2, u_6, u_9\}$. The maximum similarity value that can be found is $\mathsf{Jacc}(\{u_2, u_6, u_9\}, \{u_5\}) = \sum_{r \in \{r_2, r_1\}} |ass\_perms(r)| / \sum_{r \in \{r_2, r_5, r_1\}} |ass\_perms(r)| = (4+1)/(4+1+1) = 0.83$. Indeed, the first user-set has $\mathsf{Jacc}(\{u_2, u_6, u_9\}, \{u_1\}) = 0.63$ and then the current user-set cannot be inserted at the beginning. Moreover, the similarity between the two already-sorted items is $\mathsf{Jacc}(\{u_1\}, \{u_5\}) = 0.56$; this means that inserting the user-set between them is potentially advantageous, but this would not increase the maximum similarity found at the first position. Hence, $\sigma = \{\{u_1\}, \{u_5\}, \{u_2, u_6, u_9\}\}$.
- Similarly, $\{u_0, u_3, u_4\}$ is inserted at the beginning because the maximum similarity is $\mathsf{Jacc}(\{u_0, u_3, u_4\}, \{u_1\}) = 0.5$, thus $\sigma = \{\{u_0, u_3, u_4\}, \{u_1\}, \{u_5\}, \{u_2, u_6, u_9\}\}$.
- Finally, $\{u_7, u_8\}$ is inserted at the beginning because we have that $\mathsf{Jacc}(\{u_7, u_8\}, \{u_0, u_3, u_4\}) = 0.16$, therefore $\sigma = \{\{u_7, u_8\}, \{u_0, u_3, u_4\}, \{u_1\}, \{u_5\}, \{u_2, u_6, u_9\}\}$.

Please also note that, in this small example, all roles have been best represented. When roles are not overlapping, namely each role involves different users and permissions, the algorithm always provides to good visualization results. Notice that there is no particular strategy in positioning each role within the matrix: the algorithm only strives to reduce the number of fragments required to represent each role.

(a)   (b)

Fig. 9.4: Two typical pseudo-role settings

9.3   Visual Elicitation of Roles

In Sec. 9.1.1 we pointed out that a good matrix permutation can help role engineers elicit candidate roles. By just inspecting the matrix—that is, without analyzing the outcome of any role mining algorithm—analysts can intuitively select the more relevant roles. When we want to identify roles through visual analysis, a natural question is how a role-set for ADVISER should be made in order to facilitate this task. An approach is to first compute all possible *closed permission-sets* and later trying to best represent them (see Chap. 6). By feeding ADVISER with closed permission-sets we provide analysts with a matrix visualization that seeks to contextually best depict all identifiable patterns. However, the number of closed permission-sets is often too large when compared to the number of users and permissions [Gupta *et al.* (2008)]. Hence, leading to long running time and huge memory footprint. To reduce the overall problem complexity, we leverage the pseudo-role concept described in Sec. 5.3.2 and, in particular, the algorithm EXTRACT (see Fig. 5.6 at page 79). EXTRACT is a fast probabilistic algorithm for generating a list of pseudo-roles. Such pseudo-roles can be used to feed ADVISER in lieu of closed permission-sets. We will show that pseudo-roles and closed permission-sets lead to very similar results.

9.3.1   *Using Pseudo-Roles* ⋆

According to Sec. 5.3.2, the main idea behind pseudo-roles is that they represent interesting patterns to highlight. Hence, *by trying to best represent pseudo-roles, we group those cells that are manageable in the same roles.* This justifies why, as we will show later on in this section, visualization results obtained through pseudo-roles are very close to the representation obtained through closed permission-sets.

When using pseudo-roles in place of roles, the main objective is to best represent pseudo-roles that likely have the largest area, and have no or only few non-existing user-permission relations. The relevance concept (see Sec. 5.3.3) summarizes both these aspects. An example can support the previous statement. Figure 9.4 shows two possible submatrices of a larger user-permission matrix. All user-permission relationships have been divided in three subsets: A, B, and C. Non-existing user-permission relationships (that is, $USERS \times PERMS \setminus UP$) are indicated with D. In both figures, the same three pseudo-roles can be generated: *i*) every assignment in A generates a pseudo-role made up of A, B, C, D; *ii*) assignments in B generate A, B; and, *iii*) assignments in C generate A, C. In Fig. 9.4a, the most relevant pseudo-role—the one with the highest value for ϱ—is represented by *i*), since generating user-permission relationships belong to the largest area A. Since D is small, it likely represents missing assignments. Hence, it is advantageous to put together all the cells of A, B, C, and D. Conversely, in Fig. 9.4b the most relevant pseudo-role is *ii*). In this case, assignments in C likely represent exceptions. Hence, representing the cells of C close to A, B is probably not important.

Based on the previous observations, we propose to *represent most relevant pseudo-roles better than the less relevant ones*. This can be done by properly adapting Line 9 of Fig. 9.2 and sorting pseudo-roles by descending relevance. Moreover, a new definition for the item similarity is required, that is

$$\mathsf{Jacc}(i, i') = \frac{\sum_{R \in roles(i) \cap roles(i')} |m(R)| \times \varrho(R)}{\sum_{R \in roles(i) \cup roles(i')} |m(R)| \times \varrho(R)}, \tag{9.9}$$

where $roles(i) = \{R_{\langle u,p \rangle} \mid \langle u,p \rangle \in UP \wedge i \in ass\_users(R_{\langle u,p \rangle})\}$ when sorting permissions, while $roles(i) = \{R_{\langle u,p \rangle} \mid \langle u,p \rangle \in UP \wedge i \in ass\_perms(R_{\langle u,p \rangle})\}$ when sorting items, $R_{\langle u,p \rangle}$ is the pseudo-role generated from $\langle u,p \rangle$ (see Definition 5.14), and $\varrho(R)$ is the relevance of the pseudo-role R. Except from redefining $roles(\cdot)$, if we compare Eq. (9.9) with Eq. (9.8), the main difference is that multiplying $|m(R)|$ by the pseudo-role relevance gives more importance to relevant pseudo-roles.

Note that if the visualization quality is poor due to the approximated relevance values, it is possible to improve the quality by performing just additional samples. Suppose to have the matrix representation generated by feeding the algorithm ADVISER with the output of the algorithm EXTRACT with k samples: if we are not satisfied by this matrix, we can use k' additional samples (namely, we run the loop of Fig. 5.6 from Line 3 to

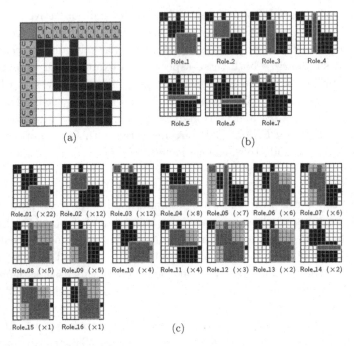

Fig. 9.5: Joint usage of EXTRACT and ADVISER

Line 21 k' more times) in order to have a more accurate relevance estimation. Section 9.5 shows an example of this approach.

9.3.2   *Example* ⋆

A simple example of the joint usage of EXTRACT and ADVISER follows. Fig. 9.5c depicts all the pseudo-roles generated through the algorithm in Fig. 5.6 when applied to the example of Fig. 9.1a and $k = 100$. Highlighted cells are user-permission relations covered by the pseudo-role. Pseudo-roles are sorted by their descending sampled relevances. The relevance is reported in Fig. 9.5c within brackets, after each pseudo-role name. Notice that the first two pseudo-roles have large areas and contextually do not have any non-existing user-permission relations, confirming our expectations.

These pseudo-roles have been used to produce Fig. 9.5a through the algorithm ADVISER. Interestingly, in this particular case we would have generated exactly the same picture if we had used closed permission-sets. Figure 9.5b shows the list of all closed permission-sets that can be identified within the given dataset. Section 9.5 practically demonstrates through a more complex case that visualization results of closed permission-sets and pseudo-roles are comparable.

9.4   A Visual Approach to Role Engineering

In the following we will show an application of the visualization and sampling algorithms finalized to a visual role engineering activity. In particular, we will illustrate how to perform role engineering upon the matrix representation obtained through ADVISER when fed by EXTRACT. Further, we will show how to identify potentially wrong or missing assignments. This methodology originates from a real case-study that has been carried out on a large private company. To protect company privacy, we will not reveal any detail of the results, but we limit ourself to summarizing the methodology.

The proposed approach is an iterative method, mainly inspired by the role-finding process proposed by Kuhlmann *et al.* (2003). First, according to Chap. 10, we simplify the role-finding task decomposing the problem into smaller sub-problems. Then, for each sub-problem, we suggest to conduct the following activities [Colantonio *et al.* (2011b)]:

(1) Select the most relevant roles by resorting to a visual inspection. Then, the corresponding user-permission assignments should be put aside. Analysts should visually recognize the most clearly visible roles, namely those corresponding to the biggest tiles, and remove them for the next iteration.

(2) Identify the business managers responsible for the involved users (typically referred to as "user managers") and the administrators within IT staff responsible for the involved data (typically referred to as "data owners") of each candidate role.

(3) In concert with user managers and data owners, understand the meaning of exceptional user-permission assignments. That is, analyze those assignments that are depicted on the "ragged edges" of the main tiles. In particular, analysts should try to understand whether such assignments are actually required or not. Further, they should verify whether "holes" within almost perfect tiles are missing user-permission relationships that could be assigned to users without violating the least-privilege principle.

After having put aside those user-permission assignments covered by

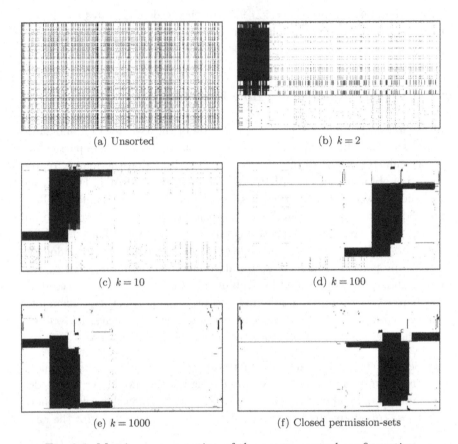

(a) Unsorted   (b) $k = 2$

(c) $k = 10$ (d) $k = 100$

(e) $k = 1000$ (f) Closed permission-sets

Fig. 9.6: Matrix representation of the access control configuration

already identified roles, the analysis can be iteratively repeated over the remaining data. Notice that discovering exceptional assignments and subsequently removing them is a good way to keep policy engineers in the work loop and still provide valuable feedback. If the feedback of the analysis is fast enough, this is a very effective technique: in real cases, we performed very few iterations (up to 4), eliciting a limited number of roles when compared to the cardinality of the assignment set.

Another important observation relates to the identification of user managers and data owners. This task is often easy whenever the divide-and-conquer approaches proposed in Chap. 10 are adopted. The reason is that the identified patterns likely reflect the actual business of the company.

9.5 Experimental Results ★

This section presents practical applications of our methodology. The testbed was a notebook equipped with an Intel Pentium Core Duo Pro processor operating at 2.40 GHz, and 3 GB RAM. The operating system was Linux Fedora 8. The algorithms were coded in Java. Since we ran the experiments in a multitasking environment, the values provided are an upper bound of the real computation time.

Figure 9.6 shows the application of our algorithms on the dataset #17 of Table 9.2. Figure 9.6a depicts the data without any sorting. Instead, figures from 9.6b to 9.6e show the results obtained when using ADVISER fed with the pseudo-roles generated by EXTRACT, respectively for $k = \{2, 10, 100, 1000\}$. Table 9.1 reports, among other data, the computation time to build each one of these pictures. For $k = 2$ (Fig. 9.6b) only some users and some permissions have been sorted, but a candidate role that could manage a large number of user-permission assignments is already clear and visible. The number of "shuffled" rows and column decreases when $k = 10$ (Fig. 9.6c). By using $k = 100$ (Fig. 9.6d), most of the main patterns become clearer. By using a larger sampling parameter, namely $k = 1000$ (Fig. 9.6e), there are very few differences when compared to Fig. 9.6d. The last example (Fig. 9.6f) shows an application of the sorting algorithm when applied to the outcome of the algorithm proposed in [Colantonio *et al.* (2008c)], which computes closed permission-sets.

To provide a quantitative analysis of the quality of visualization results, the last column of Table 9.1 indicates the cost of visualizing all possible closed permission-sets. According to our expectation, the visualization cost decreases as the number of samples increases. Moreover, the differences between Fig. 9.6f and Fig. 9.6d are minimal. Although the running time of the algorithm proposed in [Colantonio *et al.* (2008c)] is definitely greater than that of EXTRACT, it does not lead to performance bottlenecks in the case study. Yet, the advantage of adopting EXTRACT is an almost real-time representation of the data to analyze. The situation dramatically changes as the dataset becomes larger. In particular, the time required to generate all possible closed permission-sets grows exponentially as the dataset dimension increases, whereas the generation of pseudo-roles increases according to a logarithmic law. Even though large matrices cannot entirely be represented on a personal computer screen, their construction is useful anyway. For instance, visualizing a small "sliding window" and/or zooming in/out still represents a valuable way of browsing data. As stated before,

Table 9.1: Comparison among different algorithms and parameters

Figure	Algorithm	Samples	Number of (Pseudo-)Roles	Sampling/Mining Time (nsec)	Sorting Time (nsec)	Total Time (nsec)	Vis. cost $\nu_{\sigma_{UP}}$ on all closed perm-sets
9.6a	–	–	–	–	–	–	1.35×10^{15}
9.6b	Sampling	2	2	2	2	4	1.22×10^{14}
9.6c	Sampling	10	6	2	3	5	1.04×10^{13}
9.6d	Sampling	100	45	15	4	19	1.07×10^{12}
9.6e	Sampling	1000	201	149	22	171	4.55×10^{11}
9.6f	Closed permission-sets	–	315	310	23	333	2.33×10^{11}

scalability is a major problem in both automatic and visual analysis.

The main objective of the remainder of this section is to evaluate the performance of **ADVISER** and **EXTRACT**. In order to perform a fair comparison, we used publicly available datasets. Further, we decided to evaluate the quality of the algorithm outcomes by adopting both our *fragmentation* cost, represented by Eq. (9.5), and the *half-perimeter* cost, namely Eq. (9.6).

Table 9.2 reports on the results of our analysis, while Fig. 9.7 graphically represents the most significative matrices. By examining these results, the first observation is that the intuitions that constitute the basis of our heuristic definitely lead to good results. Another observation relates to the running time. In all scenarios, **ADVISER** produced its results in less than a second. This makes it possible to implement visualization tools that allows for real-time interactions, even for very large datasets.

9.6 Final Remarks

This chapter introduced the *visual role mining* problem, namely visualizing user-permission assignments in an intuitive graphical form that makes it possible to simplify the role engineering process. The proposed representation of data allows role designers to gain insight, draw conclusions, and ultimately design meaningful roles from both IT and business perspectives.

Table 9.2: Performance of ADVISER

Dataset[a]	Fig. 9.7	Users[b]	Perms	Assignments	# of Roles[c]	sec	Eq. (9.6)	Eq. (9.5)
1. Chess (sample)	(f)	250	73	9 250	20 (–)	0.42	3.99×10^3	2.74×10^7
2. Connect (sample)	(g)	250	117	10 750	20 (–)	0.24	2.59×10^3	8.90×10^5
3. Mushroom (sample)	(h)	250	108	5 750	20 (–)	0.25	1.67×10^3	3.77×10^6
4. Pumsb (sample)	(i)	250	807	18 500	20 (–)	0.29	2.20×10^3	1.07×10^6
5. Pumsb* (sample)	(j)	250	749	12 617	20 (–)	0.31	3.55×10^3	3.08×10^6
6. Retail (sample)	(k)	250	1 579	2 638	20 (–)	0.25	1.60×10^3	1.36×10^5
7. T10I4D100K (sample)	(n)	250	654	2 492	20 (–)	0.19	3.54×10^2	2.27×10^3
8. Chess	–	3 196	75	118 252	57 (0.95)	0.24	1.81×10^5	1.62×10^8
9. Connect	–	67 557	129	2 904 951	17 (0.99)	0.41	1.14×10^6	1.52×10^7
10. Mushroom	–	8 124	119	186 852	58 (0.48)	0.11	4.20×10^5	4.75×10^9
11. Pumsb	–	49 046	2 113	3 629 404	11 (0.98)	0.24	5.38×10^5	3.44×10^6
12. Pumsb*	–	49 046	2 088	2 475 947	11 (0.71)	0.26	5.08×10^5	5.61×10^6
13. Retail	–	88 162	16 470	908 576	18 (0.04)	0.27	6.56×10^5	1.85×10^8
14. T10I4D100K	–	100 000	870	1 010 228	10 (0.05)	0.16	2.65×10^5	2.12×10^7
15. APJ	(c)	2 044	1 164	6 841	148 (0.01)	0.12	3.48×10^4	3.31×10^7
16. Domino	(d)	79	231	730	71 (0.00)	0.34	5.59×10^3	1.39×10^8
17. Fire1	(e)	365	709	31 951	167 (0.03)	0.12	4.67×10^4	1.56×10^{10}
18. Fire2	(l)	325	590	36 428	21 (0.00)	0.30	3.63×10^3	9.39×10^5
19. Healthcare	(m)	46	46	1 486	30 (0.00)	0.15	1.56×10^3	8.89×10^5
20. Americas Small	(b)	3 477	1 587	105 205	214 (0.03)	0.12	8.31×10^4	2.93×10^{10}
21. Americas Large	(a)	3 485	10 127	185 294	116 (0.03)	0.14	4.64×10^4	1.27×10^9

[a] Datasets sources: 1–7 are from the authors of [Jin et al. (2008)] and can be found at http://www.cs.kent.edu/~dfuhry/order/order_version_1.zip; 8–21 represent the complete versions of 1–7 and can be found on the FIMI repository at http://fimi.cs.helsinki.fi/data/; 15–21 are real access control data used by the authors of [Molloy et al. (2009)] and located at http://www.hpl.hp.com/personal/Robert_Schreiber/data/sacmat%20relations.zip.

[b] Datasets 1–14 do not represent user-permission assignments, but we translated the term "transactions" in users and "items" in permissions.

[c] The number in brackets is the minimum user support used to generate closed permission-sets through [Colantonio et al. (2008c)], except for datasets 1–7 where we used exactly the same roles of the experiments described in [Jin et al. (2008)].

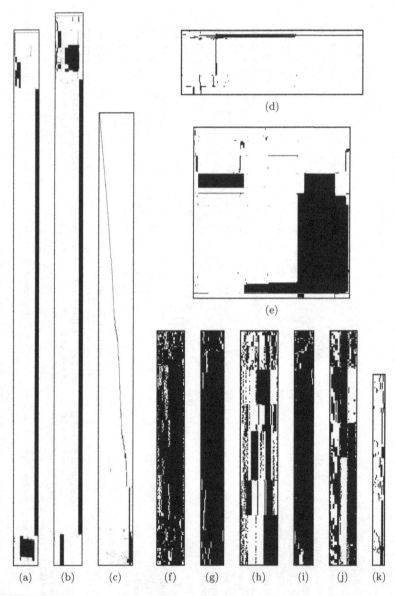

Fig. 9.7: Behavior of ADVISER on different datasets and role sets. The dataset used are described in Table 9.2

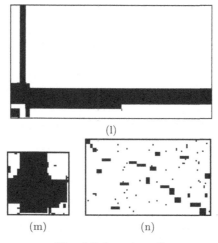

Fig. 9.7 (continued)

We provided several contributions. First, we offered a formal description of the visual role mining problem. Second, we demonstrated that constructing the binary matrix representation of user-permission relations that best represents already recognized patterns is $\mathcal{NP}$-hard. Moreover, we proposed a novel heuristic algorithm called ADVISER to generate a matrix representation starting from the outcome of any role mining algorithm or from "approximate patterns" produced by EXTRACT. Finally, extensive applications over real and public data confirm that our approach is efficient, both in terms of computational time and result quality.

PART 4

Taming Role Mining Complexity

In this part we address the problem of reducing the role mining *complexity* in RBAC systems. As a first contribution, we describe some indices that measure the level of complexity involved in identifying subsets of users that share the same permissions. Hence, allowing for a business-driven divide-and-conquer approach to role mining. Next, we describe how to identify those *exceptional* assignments (i.e., permissions exceptionally or accidentally granted or denied) which badly bias any role mining analysis. We propose a methodology to restrict the role-finding problem to user-permission assignments that lead to the elicitation of stable candidate roles, by contextually simplifying the role selection task. In case the analyzed access control system admits of missing user-permission assignments, this part also describes how to impute such missing values in a very efficient and effective way.

Chapter 10

Splitting Up the Mining Task

This chapter faces the problem of reducing the role mining burden by leveraging business information during the role mining process. Instead of performing a single bottom-up analysis on the entire organization, we advocate for *dividing the access* data into smaller parts that are homogeneous according to a business perspective. Besides reducing the problem complexity, this also eases the attribution of business meaning to roles elicited by *any* existing role mining algorithm.

To select the business information that induces the most suitable partition, we introduce two complexity measures: *minability* and *similarity*. The former measures the expected complexity in locating homogeneous subsets of data that can be managed by few "functional" roles. The latter, measures the expected complexity in locating a homogeneous set of users to manage through a single "structural" role. As a result, the decomposition with the highest minability e similarity values is the one that most likely leads to roles with a clear business meaning.

10.1 A Divide-and-Conquer Approach

Most role mining algorithms have a complexity that is not linear when compared to the number of users or permissions to analyze [Vaidya *et al.* (2006); Ene *et al.* (2008)]. When organizations have to manage thousands of users and millions of resources for which access must be controlled, RBAC can drastically reduce the burden of system administrators, but at the same time role engineering becomes harder. A possible way to tame the problem complexity is the application of a *divide-and-conquer* paradigm, also known as *divide-and-rule* [Cormen *et al.* (2009)]. It is a powerful tool for solving conceptually difficult problems. It consists in finding a way of breaking the problem into simpler sub-problems, solving the trivial cases, and then combining sub-problems to the original problem.

This strategy might be applied to the role mining case by leveraging business requirements. In particular, this section presents a viable solution to reduce the mining complexity based on *restricting the analysis to sets of data that are homogeneous from an enterprise perspective* [Colantonio et al. (2010b, 2011a)]. The key observation is that users sharing the same business attributes will essentially perform the same task within the organization. Not only does partitioning data introduce benefits in terms of execution time of role mining algorithms; it also helps role engineers ascribe business meaning to resulting roles—see also Part 3. Suppose we know, from a partial or coarse-grained top-down analysis, that a certain set of users perform the same tasks, but the analysis lacks information about which permissions are required to execute these tasks. In this scenario, restricting role mining techniques to these users only—instead of analyzing the organization as a whole—will ensure that elicited roles are related to such tasks. Consequently, it will be easier for an analyst to assign a business meaning to the roles suggested by the bottom-up approach. Moreover, elicitation of roles with no business meaning can be avoided by grouping users that perform similar tasks together first, and then analyzing each group separately. Indeed, investigating analogies among groups of users that perform completely different tasks is far from being a good role mining strategy.

To apply this divide-and-conquer strategy, several enterprise information can be used. Business processes, workflow tasks, and organization unit trees are just a few examples of business elements that can be leveraged. Notice that very often such information is already available in most companies before starting the role engineering task—for instance within HR systems. When dealing with information from several sources, the main problem is thus ascertaining which information induces the partition that improves the role engineering task the most. To this end, in the following section we introduce two indices that are able to measure the "relevance" of a high-level information with respect to access control data. For a given a high-level information (e.g., organizational units, job titles, applications, tasks, etc.) we first identify all the subsets that it naturally induces (i.e., sets of user-permission assignments where users have the same job title, or permissions belongs to the same application). Then, for each subset, we calculate the complexity measures described in Sec. 10.2, thus getting a prediction about how complex a subsequent role mining task on the subset will be. This decomposition process can be performed for each available business information, thus generating different data partitions; by selecting the one with the highest values for the indices, we choose the partition that most simplifies the subsequent role mining analysis. Furthermore, each subset might be iteratively partitioned in even smaller subsets until we reach an affordable problem complexity. Besides reducing the complexity, notice that the application of role mining algorithms on each subset will produce roles with more business meaning when compared to the outcome of the same algorithms applied on the whole data-set: since subsets are identified according to some business criteria, elicited roles will likely be aligned to business and the probability that administrators select a wrong role to assign to users will decrease, hence reducing the related risk.

10.2   Complexity Measures

In this section we describe two indices to use in conjunction with the methodology described in the previous section, hence allowing to condition existing role mining algorithms to craft roles with business meaning and to downsize the problem complexity. These indices estimate how easy it is to analyze a given set of user-permission assignments through a bottom-up approach, but using different perspectives. The first index is referred to as *similarity*, and its value is proportional to the number of permissions a given set of users share. The second one is called *minability*, and it measures the complexity of selecting candidate roles given a set of user-permission assignments.

These indices have been introduced by Colantonio *et al.* (2011a, 2010d). They both have pros and cons. To better understand the criterion for choose the index that best fits the role engineering requirements, we need to recall the role classification introduced in Sec. 3.3. In particular, roles can be classified in two main groups:

- *Organizational or Structural Roles*, which depend on employee's position within a homogeneous group of users—for instance, an organization unit or all users that have the same job title. Common permissions are usually assigned to these kinds of roles, and each user typically has only one organizational role.

- *Functional Roles*, which depend on the task that need to be performed in a particular position. Detailed permissions are usually assigned to this kind of roles. Functional roles are supposed to provide further access rights in addition to those being granted by organizational roles. Any number of functional roles can be assigned to a user.

Since the similarity index helps identify situations where all users share the majority of their permissions, its usage is most suitable when evaluating how easy it is to identify organizational roles is. Instead, the minability index indicates the level of complexity involved in identifying subsets of users that share the same permissions; thus, it is suitable to evaluate whether finding roles, both functional and organizational, is a simple task or not.

The following sections formally define these two indices, by also describing how to practically compute them.

10.3   Similarity ★

As mentioned before, the *similarity* index is a measure of the portion of permissions shared by a given set of users. Section 10.3.1 formally describes the index, then Sec. 10.3.2 offer a viable algorithm to compute the index.

10.3.1   *Similarity and Jaccard Coefficient* ★

The *Jaccard coefficient* [Jaccard (1901)] is a measure of the similarity between two sets. Given two sets S_1, S_2, the coefficient is defined as the size of the intersection divided by the size of their union:

$$J_{S_1 S_2} = |S_1 \cap S_2| / |S_1 \cup S_2| . \tag{10.1}$$

The Jaccard coefficient is widely used in statistic. In access control, it has been used by Vaidya *et al.* (2008) to offer a method to consider previously defined roles during the role mining process in order to minimize the "perturbation" introduced by new candidate roles. In this section we will use the Jaccard coefficient to measure the similarities among users of an access control configuration. In particular, referring to Eq. (10.1), we provide the following definition:

Definition 10.1 (Similarity Between Two Users). *Given two users* $u_1, u_2 \in USERS$, *the* similarity index *between them is formally defined as:*

$$s(u_1, u_2) = \frac{|\mathrm{perms}(u_1) \cap \mathrm{perms}(u_2)|}{|\mathrm{perms}(u_1) \cup \mathrm{perms}(u_2)|}. \tag{10.2}$$

The following observations about permission overlapping and inclusion are useful for the sequel:

- u_1 "contains" u_2 if $perms(u_1) \supset perms(u_2)$, namely permissions of u_1 are also possessed by u_2, but are not equal $(perms(u_1) \neq perms(u_2))$. In such a case, $s(u_1, u_2) \in (0, 1)$.

- u_1 is "equivalent" to u_2 if $perms(u_1) = perms(u_2)$, namely u_1, u_2 share the same permission set. Hence, we have that $s(u_1, u_2) = 1$.

- u_1 "overlaps" u_2 when $perms(u_1) \cap perms(u_2) \neq \emptyset$ but $perms(u_1) \not\supseteq perms(u_2)$ and $perms(u_2) \not\supseteq perms(u_1)$, namely u_1, u_2 share some permission but neither does u_1 contain u_2 nor does u_2 contain u_1. This means that $s(u_1, u_2) \in (0, 1)$.

- u_1 is "not related" to u_2 if $perms(u_1) \cap perms(u_2) = \emptyset$, namely u_1, u_2 do not share any common permissions. As a result, $s(u_1, u_2) = 0$.

Definition 10.2 (Similarity Among a Set of Users). *For a given set of users USERS, the* similarity index *is the average similarity between all possible (unordered) user pairs. Formally,*

$$
\mathcal{S}(USERS) = \begin{cases} \dfrac{1}{\binom{|USERS|}{2}} \displaystyle\sum_{\substack{u_1, u_2 \in USERS: \\ u_1 \neq u_2}} s(u_1, u_2), & |USERS| > 1; \\ 1, & otherwise. \end{cases} \tag{10.3}
$$

Notice that Eq. (10.2) and Eq. (10.3) can be extended to also consider other enterprise information. For instance, similarities can be evaluated over shared activities, involved organization units, etc.. We can define a similarity index for each kind of business data. In general, the most suitable similarity definition depends on specific organization needs and role engineering requirements. To ease exposition, in this chapter the term "similarity" indicates only the percentage of permissions shared among users, according to the previous definitions.

10.3.2 *Approximating the Similarity ⋆*

Let us analyze the computation time required to determine the exact value of $\mathcal{S}(USERS)$. In particular, according to its definition as in Eq. (10.3), it can be calculated in $\mathcal{O}(|PERMS| \, |USERS|^2)$ time. Indeed, $\mathcal{O}(|USERS|^2)$ time is required to identify all possible user pairs. For each pair $u_1, u_2 \in USERS$, the cardinality of both the intersection and the union of their granted permissions can be computed in $\mathcal{O}(|PERMS|)$. In particular, by scanning UP only once, we can build a hashtable of permissions that each user has been granted. Notice that $|UP| \leq |USERS| \, |PERMS|$. Hence,

```
 1: procedure $\tilde{S}(USERS, k)$
 2:     $\ell \leftarrow 0$
 3:     if $|USERS| = 1$ then
 4:         return 1
 5:     else
 6:         for $i = 1 \ldots k$ do
 7:             Select $u_1, u_2 \in USERS : u_1 \neq u_2$ uniformly at random
 8:             $\ell \leftarrow \ell + s(u_1, u_2)$
 9:         end for
10:         return $\ell/k$
11:     end if
12: end procedure
```

Fig. 10.1: Approximation of the similarity index

checking if a permission is in $perms(u_1)$ requires $\mathcal{O}(1)$. This check should be done for every permission in $perms(u_2)$, thus requiring $\mathcal{O}(|PERMS|)$. Altogether, the similarity index can be calculated in $\mathcal{O}(|PERMS| |USERS|^2)$.

To reduce the computation time, we propose the ε-approximated algorithm listed in Fig. 10.1. The algorithm performs uniform sampling over all possible user pairs and then computes the average similarity among them. In particular, in each of the k sampling (Line 6), a user pair u_1, u_2 is randomly chosen (Line 7). Then, the variable ℓ is incremented by the similarity value of this pair (Line 8). In accordance with our definition, the returned result is ℓ/k. We now show that the algorithm is totally correct: it terminates in a finite time and provides a correct result. First, the algorithm in Fig. 10.1 always terminates because its core is a finite loop. Then, the following theorem proves that the computed result is probabilistically correct [Colantonio *et al.* (2011a)]:

Theorem 10.1. *The value $\tilde{S}(USERS, k)$ computed by a run of the algorithm in Fig. 10.1 satisfies:*

$$\Pr\left(\left|\tilde{S}(USERS, k) - S(USERS)\right| \geq \varepsilon\right) \leq 2\exp\left(-2k\varepsilon^2\right).$$

For practical applications of the algorithm in Fig. 10.1, it is possible to calculate the number of loops needed to obtain an expected error that is less than ε with a probability greater than p. The following is an application of Theorem 10.1:

$$k > -\frac{1}{2\varepsilon^2}\ln\left(\frac{1-p}{2}\right). \tag{10.4}$$

For instance, if we want an error $\varepsilon < 0.05$ with probability greater than 98.6%, it is enough to choose $k \geq 993$.

Finally, we shall demonstrate that the computational complexity of the algorithm in Fig. 10.1 is $\mathcal{O}\left(|UP|\,|PERMS|\right)$. Indeed, according to the observation made at the beginning of this section, we can build a hashtable of permissions possessed by users in $\mathcal{O}(UP)$. The loop in Line 6 is repeated k times, and we reasonably assume that $k \in \mathcal{O}(|UP|)$. Computing the similarity of two users in each loop requires $\mathcal{O}(|PERMS|)$ thanks to the hashtable. Therefore, the total complexity is $\mathcal{O}\left(|UP|\,|PERMS|\right)$, that is advantageous when compared to the exact similarity calculation if the number of users is greater than the number of permissions and, most of all, when the user set is large.

10.4 Minability⋆

In this section we describe the *minability* index, namely a measure of the complexity of identifying and selecting the roles required to manage existing user-permission assignments. We offer both a formal description of the index and its relation with the *clustering coefficient* (through section from 10.4.1 to Sec. 10.4.2) and a practical way to compute it (see Sec. 10.4.3).

10.4.1 *Clustering Coefficient⋆*

The so-called *clustering coefficient* was first introduced by Watts and Strogatz (1998) in the social network field, to measure the "cliquishness" of a typical neighborhood. Given a graph $G = \langle V, E \rangle$ (see Sec. 5.2.1), we indicate with $\delta(v)$ the number of *triangles* of v, formally:

$$\delta(v) = \left|\left\{\langle u, w \rangle \in E \mid \langle v, u \rangle \in E \,\wedge\, \langle v, w \rangle \in E\right\}\right|. \tag{10.5}$$

A path of length two for which v is the center node is called a *triple* of the vertex v. We indicate with $\tau(v)$ the number of triples of v, namely:

$$\tau(v) = \left|\left\{\langle u, w \rangle \in V \times V \mid \langle v, u \rangle \in E \,\wedge\, \langle v, w \rangle \in E\right\}\right|. \tag{10.6}$$

The *clustering coefficient* of a graph G is defined as:

$$C(G) = \frac{1}{|V|} \sum_{v \in V} c(v), \tag{10.7}$$

where

$$c(v) = \begin{cases} \dfrac{\delta(v)}{\tau(v)}, & \tau(v) \neq 0; \\ 1, & \text{otherwise} \end{cases} \tag{10.8}$$

quantifies how close the vertex v and its neighbors are to being a clique. The quantity $c(v)$ is also referred to as the *local* clustering coefficient of v, while $C(G)$ is average of all local clustering coefficients, and it is also referred to as the *global* clustering coefficient of G. Thus, $C(G)$ can be used to quantify "how well" a whole graph G is partitionable in cliques. Another possible definition for the clustering coefficient is to set to 0 when there are no triples. Anyway, our definition is more suitable for our purposes.

10.4.2   *The Minability Index*⋆

We now redefine the clustering coefficient to be used with bipartite graphs that represent the user-permission assignments of an organization according to Eq. (5.3) at page 68. In particular, given a user-permission assignment $\omega \in UP$, we define the function *triples*: $UP \to 2^{UP \times UP}$ (derived from Eq. (10.6)) as

$$triples(\omega) = \big\{ \langle \omega_1, \omega_2 \rangle \in UP \times UP \mid \omega_1, \omega_2 \in \mathcal{B}(\omega) \wedge \omega_1 \neq \omega_2 \big\}, \tag{10.9}$$

namely the set of all possible pairs of elements in UP that both induce a biclique with ω. We also define the function *triangles*: $UP \to 2^{UP \times UP}$ (derived from Eq. (10.5)) as

$$triangles(\omega) = \big\{ \langle \omega_1, \omega_2 \rangle \in triples(\omega) \mid \omega_1 \in \mathcal{B}(\omega_2) \big\}, \tag{10.10}$$

namely the set of all possible pairs of elements in UP that both induce a biclique with ω, and that also induce a biclique with each other.

The clustering coefficient of Eq. (10.7) thus becomes:

Definition 10.3 (Minability). *The minability index of an access control system configuration represented by the set UP is defined as*

$$\mathcal{M}(UP) = \frac{1}{|UP|} \sum_{\omega \in UP} m(\omega), \tag{10.11}$$

where

$$m(\omega) = \begin{cases} \dfrac{|triangles(\omega)|}{|triples(\omega)|}, & triples(\omega) \neq \emptyset; \\ 1, & \text{otherwise.} \end{cases} \tag{10.12}$$

The value of $m(\omega)$ is also referred to as the *local* minability index of ω, and it quantifies how close ω, together with all the edges which induce a biclique with it, are to being a biclique. Instead, $\mathcal{M}(UP)$ is also referred to as the *global* minability index. Equation (10.11) can be alternatively written as

$$\mathcal{M}(UP) = \frac{1}{|UP|} \sum_{\omega \in UP} \sum_{\langle \omega_1, \omega_2 \rangle \in triples(\omega)} \frac{Y(\omega, \omega_1, \omega_2)}{|triples(\omega)|} +$$

$$\frac{|\{\omega \in UP \mid triples(\omega) = \emptyset\}|}{|UP|}, \quad (10.13)$$

where $Y: UP \times UP \times UP \to \{0,1\}$ returns 1 if their parameters induce a biclique, and 0 otherwise. Formally:

$$Y(\omega, \omega_1, \omega_2) = \begin{cases} 1, & \langle \omega_1, \omega_2 \rangle \in triangles(\omega); \\ 0, & \text{otherwise.} \end{cases}$$

With the above formulation, the minability index $\mathcal{M}(UP)$ can be computed by considering each tuple $\langle \omega, \omega_1, \omega_2 \rangle \in UP \times UP \times UP$ such that $\omega_1, \omega_2 \in \mathcal{B}(\omega)$, and checking whether the condition $\omega_1 \in \mathcal{B}(\omega_2)$ holds true.

In the remainder of this section we introduce definitions and prove theorems that help to better understand the relationship between the minability index and the complexity of the role mining problem. In particular, in Definition 5.10 at page 72 we introduced the *maximal role* concept, that is a role "representative" of all possible subsets of permissions shared by a given set of users. The key observation which is made regarding a maximal role is that two permissions which always occur together among users should simultaneously belong to the same candidate roles. Without further business semantics of access control data, a bottom-up approach to role engineering cannot differentiate between a role made up of two permissions and two roles that contain individual permissions. Moreover, defining roles made up of as many permissions as possible likely minimizes the administration effort of the RBAC system by reducing the number of required role-user assignments.

The following theorem relates the minability index to the complexity of the role mining problem in terms of number of maximal roles [Colantonio *et al.* (2010d, 2011a)]:

Theorem 10.2. *Let M be the set of all possible maximal roles that can be derived from UP. Given a user-permission assignment $\omega \in UP$, let M_ω be the set of all maximal roles that "cover" the given user-permission assignment, that is $M_\omega = \{r \in M \mid \omega \in ass\_users(r) \times ass\_perms(r)\}$. Then, the followings holds:*

- $m(\omega) = 1 \iff |M_\omega| = 1;$
- $m(\omega) = 0 \iff |M_\omega| = |\mathcal{B}(\omega)|;$
- $m(\omega) \in (0,1) \iff 1 < |M_\omega| < |\mathcal{B}(\omega)|.$

The previous theorem allows us to make some consideration on the complexity of the role mining problem. Given a user-permission assignment ω, the higher its local minability is, the less the number of possible maximal roles to analyze is. Section 10.5 and Sec. 10.7 offer practical examples of this property.

10.4.3 *Approximating the Minability* ⋆

Here we will show that the computational complexity of calculating $\mathcal{M}(UP)$ is $\mathcal{O}(|UP|^3)$. In the case of a large-size organization, computation may be unfeasible since UP can count hundreds of thousands of user-permission assignments. For this reason, we propose an approximation algorithm for $\mathcal{M}(UP)$ that has a computational complexity of $\mathcal{O}(k\,|UP|)$.

First, let us consider the complexity of computing the exact value of $\mathcal{M}(UP)$. In Eq. (10.13), the first sum is over all the user-permission assignments $\omega \in UP$, while the second one is over all the triples $\langle \omega_1, \omega_2 \rangle \in triples(\omega)$—that, for a given ω, are $(|UP| - 1)(|UP| - 2)$ in the worst case. Each addendum of the sum corresponds to checking whether the selected triple is also a triangle. It is a triangle if the two outer nodes $\omega_1 = \langle u, p \rangle$ and $\omega_2 = \langle u', p' \rangle$ of the selected triple induce a biclique. This occurs if $u = u'$, or $p = p'$, or other two edges $\omega_3 = \langle u, p' \rangle$ and $\omega_4 = \langle u', p \rangle$ exist in UP. It is possible to check if $u = u'$ or $p = p'$ in a constant time. Instead, the search for the pair ω_3, ω_4 can be executed in $\mathcal{O}(1)$ after having built a hashtable of all possible user-permission assignments in $\mathcal{O}(|UP|)$. The total computational cost is thus $\mathcal{O}(|UP|^3)$.

To reduce the computation time, we propose the ε-approximated algorithm listed in Fig. 10.2, that is inspired by [Schank and Wagner (2005)] but adapted to the bipartite graph case. In each of the k steps, a user-permission assignment ω is randomly chosen (Line 4). Then, two random user-permission pairs among those that induce a biclique together with ω (if any) are selected (Line 6). If these two user-permission assignments induce a biclique, the counter ℓ is incremented by 1 since we have found a triple that is also a triangle (Line 7). The ratio of the number of found triangles ℓ to the number of sampled triples k (Line 14) represents the approximated minability value.

```
 1: procedure M̃(UP, k)
 2:     ℓ ← 0
 3:     for i = 1 … k do
 4:         Select ω ∈ UP uniformly at random
 5:         if triples(ω) ≠ ∅ then
 6:             Select ⟨ω₁, ω₂⟩ ∈ triples(ω) uniformly at random
 7:             if ω₁ ∈ B(ω₂) then
 8:                 ℓ ← ℓ + 1
 9:             end if
10:         else
11:             ℓ ← ℓ + 1
12:         end if
13:     end for
14:     return ℓ/k
15: end procedure
```

Fig. 10.2: Approximation of the minability index

In the following, we show that the algorithm terminates and returns a correct result. First, notice that the core of the algorithm in Fig. 10.2 is a finite loop, thus it always outputs a result in a finite amount of time. The following theorem proves that this answer is probabilistically correct [Colantonio *et al.* (2011a)]:

Theorem 10.3. *The value* $\widetilde{\mathcal{M}}(UP, k)$ *computed by a run of the algorithm in Fig. 10.2 satisfies:*

$$\Pr\left(\left|\widetilde{\mathcal{M}}(UP, k) - \mathcal{M}(UP)\right| \geq \varepsilon\right) \leq 2\exp\left(-2k\varepsilon^2\right).$$

In the same way as the similarity index, it is possible to calculate the number of times it takes the loop in Fig. 10.2 to obtain an expected error which is less than ε with a probability greater than p. By analyzing Theorem 10.3 it can be seen that the same result Eq. (10.4) holds for this case.

As for computational complexity, we will now show that the algorithm in Fig. 10.2 requires a time $\mathcal{O}(k|UP|)$ to run. The loop in Line 3 is repeated k times. In each loop, a random user-permission relationship $\omega \in UP$ can be selected in constant time (Line 4). Let us consider $\omega = \langle u, p \rangle$. In order to randomly select a pair $\langle \omega_1, \omega_2 \rangle$ that belongs to $triples(\omega)$, we have to calculate the set $\mathcal{B}(\omega)$, then every possible pair of this set is in $triples(\omega)$ (Line 5). Equation (5.2) at page 68 states that $\mathcal{B}(\langle u, p \rangle) = \{\langle u', p' \rangle \in UP \mid$

$\langle u, p' \rangle, \langle u', p \rangle \in UP \wedge \langle u, p \rangle \neq \langle u', p' \rangle \}$. The number of elements of $\mathcal{B}(\omega)$ is at most $|UP| - 1$, and each element can be found in $\mathcal{O}(1)$ after having built a hashtable of all possible user-permission assignments in $\mathcal{O}(|UP|)$. Then, the computational cost incurred to identify a biclique is at most $\mathcal{O}(|UP|)$. Line 7 can be executed in $\mathcal{O}(1)$ since it represents a search in the hashtable to verify the conditions in Eq. (5.2). Therefore, the computational complexity of the algorithm listed in Fig. 10.2 is $\mathcal{O}(k|UP|)$, which greatly improves over the time required to calculate the exact value $\mathcal{M}(UP)$. This improvement is traded-off with a slight (tunable) decrease in the precision of the computed value $\widetilde{\mathcal{M}}(UP, k)$.

10.5   Considerations About Minability and Similarity ⋆

We now provide some considerations that demonstrate how minability and similarity indices can actually provide role mining engineers with the expected complexity to find functional and/or organizational roles. A first relevant observation correlates these two indices, and it is represented by the following lemma [Colantonio *et al.* (2011a)]:

Lemma 10.1. *Given a set of users USERS that have been granted permissions in PERMS through the corresponding assignments UP, then* $\mathcal{S}(USERS) = 1 \implies \mathcal{M}(UP) = 1$.

The previous lemma states that the similarity index is tighter than the minability index. Indeed, a similarity index equal to 1 requires that all users share the same set of permissions, whereas minability can be equal to 1 even if the users do not share all the same permissions. Further, notice that the inverse of Lemma 10.1 does not hold. The example depicted in Fig. 10.3a is one possible case of $\mathcal{M}(UP) = 1$ and $\mathcal{S}(USERS) < 1$.

We now show some examples to better understand the behavior of minability and similarity indices. In Fig. 10.3, three different and simple access control configurations are depicted. In each one, we have 4 users and 6 permissions, but with different user-permission assignments. To better illustrate these indices, we also report the corresponding unipartite graphs constructed according to Eq. (5.3) at page 68.

In Fig. 10.3a the minability index is 1. In this case, it is straightforward to verify that a possible clique cover of the unipartite graph is represented by cliques $C_1 = \{\langle A, 1 \rangle, \langle A, 2 \rangle, \langle A, 3 \rangle, \langle B, 1 \rangle, \langle B, 2 \rangle, \langle B, 3 \rangle\}$ and $C_2 = \{\langle C, 4 \rangle, \langle C, 5 \rangle, \langle C, 6 \rangle, \langle D, 4 \rangle, \langle D, 5 \rangle, \langle D, 6 \rangle\}$. In RBAC terms, C_1 and C_2

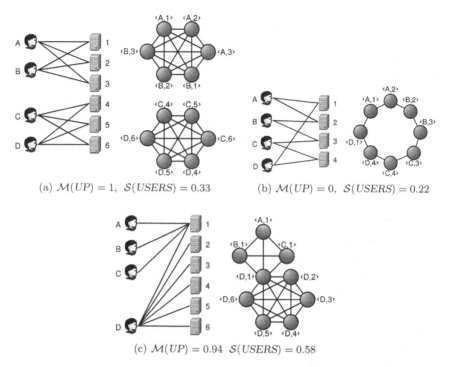

(a) $\mathcal{M}(UP) = 1,\ \ \mathcal{S}(USERS) = 0.33$ (b) $\mathcal{M}(UP) = 0,\ \ \mathcal{S}(USERS) = 0.22$

(c) $\mathcal{M}(UP) = 0.94\ \ \mathcal{S}(USERS) = 0.58$

Fig. 10.3: Access control configurations as bipartite graphs and corresponding unipartite graphs

correspond to two maximal roles: the first one made up of permissions $\{1, 2, 3\}$ and it is assigned with users $\{A, B\}$, the second one made up of permissions $\{4, 5, 6\}$ and assigned with users $\{C, D\}$. As for the similarity index, $\mathcal{S}(\{A, B, C, D\}) = 1/3$.

Figure 10.3b shows another access control configuration such that the minability index equals 0. According to Theorem 10.2, it represents the most ambiguous case. Indeed, in this example we have two possible maximal roles to manage each user-permission assignment (one is composed by one user and two permissions, the other one is made up of one permission and two users). Yet, without further business semantics of access control data, it is not clear which is the best choice. Another observation is that in Fig. 10.3b the similarity index is smaller than in Fig. 10.3a. Indeed, since each permission is used by 2 users, it is impossible to define a role that has to be assigned to the majority of users.

Fig. 10.3c shows a slightly more complicated configuration, where the minability index is between 0 and 1, while the similarity is higher than in all previous cases. It is quite clear that the unipartite graph can be covered with two cliques (i.e., two maximal roles), and this suggests that the minability must be very close to 1. Indeed, we have an ambiguity only for the user-permission assignment $\langle D, 1 \rangle$: it can belong to both the cliques $C_1 = \{\langle A, 1 \rangle, \langle B, 1 \rangle, \langle C, 1 \rangle, \langle D, 1 \rangle\}$ and $C_2 = \{\langle D, 1 \rangle, \langle D, 2 \rangle, \langle D, 3 \rangle, \langle D, 4 \rangle, \langle D, 5 \rangle, \langle D, 6 \rangle\}$. $\mathcal{M}(UP) = 0.94$ is in line with the previous observation.

10.6   Conditioned Indices ⋆

As mentioned earlier in Sec. 10.1, minability and similarity can be used to identify the best partition pertaining the given access control data and business information. As a matter of fact, grouping users that share the same job title likely identify homogeneous access control data with high values for the minability and similarity indices. Instead of computing the indices on each subset of a given partition, it is more advantageous to have a value for both indices that "summarizes" the simplification introduced by the partition. To this aim, we need to review all the aforementioned indices to *condition* them by the given partition. The conditioning concept will apply on both similarity and minability indices. We therefore speak of *conditioned similarity and minability*.

The reason why minability and similarity change after decomposing the problem can be analyzed in terms of the graph model. As a matter of fact, partitioning the set UP is equivalent to partitioning the unipartite graph G constructed according to Eq. (5.3) in subgraphs, since each element in UP corresponds to a node in G. Hence, partitioning UP means discarding all the relationships between user-permission assignments that are in two different subsets of the partition—they will no longer induce a biclique—namely removing edges in G that connect distinct subgraphs. In other words, the partition "breaks" roles that spread across multiple subsets into more parts; that is, roles without a clear meaning according to the business information that induced the partition.

10.6.1   *Conditioned Similarity* ⋆

Let $\Omega = \{\Omega_1, \ldots, \Omega_k\}$ be a k-partition of UP such that $\Omega_i \subseteq UP$ and $UP = \bigcup_{i=1}^{k} \Omega_i$. Each subset Ω_i induces a set of users Υ_i, such that $\Upsilon_i =$

$\{u \in USERS \mid \exists p \in PERMS, \langle u, p \rangle \in \Omega_i\}$. According to Eq. (10.3), we can define the similarity of Υ_i in the following way:

$$
S(\Upsilon_i) = \begin{cases} \dfrac{1}{\binom{|\Upsilon_i|}{2}} \displaystyle\sum_{\substack{u_1, u_2 \in \Upsilon_i: \\ u_1 \neq u_2}} s_{\Omega_i}(u_1, u_2), & |U| > 1; \\ 1, & \text{otherwise.} \end{cases} \tag{10.14}
$$

where $S_\Omega(u_1, u_2)$ is the similarity of the users u_1 and u_2 obtained by only considering the permissions that are involved in Ω_i. Equation (10.14) can also be rewritten in the following way:

$$
S(\Upsilon_i) = \frac{1}{\sigma_i + \binom{|\Upsilon_i|}{2}} \left(\sigma_i + \sum_{\substack{u_1, u_2 \in \Upsilon_i: \\ u_1 \neq u_2}} s_{\Omega_i}(u_1, u_2) \right),
$$

where

$$
\sigma_i = \begin{cases} 1, & |\Upsilon_i| = 1; \\ 0, & \text{otherwise.} \end{cases}
$$

We can then offer the following definition:

Definition 10.4 (Conditioned Similarity). *Given a partition* $\Omega = \{\Omega_1, \ldots, \Omega_k\}$ *for UP such that* $UP = \bigcup_{i=1}^{k} \Omega_i$ *and the induced sets of users* $\Upsilon_i = \{u \in USERS \mid \exists p \in PERMS, \langle u, p \rangle \in \Omega_i\}$, *we define the similarity index conditioned by* Ω *as*

$$
S_\Omega(USERS) = \frac{\sum_{i=1}^{k} S(\Upsilon_i)\left(\sigma_i + \binom{|\Upsilon_i|}{2}\right)}{\sum_{i=1}^{k}\left(\sigma_i + \binom{|\Upsilon_i|}{2}\right)} = \frac{\sum_{i=1}^{k}\sigma_i + \sum_{i=1}^{k} S(\Upsilon_i)\binom{|\Upsilon_i|}{2}}{\sum_{i=1}^{k}\sigma_i + \sum_{i=1}^{k}\binom{|\Upsilon_i|}{2}}. \tag{10.15}
$$

Notice that Eq. (10.15) holds since $S(\Upsilon_i) = 1$ when $\sigma_i = 1$. Another important observation is that the conditioned index Eq. (10.15) is a sort of "modified" version of Eq. (10.3), where the pairs of users that belong to different subsets are discarded.

10.6.2 *Conditioned Minability ★*

Given a k-partition $\Omega = \{\Omega_1, \ldots, \Omega_k\}$ of *UP*, according to Eq. (10.11) the minability index of each subset Ω_i is

$$
\mathcal{M}(\Omega_i) = \frac{1}{|\Omega_i|} \sum_{\omega \in \Omega_i} m_{\Omega_i}(\omega),
$$

where $m_{\Omega_i}(\omega)$ indicates the local minability of ω obtained considering only the user-permission assignments belonging to Ω_i. This leads to the following definition:

Definition 10.5 (Conditioned Minability). *Given a k-partition $\Omega = \{\Omega_1, \ldots, \Omega_k\}$ for UP, the minability index* conditioned by Ω *is*

$$\mathcal{M}_\Omega(UP) = \frac{\sum_{i=1}^{k} \mathcal{M}(\Omega_i) |\Omega_i|}{\sum_{i=1}^{k} |\Omega_i|} = \frac{1}{|UP|} \sum_{i=1}^{k} \sum_{\omega \in \Omega_i} m_{\Omega_i}(\omega)$$

$$= \frac{1}{|UP|} \sum_{\omega \in UP} m_{\Omega_i}(\omega).$$

(10.16)

It is possible to note that the conditioned index Eq. (10.16) is similar to the basic minability index Eq. (10.11), except that relationships between user-permission assignments that belong to different subsets are no longer considered.

10.6.3   *Examples*⋆

In this section we show a simple application of our conditioned indices. Let us assume that the access control configuration to analyze is the one depicted in Fig. 10.4a. The unipartite graph corresponding to the analyzed access control configuration is shown in Fig. 10.4b. The values of the indices are reported in the caption. We now try to split the problem into several sub-problems by leveraging some available business information in order to check whether the minability and similarity values increase. For this purpose, suppose that we have two different business information at our disposal: the organization unit the user belongs to, and the applications involved by the given permission set. This information is depicted in Fig. 10.4a. In particular, the organization unit U_1 is composed of the users A, B, and C, while the organization units U_2 and U_3 are composed of the users D and E, respectively. As for the applications, A_x is composed of the permissions 1,2,3, and 4; A_y is composed of the permissions 5 and 6; while A_z is made up of permissions 7,8, and 9.

Given these pieces of information, we have to choose which one induces the partition that most simplifies the successive role mining steps. To ease exposition, we assume that all the subsets have the same importance. Figure 10.4c shows the subsets generated by partitioning according to the organization units. Notice that both minability and similarity indices are

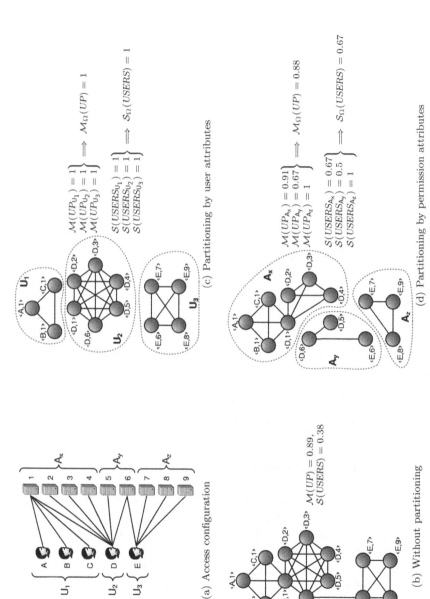

Fig. 10.4: A partitioning example

equal to 1 for each subset. Hence, both the conditioned indices equal 1. Figure 10.4d shows the subsets generated by partitioning according to applications and the corresponding minability and similarity values for each subset.

When comparing the conditioned indices of the two partitions, it can be easily noticed that the organization-units based partition is preferable to the applications-based partition. Indeed, the minability conditioned by applications is 0.88, which is even worse than the not-conditioned minability. Partitioning by organization units is also preferable when evaluating other conditioned indices.

10.6.4 *Approximation of Conditioned Indices* ⋆

We now demonstrate that the amount of approximation introduced by the proposed randomized algorithms, when applied to the calculation of conditioned indices, is comparable to the approximation of the non-conditioned indices [Colantonio *et al.* (2011a)].

Theorem 10.4. *Let* $\mathcal{S}_\Omega(USERS)$ *and* $\mathcal{M}_\Omega(UP)$ *be the exact indices conditioned by a given partition* Ω *according to Definitions 10.4 and 10.5, respectively. Let* $\widetilde{\mathcal{S}}_\Omega(USERS, k)$ *and* $\widetilde{\mathcal{M}}_\Omega(UP, k)$ *be the corresponding approximated values computed by adopting the algorithms in Fig. 10.1 and Fig. 10.2 for each subset* $\Omega_i \in \Omega$. *Then:*

$$\Pr\left(\left|\widetilde{\mathcal{S}}_\Omega(USERS, k) - \mathcal{S}_\Omega(USERS)\right| \geq \varepsilon\right) \leq 2\exp\left(-2k\varepsilon^2\right),$$
$$\Pr\left(\left|\widetilde{\mathcal{M}}_\Omega(UP, k) - \mathcal{M}_\Omega(UP)\right| \geq \varepsilon\right) \leq 2\exp\left(-2k\varepsilon^2\right).$$

10.7 Application to a Real Case

To demonstrate the usefulness of the proposed indices, we show how they have been applied to a real case. Our case study has been carried out on a large private organization. We examined a representative organization branch that contained 1,363 users with 5,319 granted permissions, resulting in a total of 84,201 user-permission assignments. To apply our approach we used two information sources: the organization unit (OU) chart, and a categorization of the users based on their job titles. In order to protect organization privacy, all names reported in this section for organization units and job titles are slightly different from the original ones. We calculated the indices described in the previous sections by adopting the algorithm in

Figs. 10.1 and 10.2 with $k = 5,000$, hence obtaining an error of less than 0.02 with a probability higher than 96%.

The remainder of this section is organized as follows. In Sec. 10.7.1 we will show two examples that have different values for minability and similarity, thus making it possible to better understand the meaning of having high or low values associated to these indices. In turn, in Sec. 10.7.2 we will apply our methodology in order to select the best available top-down information to decompose the problem. To further demonstrate the reliability of the methodology, we borrow from biology the methodology of introducing a *control test*. That is, we try to categorize users according to the first character of their surname. Since this categorization does not reflect any access control logic, we will analytically show that—as expected—it never helps the mining phase. Finally, in Sec. 10.7.3 we will use the proposed methodology in conjunction with the organizational unit chart to "drill-down" into smaller role mining problems.

10.7.1   *High and Low Values of Minability and Similarity*

Figure 10.5 shows the user-permission assignments for two distinct sets of users that belong to two chosen branches of the analyzed organization. The two OUs are comparable in terms of number of users, permissions, and user-permission assignments: Fig. 10.5a is related to 54 users who possess 285 permissions through 2,379 user-permission assignments; Fig. 10.5b represents 48 users who possess 299 permissions through 2,081 user-permission assignments. Assignments are depicted in a matrix form through the algorithm described in Chap. 9, where each row represents a user, each column represents a permission, and a black cell indicates a user with a given permission granted. By using the role mining algorithm described in [Colantonio *et al.* (2008c)], we computed all possible maximal equivalent roles.

Fig. 10.5a is an example of high values for minability (0.84) and similarity (0.43). It visually demonstrates how, in this case, it is easy to identify candidate roles—few groups of contiguous cells that cover most of the assignments can be easily identified via a visual inspection. The role identification task clearly requires more effort in Fig. 10.5b, in line with lower values for minability (0.66) and similarity (0.21). Indeed, it is impossible to define an organizational role composed of as many users and permissions as in the previous case, and it is harder to identify roles in general. This intuition is also supported by Fig. 10.5e and Fig. 10.5f. In these pictures we show the number of possible maximal roles that can be used to manage

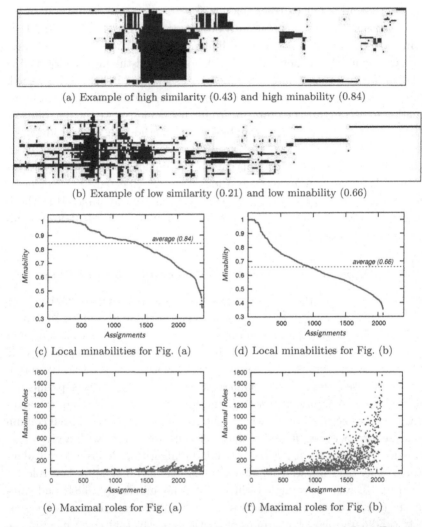

(a) Example of high similarity (0.43) and high minability (0.84)

(b) Example of low similarity (0.21) and low minability (0.66)

(c) Local minabilities for Fig. (a)

(d) Local minabilities for Fig. (b)

(e) Maximal roles for Fig. (a)

(f) Maximal roles for Fig. (b)

Fig. 10.5: Examples of different values for similarity and minability. Figures (a) and (b) depict user-permission assignments in a matrix form, where each black cell indicates a user (row) that has a certain permission (column) been granted. Figures (e) and (f) show the number of maximal roles which cover each user-permission assignment, sorted by the descending local minability values reported in (c) and (d)

each user-permission assignment of Fig. 10.5a and Fig. 10.5b, respectively. Assignments are sorted by descending local minabilities, and the corresponding minability values are reported in Fig. 10.5c and Fig. 10.5d. In the first case, the number of assignments with a local minability close to 1 is higher than in the second case. This is reflected by the number of maximal roles that cover each user-permission assignment, that is lower in the first case. Put another way, the ambiguity of selecting the role to manage each user-permission assignment is lower in the first example. This is in line with Theorem 10.2, which states that when the local minability of an assignment is equal to 1, there is only one maximal role to choose. The more the minability is far from 1, the more the number of maximal roles that can be used to manage that assignment increases, indicating that the identification of the "best" role-set requires more effort and, consequently, it is more error prone.

10.7.2 *Selection of the Best Business Information*

In this section we summarize an implementation of our divide-and-conquer approach. As anticipated before, we had at our disposal two top-down pieces of information—OU and job titles—and we wanted to choose the one that mostly simplifies the subsequent mining steps. As a *control*, we also introduced a third "artificial" information without any relation to the business—the first letter of user's surname. We generated three groups of users: A–G, H–P, and Q–Z. Obviously, we did not expect that this information would help the identification of roles. Indeed, experimental results confirmed our expectations, as shown later on.

The information about job titles was only available inside OU branches at the second level of the OU tree. Therefore, we first decomposed the problem by using the first OU level. For each index, the best values among all available partitions is highlighted in gray in Table 10.1. First, notice that alphabetical groups are never preferred, since they do not capture any pattern or commonality among users within access control data. For the other pieces of information, different cases can be identified:

- Within Manufacturing, partitioning by job titles is the best choice according to both indices. This means that job title is a good user's attribute to use when defining administration rules for the assignment of roles with users belonging to Manufacturing.
- Even though the job title concept is closer to the "role" concept, parti-

Table 10.1: Conditioned indices for the sample organization branch

Organization Unit	Index Type	Similarity	Minability	Roles
Operations				
Manufacturing				
	Not Conditioned	0,08	0,68	10.001
	Conditioned by Alphabetical Groups	0,08	0,74	4.422
	Conditioned by Organization Units	0,10	0,78	4.424
	Conditioned by Job Titles	0,29	0,89	918
Product Development				
	Not Conditioned	0,20	0,82	4.007
	Conditioned by Alphabetical Groups	0,20	0,84	2.511
	Conditioned by Organization Units	0,37	0,86	2.080
	Conditioned by Job Titles	0,38	0,90	818
Material Management				
	Not Conditioned	0,28	0,76	36.620
	Conditioned by Alphabetical Groups	0,28	0,80	3.504
	Conditioned by Organization Units	0,33	0,85	1.224
	Conditioned by Job Titles	0,28	0,82	21.614
Sales				
	Not Conditioned	0,07	0,63	61.933
	Conditioned by Alphabetical Groups	0,08	0,72	11.659
	Conditioned by Organization Units	0,11	0,67	50.314
	Conditioned by Job Titles	0,11	0,80	1.757
Quality				
	Not Conditioned	0,08	0,89	40
	Conditioned by Alphabetical Groups	0,08	0,94	36
	Conditioned by Organization Units	0,12	0,94	24
	Conditioned by Job Titles	0,21	0,96	25
Logistics				
	Not Conditioned	0,24	0,71	1.677
	Conditioned by Alphabetical Groups	0,24	0,80	642
	Conditioned by Organization Units	0,33	0,80	854
	Conditioned by Job Titles	0,64	0,83	357

tioning by job titles is not always the best choice. Material Management shows a case where the best partition is based on OUs. In this case, this is justified by the fact that the majority of the users have the same job title. Hence, partitioning does not actually improve the mining complexity.

- As for the mining complexity, the number of maximal roles is in line with the minability and similarity indices. Few roles also means less elaboration time, thus resulting in faster algorithm runs.

The previous examples also demonstrate that, in general, the choice of the best index to use depends on the main role engineering objectives.

Table 10.2: Further decomposition of the sample organization branch

Organization Unit	Users	Permissions	User-Perm Assignments	Similarity	Mirability	Roles
Operations	**946**	**3.647**	**56.905**	**0,07**	**0,65**	**219.086**
Manufacturing	**379**	**1.810**	**20.400**	**0,08**	**0,68**	**10.001**
Parent	1	64	64	1,00	1,00	1
Technology	49	323	2.342	0,35	0,92	127
Control	26	577	2.396	0,30	0,81	254
Test & Quality	8	226	301	0,09	0,92	17
Production	288	1.452	15.226	0,09	0,75	4.013
Plants	7	39	71	0,12	0,83	12
Product Development	**319**	**1.341**	**14.222**	**0,20**	**0,82**	**4.007**
Parent	2	32	33	0,03	0,98	3
Engineering	77	559	2.898	0,36	0,82	564
Design #1	88	361	3.275	0,41	0,84	10
Design #2	121	739	6.965	0,35	0,87	232
Design #3	6	115	214	0,14	0,93	1.205
Marketing	17	404	663	0,08	0,91	57
Innovation	8	92	174	0,23	0,97	9
Material Management	**58**	**1.038**	**8.670**	**0,28**	**0,76**	**36.620**
Parent	3	286	368	0,17	0,95	6
Purchase Dept #1	23	549	3.043	0,27	0,80	745
Purchase Dept #2	13	407	2.136	0,49	0,89	382
Purchase Dept #3	7	406	1.054	0,29	0,77	56
Purchase Dept #4	5	311	972	0,69	0,91	15
Saving Control	3	203	303	0,32	0,86	7
Analysis & Reporting	4	376	794	0,35	0,87	13
Sales	**100**	**1.531**	**9.483**	**0,07**	**0,63**	**61.933**
Parent	1	68	68	1,00	1,00	1
Logistics	36	1.142	6.836	0,24	0,63	49.256
Support	63	795	2.579	0,07	0,76	1.057
Quality	**16**	**272**	**697**	**0,08**	**0,89**	**40**
Parent	1	20	20	1,00	1,00	1
Certification	2	40	46	0,15	0,92	3
Audit	6	188	352	0,20	0,94	7
Quality Center	7	151	279	0,07	0,93	13
Logistics	**73**	**1.078**	**3.432**	**0,24**	**0,71**	**1.677**
Parent	0	0	0	-	-	0
Methodologies	2	350	549	0,57	0,92	3
Planning	7	311	682	0,41	0,88	38
Distribution #1	62	464	1.780	0,32	0,70	810
Distribution #2	2	351	421	0,20	0,93	3

10.7.3 *Drill Down*

We now show an application of the proposed methodology when hierarchical information is available. Suppose that the only available top-down information is the organizational unit chart. Table 10.2 shows index values obtained by iteratively applying a decomposition based on OUs for the unit Operations. First, notice that partitioning users according to the second level of the OU tree raised the values of both indices for most OUs. For instance, Product Development, which holds approximately one third of the branch Operations, has a minability of 0.82 and a similarity of 0.20. Conversely, Manufacturing still has low values for those indices. This means that it would be easier to find optimal organizational and functional roles for Product Development rather than for Manufacturing. Moreover, the average increase of minability is reflected by a lower number of possible maximal roles, dropped down from 219,086 to 114,278.

Another observation is that partitioning always reduces the number of users, permissions, and user-permission assignments to analyze, but the values of minability and the similarity do not rise proportionally. For example, Logistics has a minability of 0.71, but his child Distribution #1 has a minability of 0.70, indicating that the "mess" of Logistics is likely concentrated in Distribution #1, as confirmed by the number of maximal roles. Further, Product Development has much more users than Logistics, but it also has a higher minability. Moreover, high values for similarity imply high minability as well, but the inverse does not hold. If similarity is close to 1, then all users possess the same permissions; thus, minability is also close to 1. The opposite is false. For example, Distribution #2 shows a high minability (0.93) and a low similarity (0.20).

There are other examples of different trends for minability and similarity when compared to the number of users or permissions. For instance, let us consider Marketing and Purchase Dept #2 which have similar number of users and permissions. In the first case, we have 0.91 for minability and 0.08 for similarity, while in the second case we have 0.89 for minability (less than the previous case) and 0.49 for similarity (more than the previous case). This confirms that there is no direct relation between these two indices, but both are helpful to address role elicitation by highlighting two different aspects of the user-permission set. Indeed, if the objective of role engineers is to elicit organizational roles, the similarity helps to identify the OUs where an organizational role that covers a relevant number of user-permission assignment exists. This happens, for instance, for

Purchase Dept #4 because of the similarity of 0.69. On the other hand, if the objective of role engineers is to find functional roles, they have to consider the minability index. For example, the sub-branch Innovation is likely to be an easily solvable sub-problem due to a minability of 0.97, as confirmed by the low number of possible maximal roles.

10.8 Final Remarks

We described a methodology that helps role engineers to leverage business information during the role mining process. In particular, we demonstrated that by dividing data into smaller, more homogeneous subsets, it practically leads to the discovery of more meaningful roles from a business perspective, reducing the complexity of the mining task, and decreasing the risk factor of making errors in managing them. To drive this process, the minability and similarity indices were introduced to measure the expected complexity in locating homogeneous set of users and permissions that can be managed through roles. Leveraging these indices allows to identify the decomposition that increases business meaning in elicited roles in subsequent role mining steps, thus simplifying the analysis. The quality of the indices was also guaranteed by analysis.

Please also note that minability and similarity are also metrics for the likelihood of making administration errors when managing roles throughout their lifecycle. For instance, given a group of users, when the minability index equals 1 for user-permission assignments involved in the group, according to Theorem 10.2 there will be just one possible maximal role for managing those assignments. This means, for example, that new permissions introduced within the system will likely be assigned to all users of the group (via the single role) or to none of them, and new users that join such a group will likely be granted the same permissions of other users (namely, all the permissions contained within the single role). Moreover, the business meaning of the role is strictly related to business aspects that users within the group have in common. Therefore, the probability of making wrong access control decisions is low. Chapter 13 further discusses this application of minability and similarity.

Chapter 11

Stable Roles

This chapter proposes a methodology that helps role engineers to identify roles that are stable and minimize the effort required to select the most meaningful roles for the organization. The proposed approach allows to *prune* user-permission assignments which lead to unstable roles and that increase the complexity of the role mining task. In this way, we are able to build a core set of roles that have the above mentioned features. In particular, we leverage the mapping between role mining and some well-known graph problems described in Chap. 5. Finally, applications of the methodology to real-world data are shown.

11.1 Stable Assignments and Stable Roles ⋆

Chapter 2 pointed out that RBAC can drastically reduce the costs of administering and monitoring permissions when compared to antecedent access control models. RBAC allows for greater automation while adhering to the specified access control policy. Changes to permissions are automated through role assignment rather than being manually assigned whenever a new user is hired, an existing user changes positions, or new applications or IT systems are adopted. However, by introducing new users, new permissions, or new user-permission assignments within an RBAC-based access control system, there might be the need to reassess the role-set in use.

In such a scenario, roles could be *unstable*, in the sense that the introduction of few users or few permissions could require a complete re-design of such roles in order to reduce the overall administration cost [Colantonio *et al.* (2009b, 2010d)]. Unstable roles are thus difficult to manage as they likely change during their life-cycle. Conversely, a role is *stable* if it is not greatly affected by the introduction of new users, new permissions, or new user-permission assignments, namely it still remains optimal according to organization's requirements. That is why, when dealing with automated role mining algorithms, the stability of elicited candidate roles is a desirable property.

In the following we formalize the "stability" concept described above.

11.1.1   *Problem Formalization* ⋆

For the purposes of this chapter, we introduce the following metric for roles:

Definition 11.1 (Role Weight). *Given a role* $r \in ROLES$, *let* P_r *and* U_r *be the sets of permissions and users associated to* r, *that is* $P_r = \{p \in PERMS \mid \langle p, r \rangle \in PA\}$ *and* $U_r = \{u \in USERS \mid \langle u, r \rangle \in UA\}$. *We indicate with* $w \colon ROLES \to \mathbb{R}$ *the weight function of roles, defined as*

$$w(r) = c_u \, |U_r| \oplus c_p \, |P_r|, \tag{11.1}$$

where the operator "$\oplus$" represents a homogeneous[1] binary function of degree 1, while c_u *and* c_p *are real numbers greater than 0.*

In the following, we use the role weight as an indicator of the "stability" of a role:

Definition 11.2 (Role Stability). *Let* $r \in ROLES$ *be a given role,* w *be the role weight function, and* $t \in \mathbb{R}$ *be a real number that we refer to as a "threshold." We say that* r *is* stable *with respect to* t *if* $w(r) > t$. *Otherwise,* r *is* unstable.

Definition 11.3 (Assignment Stability). *Let the pair* $\langle u, p \rangle \in UP$ *be a given assignment, and* $t \in \mathbb{R}$ *be a real number that we refer to as a "threshold." Let* $R_{\langle u,p \rangle}$ *be the set of roles that contains the assignment* $\langle u, p \rangle$, *namely* $R_{\langle u,p \rangle} = \{r \in ROLES \mid \langle u, r \rangle \in UA, \langle p, r \rangle \in PA\}$, *and let* w *be the role weight function. We say that* $\langle u, p \rangle$ *is* stable *with respect to*

---

[1]A function is *homogeneous* when it has a multiplicative-scaling behavior, that is if the argument is multiplied by a factor, then the result is multiplied by some power of this factor. Formally, if $f \colon V \to W$ is a function between two vector spaces over a field F, then f is said to be homogeneous of degree k if $f(\alpha \mathbf{v}) = \alpha^k f(\mathbf{v})$ for all nonzero $\alpha \in F$ and $\mathbf{v} \in V$. When the vector spaces involved are over the real numbers, a slightly more general form of homogeneity is often used, requiring only that the previous equation holds for all $\alpha > 0$. Note that any linear function is homogeneous of degree 1, by the definition of linearity. Since we require functions with two parameters, we can alternatively state that the multiplication must be *distributive* over "$\oplus$." Thus, an example of valid "$\oplus$" operator is the sum, as shown in Sec. 11.4.3.

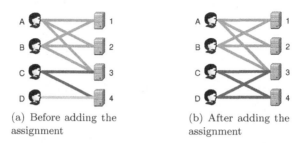

(a) Before adding the
assignment

(b) After adding the
assignment

Fig. 11.1: Behavior of stable and unstable assignments when new assignments are added. Candidate roles are highlighted with different colors.

t *if it belongs to at least one stable role, namely* $\exists r \in R_{\langle u,p \rangle} : w(r) > t$. *Otherwise, the assignment is* unstable, *that is* $\forall r \in R_{\langle u,p \rangle} : w(r) \leq t$.

If a role is composed by few user-permission relationships, its weight will be limited, and subsequently it will be unstable. Indeed, when a change of the access control configuration happens, there is the need to recalculate the optimal candidate role-set. In this case, the introduction of a new user-permission assignment could drastically change the configuration of an unstable role, according to the specific cost function considered. To better understand this concept, Fig. 11.1 shows an example of assignment addition in a context where assignments that belong to roles with different weights are present. In particular, Fig. 11.1a shows a possible system configuration. On the left side there are users $\{A, B, C, D\}$, while on the right side there are permissions $\{1, 2, 3, 4\}$. A "link" between a user and a permission indicates that the given user is granted the given permission. The picture also highlights a candidate role-set, represented by the roles:

- Role r_1: users $U_{r_1} = \{A, B\}$, permissions $P_{r_1} = \{1, 2, 3\}$;
- Role r_2: users $U_{r_2} = \{C\}$, permissions $P_{r_2} = \{3, 4\}$;
- Role r_3: users $U_{r_3} = \{D\}$, permissions $P_{r_3} = \{4\}$.

Suppose that we want user D to be granted permission 3. Figure 11.1b shows the resulting new configuration and proposes a new candidate role-set, represented by the following roles:

- Role r_1: users $\{A, B\}$, permissions $\{1, 2, 3\}$;
- Role r_4: users $\{C, D\}$, permissions $\{3, 4\}$.

Intuitively, by replacing roles r_2 and r_3 with the new role r_4 we get more advantages than creating a new role to manage the newly introduced assignment. Instead, role r_1 exists in both the solutions, due to the high number of users and permissions involved. Thus, it is not advantageous to modify the definition of r_1 in order to manage the new assignment. As a consequence of the previous observation, the administration of unstable assignments through roles requires more effort. Hence, the direct assignment of permissions to users could be more profitable.

In general, once an optimal set of roles has been found, the introduction of a new user or a new permission may change the system equilibrium whenever roles with limited weight exist. This translates in higher administration cost, which is something that RBAC administrators tend to avoid. Therefore, roles with a consistent weight are preferable, since they are more stable and less affected by the modifications of the existing user-permission assignments. The main idea is thus to identify and "discard" the user-permission relationships that only belong to roles with a limited weight—that is, unstable assignments. Put another way, we do not manage unstable assignments with any roles. Equivalently, we can create as many single-permission roles as the permissions involved with unstable assignments. Thus, restricting the role mining problem to the remaining user-permission assignments only. In this way, the elicited roles are *representative* and *stable*. Representative since they are used by several users or they cover several permissions. Stable because they are not greatly affected by the introduction of new users or new permissions.

11.2   Pruning Unstable Assignments ⋆

This section formally describes a strategy for the reduction of the role mining complexity by pruning unstable assignments. We first explain the mapping between the role engineering problem, the biclique cover and the clique partition problems, as in [Ene *et al.* (2008)]. Then we introduce our three-step methodology. Moreover, we prove the relation between the degree of a graph nodes and their instability.

11.2.1   *Methodology* ⋆

To generate a candidate role-set that is stable and easily analyzable, we split the problem in three steps:

- *Step 1*: Define a weight-based threshold.
- *Step 2*: Catch the unstable user-permission assignments.
- *Step 3*: Restrict the problem of finding a set of roles that minimizes the administration cost function by only using stable user-permission assignments.

In particular, we introduce a pruning operation on the vertices of the graph $\overline{G}'$ (see Eq. (5.5) at page 69) that corresponds to identifying unstable user-permission assignments. We suggest to not manage these assignments with roles, but to directly assign permission to users or, equivalently, to create "special" roles composed by only one permission. In this way, we are able to limit the presence of unstable roles. Moreover, we will show that the portion of the graph that survives after the pruning operation can be represented as a graph $\overline{G}'$ with a limited degree. Since the third step corresponds to coloring $\overline{G}'$, the information about the degree can be leveraged to select an efficient coloring algorithms among those available in the literature that make assumptions on the degree. The choice of which algorithm to use depends on the definition of the administration cost function.

It is also important to note that when the graph G is not connected, it is possible to consider any connected component as a separate problem. Hence, the union of the solutions of each component will be the solution of the original graph, as proven in the following lemma [Colantonio *et al.* (2010d)]:

Lemma 11.1. *A biclique cannot exist across two or more disconnected components of a bipartite graph* G.

Since a biclique corresponds to a role, the previous lemma states that a role r, made up of users U_r and permissions P_r, cannot exist if all the users in U_r do not have all the permissions in P_r. If this were the case, we would have introduced some user-permission relationships that were not in the configuration $\varphi = \langle USERS, PERMS, UP \rangle$. This lemma has an important implication [Colantonio *et al.* (2010d)]:

Theorem 11.1. *If* G *is disconnected, the union of the biclique covers of each component of* G *is a biclique cover of* G.

As a main consequence of the theorem, if the graph G is disconnected, we can study each component independently. In particular, we can use the union of the biclique cover of the different components to build a biclique cover of G. According to what we will see in the next section, we can use this result to limit the degree of $\overline{G}'$ when the bipartite graph G is disconnected.

11.2.2 *Unstable Assignment Identification* ⋆

In our model, the role mining problem corresponds to finding a proper coloring for the graph $\overline{G}'$. Depending on the organization's requirements, the optimal coloring can change. For instance, if we want to minimize the total number of roles, the optimal coloring is the one which uses the minimum number of colors. In this section we will analyze the degree of the graph $\overline{G}'$ by highlighting how this information can affect the assignment stability and, as a consequence, the administration effort.

According to Eq. (5.5) at page 69, the degree of $\overline{G}'$ can be expressed as:

$$\Delta(\overline{G}') = \max_{\omega \in UP} |\overline{\mathcal{B}}(\omega)|. \qquad (11.2)$$

To understand the relation between the graph degree and the stable assignment identification problem, it is useful to recall the graph meaning in terms of RBAC semantic. A vertex of $\overline{G}'$ is a user-permission relationship in the set UP. An edge in $\overline{G}'$ between two vertices ω_1 and ω_2 exists if the corresponding user-permission relationships cannot be in the same role, due to the fact that the user in ω_1 does not have the permission in ω_2, or the user in ω_2 does not have the permission in ω_1. Consequently, a vertex of $\overline{G}'$ that has a high degree means that this vertex cannot be colored using the same colors of a high number of other vertices. In other words, this user-permission relationship cannot be in the same role together with a high number of other user-permission relationships.

The previous considerations have an important aftermath: if a user-permission relationship cannot be in the same role together with a high number of other user-permission relationships, it will belong to a role with few user-permission relationships, and we can estimate the maximal weight of such a role. Hence, we can prune those user-permission relationships which can only belong to roles with a weight that is lower than a fixed threshold. In particular, suppose that for each edge $\omega \in UP$ of the bipartite graph G there are at least d other edges such that the corresponding endpoints induce a biclique together with the endpoints of ω. In this case, every edge of G will not be in biclique with less than $|UP| - d$ other edges, according to the following lemma [Colantonio *et al.* (2010d)]:

Lemma 11.2. *Let UP be the set of edges of the bipartite graph G. Then:*

$$\forall \omega \in UP, \; |\mathcal{B}(\omega)| > d \implies \Delta(\overline{G}') \leq |UP| - d$$

Thus, given a suitable value for d, the idea is to prune the graph $\overline{G}'$ by deleting the vertices that have a degree higher than $|E(G)| - d$. This corresponds to pruning edges in G that induce a biclique with at most d other edges. Moreover [Colantonio *et al.* (2010d)]:

Theorem 11.2. *The pruning operation based on removing from $\overline{G}'$ vertices ω such that $|\mathcal{B}(\omega)| \leq d$ will prune only user-permission assignments that cannot belong to any role $r \in ROLES$ such that $w(r) > d \times (c_U \oplus c_P)$.*

Note that many coloring algorithms known in the literature make assumptions on the degree of the graph. Since our pruning approach limits the degree of $\overline{G}'$, it allows for an efficient application of this class of algorithms. Without our pruning operation, the degree of the graph $\overline{G}'$ could be high, up to $|UP| - 1$. This is the case when a user-permission assignment that must be managed alone in a role exists. Note also that when the graph G is disconnected in two or more components, any edge of one component does not induce a biclique together with any edge of the other components. Thus, in these cases $\Delta(\overline{G}')$ is very high. But, for Theorem 11.1, we can split the problem by considering the different components distinctly, and then join the results of each component.

As for practical application of the pruning strategy, in Sec. 5.3 we demonstrated that the function $\mathcal{B}(\cdot)$ is equivalent to the relevance of pseudo-roles. In particular, the output of the algorithm EXTRACT listed in Fig. 5.6 is an approximation for $\mathcal{B}(\cdot)$. It is very important to note that the neighbor-counters are inferred with only one run of EXTRACT. Changing a threshold d does not require the complete re-imputation of neighbor-counters: Each run can be subsequently analyzed by trying to find the one that best reaches a certain target function. The tuning of the threshold d depends on the final objective of the data analysis problem. First, we can define a metric that measures how well the objective has been reached. Then, this metric can be used to evaluate the imputed dataset. This can be an iterative process, executed several times with different thresholds, thus choosing the threshold value that provides the best result. Section 11.4 shows a practical application of this methodology in a real case.

11.3 Stability and Mining Complexity ⋆

In this section we will show that not only does the pruning operation proposed in Sec. 11.2.2 identify the user-permission assignments that are unstable, but it is also able to simplify the identification and selection of stable roles among all the candidate roles. The main result is that stable assignments may have a low value for the minability index described in Sec. 10.4 due to the presence of unstable assignments. A low value for the minability index is a synonym for high role engineering complexity. This can be summarized with the following statement:

assignments with unstable neighbors
$$\implies \text{ low minability index}$$
$$\implies \text{ complex role engineering task.}$$

In Sec. 10.4 we demonstrated that the local minability index of a given assignment expresses the ambiguity in selecting the best maximal role to cover it. Hereafter, we show that the local minability index and the number of assignments that induce a role are bound. In particular, we prove that the presence of unstable assignments decreases the maximum local minability value allowed for stable assignments. Therefore, keeping unstable assignments within the data to analyze hinders the role engineering process by increasing the ambiguity in selecting the best roles used to cover stable assignments. In particular [Colantonio *et al.* (2010d)]:

Theorem 11.3. *Let* $\omega \in UP$ *be a user-permission assignment such that* $|\mathcal{B}(\omega)| > 1$. *Then, the following holds:*

$$m(\omega) \leq \frac{\underset{\omega' \in \mathcal{B}(\omega)}{\text{avg}} |\mathcal{B}(\omega')| - 1}{|\mathcal{B}(\omega)| - 1}. \tag{11.3}$$

Notice that $m(\omega) = 1$ means that all the neighbors of ω in the graph G' built according to Eq. (5.3) have, among their neighbors, all the neighbors of ω. Thus, the right side of the inequality in Eq. (11.3) is equal to or greater than 1. Similarly, $m(\omega) = 0$ means that each pair of neighbors of ω are not neighbors among them. Thus, the right side of the inequality in Eq. (11.3) is equal to or greater than 0.

Finally, let us assume that all the neighbors of ω have a degree that is lower than the degree of ω, namely $\forall \omega' \in \mathcal{B}(\omega) : |\mathcal{B}(\omega')| < |\mathcal{B}(\omega)|$. Then, $m(\omega) < 1$. This likely happens to assignments that have a high degree and many unstable assignments as neighbors. Hence, unstable assignments make the task of selecting the best maximal role used to cover stable assignments more difficult. From this point of view, unstable assignments are a sort of "noise" within the data, that badly bias any role mining analysis. Indeed, the number of elicited roles may be large when compared to the number of users and permissions, mainly due to noise within the data—namely, permissions exceptionally or accidentally granted or denied. In such a case, classical role mining algorithms discover multiple small fragments of the true role, but miss the role itself [Liu *et al.* (2006)]. The problem is even worse for roles which cover many user-permission assignments, since they are more vulnerable to noise [Mahfouz and Ismail (2009)].

In the next section we will show through experiments on real data that the minability index increases when pruning unstable assignments.

11.4 Pruning Examples

To prove the viability of our approach, we applied it to several real-world datasets at our disposal. In the following, we first report the application of our model to the access control configuration related to users of an organization unit of a large company. Then, by using the previous dataset, we highlight the effect of the pruning operation on the role mining complexity. Finally, we show how it is possible to compute the optimal threshold to use with our pruning strategy. In all the tests we used the pruning strategy in conjunction with the algorithm EXTRACT (with $k = 1000$).

11.4.1 *A Real Case*

Fig. 11.2 shows an example of our strategy when applied to a real dataset. Figure 11.2a represents the bipartite graph G built from the access control configuration relative to users of an Organization Unit (OU) of a large company. The OU analyzed counts 7 users (nodes on the left) and 39 permissions (nodes on the right), with a total of 71 user-permission assignments. We have chosen an OU with few users and permissions to ease graph representation. According to a pruning threshold equal to 0.39, stable assignments are depicted with thicker edges, while unstable assignments with thinner edges. Figure 11.2b depicts the unipartite graph G', built according to Eq. (5.3). The user-permission assignments of G correspond to the vertices of G', and two vertices are connected by an edge if they induce a biclique. Dashed edges indicate that one of the two endpoints will be pruned. Figure 11.2c shows only the stable assignments, namely the ones that will survive to the pruning operation. By comparing these last two figures it is possible to see that the main component of the whole graph survives after the pruning, while pruned assignments correspond to "noise."

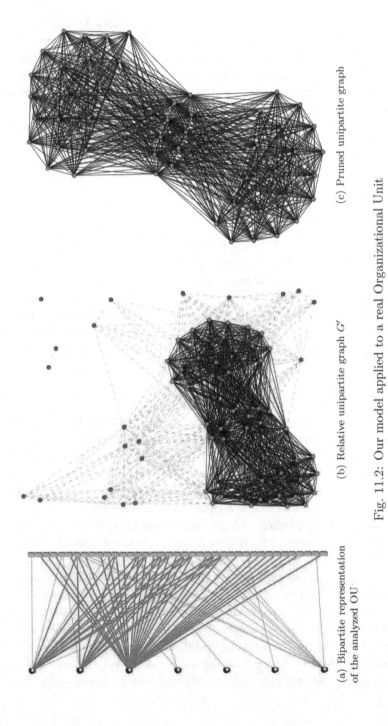

(c) Pruned unipartite graph

(b) Relative unipartite graph G'

Fig. 11.2: Our model applied to a real Organizational Unit

(a) Bipartite representation of the analyzed OU

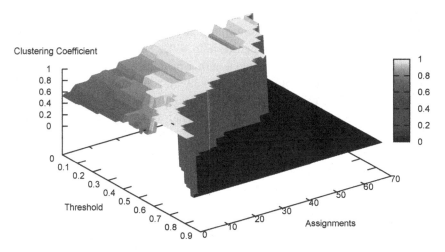

Fig. 11.3: Pruning effect on local minability index

Indeed, the pruned vertices induce a biclique with only a small fraction of nodes of the main component.

11.4.2 Effects of the Pruning on the Mining Complexity

Theorem 11.3 states that the local minability index of a vertex is upper bounded by the ratio of the average neighborhoods degrees and its own degree. As a consequence, stable assignments have a limited minability index because of the low degree of their neighbors. This means that these assignments are difficult to manage in a role mining process. Yet, they also are the most "interesting" one since they are stable assignments. Our pruning operation is able to increase the average degrees of neighbors, and, at the same time, to decrease the degree of stable assignments. Thus, it is able to increase the above limitation of the local minability index. In the following, we will experimentally show that when the pruning is executed, not only does the above local minability index limit increase, but even the minability index grows.

Fig. 11.3 graphically shows this behavior. The dataset analyzed is the same that has been used in Sec. 11.4.1. The minability index has been reported for all the assignments, which are ordered by *descending* degree (i.e., descending stability), and for different pruning thresholds. For representation purposes, we have assigned 0 to the minability index of pruned assignments. By analyzing Fig. 11.3, it turns out that originally stable assignments have a limited minability index. Indeed, all the assignments numbered between 0 and 20 have a minability index lower than 0.73 when no pruning operation is executed (threshold = 0). Further, it turns out that the minability index increases when a higher pruning threshold is used. For example, when the threshold is equal to 0.39, all the assignments numbered between 10 and 50 have a minability index equal to 1. Note that, according to Theorem ?? in these cases only one maximal role which they can belong to exists. In terms of RBAC, there exists only one role (represented by a maximal role) that they can belong to. Furthermore, the pruned assignments are only 20 out of 71, the assignments with a minability index equal to 1 are 40, while only 10 assignments have a minability index between 0 and 1. Anyway, the minability index of 5 out of these 10 assignments increased from 0.52 to 0.65, while it was almost steady for the other 5 assignments. This means that the mining complexity has been actually reduced.

11.4.3 *Threshold Tuning*

The tuning of the threshold to use in our pruning algorithm depends on the final objective of the data analysis problem. In particular, we first need to define a metric that measures how well the objective has been reached. Then, it is possible to use this metric to choose the best threshold. The metric that we used in our tests is a *multi-objective* function that considers different aspects of the role engineering problem. Multi-objective analysis often means to trade-off conflicting goals. In a role engineering context, for example, we execute the pruning while requiring to minimize the complexity of the mining, minimize the number of pruned assignments, and maximize the stability of the candidate role-set.

A viable approach to solve a multi-objective optimization problem is to build a *single aggregated objective function* from the given objective functions [Deb (2001)]. One possible way to do this is combining different functions in a *weighted sum*, with the following general formulation:

$$\sum_{f_i \in F} \alpha_i f_i. \tag{11.4}$$

F is the set of the functions to optimize, and α_i is a scale parameter that can be different for each function $f_i \in F$. Put another way, one specifies scalar weights for each objective to be optimized, and then combines them into a single function that can be solved by any single-objective optimizer. Once we defined the aggregated objective function, the problem of finding the best trade-off corresponds to the minimization of this function. The weight parameters can be negative or positive, according to the need of minimizing or to maximizing the corresponding function. Clearly, the solution obtained will depend on the values (more precisely, the relative values) of the specified weights. Thus, it may be noticed that the weighted sum method is essentially subjective, in that an analyst needs to supply the weights.

As for the practical computation of the best threshold, we identified the following objective functions:

- Minability Index, that indicates the global minability index of the unipartite graph G' built from UP. It is a measure of the mining complexity.
- Pruned Assignments, that is the number of assignments that are pruned by our algorithm.
- Maximal Roles, namely the number of maximal roles identifiable in G. They represent the number of maximal roles of the underlying access control configuration.
- Average Weight, that is the average weight of the roles relative to the set of maximal roles. The weight of a role r is defined as $|U_r| \times |P_r|$.

These objectives have been combined in the following multi-objective function:

$$\mathsf{Index} = -\mathsf{Minability\ Index} + \frac{0.3 \times \mathsf{Pruned\ Assignments}}{max(\mathsf{Pruned\ Assignments})}$$

$$+ \frac{0.8 \times \mathsf{Maximal\ Roles}}{max(\mathsf{Maximal\ Roles})} - \frac{0.8 \times \mathsf{Average\ Weight}}{max(\mathsf{Average\ Weight})}$$

Finding the "best" threshold means to minimize the previous equation. Weights have been chosen by giving a higher relevance to the minability index; an intermediate relevance to the maximal roles number and to the average weight; and finally, a low relevance to the number of pruned assignments. Thus, we are willing to reduce the number of pruned assignments, by contextually reducing the complexity of the role mining task, the number of maximal roles, and maximizing the average weight.

In Fig. 11.4, we report two examples of the threshold tuning applied to two real datasets at our disposal. The two analyzed cases concern two organization units of a large company. They are comparable with respect to their size: the first one counts 54 users and 285 permissions, with a total of 2,379 assignments; the second one is composed of 48 users, 299 permissions, and a total of 2,081 assignments. The difference between them mainly lies

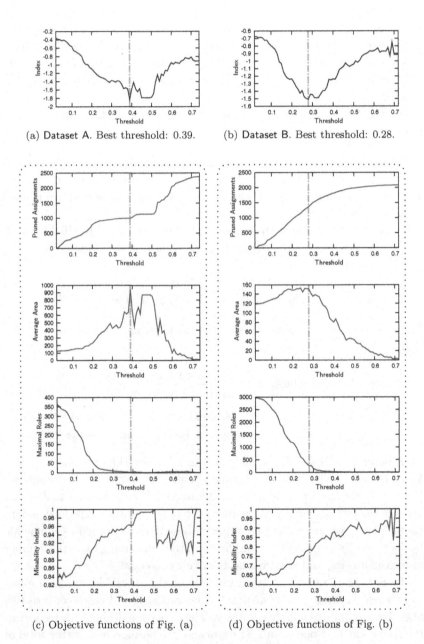

(a) Dataset A. Best threshold: 0.39. (b) Dataset B. Best threshold: 0.28.

(c) Objective functions of Fig. (a) (d) Objective functions of Fig. (b)

Fig. 11.4: Finding the best threshold

on the mining complexity: the first one has a global minability index higher than the second one (0.84 vs. 0.66). In particular:

- Dataset A: high minability index (0.84), 54 users, 285 permissions, and 2,379 assignments.
- Dataset B: low minability index (0.66), 48 users, 299 permissions, and 2,081 assignments.

By using the given cost function, a high relevance is given to Minability Index, a medium one is given to Average Weight and Maximal Roles, while less relevance is given to Pruned Assignments. In this way, we are willing to prune a high number of assignments to reduce the complexity of the role mining task, by contextually minimizing the number of maximal roles and maximizing the average weight. Figures 11.4a and 11.4b represent the aggregated functions for these two organization unit. Figures 11.4c and 11.4d show the four functions that compose the aggregated one. In both cases, the minimum of the aggregated function is highlighted with a vertical dashed line.

As for the first organization unit, the minimum is reached when the threshold is equal to 0.39. Indeed, in Fig. 11.4c it can be seen that this is a good trade-off among all the four single functions: the pruned assignments are 1,001 out of 2,379; the average weight (that indicates the average stability) has grown almost 9 times from the original average weight; the number of maximal bicliques has been decreased from 350 to 2; finally the minability index has been increased from 0.84 to 0.96. Note that, since we have only 2 maximal bicliques, we are able to manage all the assignments survived to the pruning with only 2 roles. Put another way, we found two stable roles that together are able to manage 1,378 out of 2,379 assignments.

As for the second organization unit, the minimum of the multi-objective function is reached when the threshold is equal to 0.28 (see Fig. 11.4b). In this case, the pruned assignments are 1,367, the average weight increased from 120 to 151, the number of maximal roles has been decreased from 3,000 to 266, while the minability index has been increased from 0.66 to 0.78. At first sight, it seems that we pruned too much assignments, but these results depend both on the dataset we are analyzing and on the targets that role engineers want to reach. Indeed, this dataset has a higher complexity with respect to the first one, and we provided high weights for Minability Index and Maximal Roles. If we gave less relevance to these two parameters, a lower threshold would have been a good trade off. In that case, the pruned assignments would have been less than 1,367, and the average weight would have been higher than the original one. In general, the role engineers mission is to establish the weights of the multi-objective aggregated function in such a way to get as close as possible to the target that they want to reach.

11.5 Final Remarks

In this chapter we proposed a three steps methodology, rooted on sound graph theory, to reduce the role mining complexity in RBAC systems. To show the viability of the proposal, the methodology is applied to a concrete case. Extensive experiments on real data set do confirm its viability, as well as the quality of the results achieved by the related algorithms.

Chapter 12

Imputing Missing Grants

A typical problem affecting the majority of existing role mining algorithms is that the number of automatically elicited roles is often very large. This is mainly due to "noise" within the data, namely permissions exceptionally/accidentally granted (e.g., unstable user-permission assignments, as discussed in the previous chapter) or denied (e.g., "missing" assignments). In both cases, classical role mining algorithms elicit multiple small fragments of the true role. Recently, a number of methods have been proposed to discover approximate patterns in the presence of noise. However, they usually require tuning several parameters that can greatly affect algorithm performances and the quality of results. Further, the number of exceptions may be so high to make it difficult to navigate and analyze them.

In this chapter we address the problem of identifying missing assignments in access control systems. The problem is analyzed in terms of binary matrix representation of user-permission assignments. We also introduce an algorithm that is able to impute missing data by leveraging identifiable patterns within available data.

12.1 Missing Values

When dealing with binary matrices (see Sec. 5.3), a fundamental problem that analysts need to deal with is *incomplete data*, namely portions of data that are unavailable or unobserved. We refer to this data as *missing values*. Since the seminal paper of Rubin Rubin (1976), much work has been done about imputing missing values,[1] mainly in the statistical field [Little

---

[1]The study of missing values is relevant in several data mining areas. Indeed, missing values arise in many practical situations. For example, in almost all medical studies important data may be missing for some subjects for a variety of reasons: from malfunc-

and Rubin (1987); Schafer (1997); Schafer and Graham (2002)]. In access control, a binary matrix is such that rows represent users and columns represent permissions. A cell representing a user-permission assignment is then set to 1 if the user must have the permission granted, 0 if not, and '*' in the case that he could have that permission granted but it is not strictly needed to accomplish his work, or in the case that it is not clear whether he should have that permission granted or not. In general, missing values in a binary matrix can be classified in two categories: *flagged* and *non-flagged*. In the first case, missing values are explicitly "highlighted" with a special value (e.g., with a '*'). In the second case, missing values are not explicitly flagged, but they are embedded in the 0's data—namely each 0 is potentially a missing value.

Typically, missing values in an access control scenario are neglected since having less privileges than strictly required is not considered a risk. However, having few permissions is not always desirable. For instance, in Chap. 2 we pointed out that RBAC can help reduce new employee downtime from more efficient provisioning. In this case, recently hired employees might be only marginally productive because they are underentitled. Moreover, the quality of role mining results is severely biased by missing values [Colantonio *et al.* (2010a)]. For these reasons, it is desirable to replace potential missing values with "certain" values.

When a complete dataset is required, as is the case of most role mining tools, data analysts typically have three options before performing the analysis: discarding the user/permission that contain missing data, replacing missing data values (i.e., granting the corresponding permission), or estimating values of missing data entries [Tuikkala *et al.* (2008)]. The inappropriate handling of missing values can pose serious problems. It may introduce bias on the final results, and sometimes it can also affect the generalization of the analysis. For instance, when missing values are present,

---

tioning hardware components, to indecision due to the rounding of some measurement values, from mistakes made by the medical personnel, to refusal or inability of the patients to provide information. Another example of flagged missing values comes from biology. In DNA micro-array experiments, we would like to translate hybridization intensity values into binary values where 1 indicates hybridization and 0 indicates the opposite. Unfortunately, given the intensity values provided by the scanned array, it is not always easy to determine which clones hybridized and which did not, so in the final data set we will not only have 1's and 0's but also some '*'. Additionally, consider the presence/absence data from paleontology or ecology. Rows represent sites, columns represent species, and 1 indicates that the corresponding species have been found in that site. In this case, we often have the situation where the 1's are reasonably certain, but the 0's can be missing values.

classical role mining algorithms discover multiple small fragments of the real pattern (i.e., elicited role), neglecting the pattern itself [Liu *et al.* (2005)]. The problem is even worse for patterns which cover many rows and columns, since they are more vulnerable to this kind of "noise" [Mahfouz and Ismail (2009)].

Automatically switching all the imputed values might not always be appropriate. Rather, it would be advisable to submit these results to a checker. In our example, we should not forget that security still remains the main objective. Hence, the system administrator should carefully check the missing values, one by one. Checking all possible missing values could be an unfeasible task. By having a sorted list of the missing user-permission relations based on the computed relevance index, a system administrator can only focus on the most relevant ones, evaluating them in the reverse order. To make this approach feasible, one solution to solve the missing value problem could be further investigating the meaning of identified missing values. One possibility is to *impute* them by analyzing uncovered structures that reveal the nature of the relationship among the rows and the columns of the binary dataset. This approach is rooted on the consideration that in a dataset many rows and many columns are implicitly bound to one another. In access control this observation is particularly true: if an organization has several users performing the same tasks, it is likely that they share the same permission set.[2] However, caution should be taken: a missing value imputed in this way is *not* real data. It is only an estimation, and it could not reflect the real value. A conservative approach consists in suggesting which missing values should be analyzed first in order to improve the subsequent mining analysis. Indeed, checking all possible missing values could be an unfeasible task. By having a sorted list of the missing user-permission relations based on some "relevance" index, we can focus on the most relevant missing values, thus further analyzing only the most suspicious values.

An approach that is often used to impute missing values is the k-*nearest neighbors* (KNN) [Troyanskaya *et al.* (2001)]: for each row (i.e., user) that has a missing value in the column i, the k-nearest rows that do not have a missing value in the column i are used to impute the missing value. This

---

[2]In other contexts, uncovered structures are common as well. For example, in a paleontology dataset many sites (rows) are geographically close to each other, so that it is predictable that they host the same species (columns), even if physical evidences have not been found. Therefore, looking at the data makes it possible to uncover their embedded relationships and leverage them to impute missing values.

set of k-nearest rows is found according to some similarity metric. In turn, the missing value is replaced with the average value for the cells on the column i within the k-nearest rows. One of the critical issues using the KNN is the choice of the parameter k. On one hand, if parameter k has a high value, rows that are significantly different from the analyzed ones can decrease the imputing accuracy. Indeed, a "neighborhood" that is too large could decrease the imputing accuracy. On the other hand, if k is too small, an overemphasis is given to small patterns. In fact, the optimal selection of k likely depends on the size of the identifiable clusters within the given dataset. Another aspect of applying KNN is the choice of a threshold t to decide if the imputed value has to be a 0 or a 1. Once each missing value has been imputed, it assumes a value between 0 and 1: the threshold t is used to switch it to 1 or to 0. To the best of our knowledge, the most frequently used approaches for missing value imputation in binary matrices always require that a parameter comparable to k is fixed *a-priori* [Kim *et al.* (2005); Oba *et al.* (2003); Troyanskaya *et al.* (2001)].

In the rest of this chapter we address the challenge posed by the imputation of flagged and non-flagged missing grants in an access control system. In particular, we propose an algorithm referred to as ABℲA (*Adaptive Bicluster-Based Approach*,[3] [Colantonio *et al.* (2010a)]) that leverages the identifiable patterns within the data to infer missing values in binary matrices. Our approach provides several distinguishing features when compared to the other approaches similar to KNN. The most important one is that ABℲA does not require to fix any parameter a-priori. Indeed, the main issue in KNN-like approaches is that a fraction of the rows, *fixed before* running the algorithm, is used to impute a missing value, regardless of the identifiable patterns within the data. Further, ABℲA shows a better computational complexity. Moreover, the relevance of missing values are inferred by only one algorithm run. Another distinguishing feature is that ABℲA leverages the actual patterns that are identifiable within the available data, thus making it *adaptive*.

12.2   ABℲA: Adaptive Bicluster-Based Approach ⋆

To solve the problem of imputing missing user-permission assignments access control systems, we leverage the maximal pseudo-role concept discussed

---

[3]In [Colantonio *et al.* (2010a)], the term "pseudo-bicluster" is actually used as a synonym for the pseudo-role concept introduces in Sec. 5.3.2.

in Sec. 5.3.2. The reason why we introduce maximal pseudo-roles is that they can be used to impute missing data, for both flagged and non-flagged missing values. Given a matrix representation A for the user-permission assignments to analyze, for each element $a_{ij} \in A$ that is equal to 1, it is possible to generate a maximal pseudo-role $R = \langle U, P \rangle$ from a_{ij} by setting $U = \{\ell \in [n] \mid a_{\ell j} = 1\}$ and $P = \{k \in [m] \mid a_{ik} = 1\}$. As we have seen before, a role can contain 0, 1, and '*' in the case of matrices with flagged missing values. The intuition is that the cells of a maximal pseudo-role equal to 0 (in the non-flagged matrices) or equal to '*' (in the flagged matrices) are likely to be '1' since they belong to a pattern. Note that the less cells are equal to 0 and/or '*' within a maximal pseudo-role R, the more R is close to being a role, and the more the missing values contained in R are likely to be 1's. This is the rationale that we will use to impute missing data in binary matrices.

By evaluating the *relevance* $\sigma(a_{ij})$ for a given user-permission assignment a_{ij} (see Definition 5.16) that is equal to '*' (flagged matrix) or 0 (non-flagged matrix) we can impute the missing value according to the identified patterns within the available data. In this way, each missing value is imputed considering *all* and *only* those patterns that could involve it. This does not happen in other approaches such as KNN. Indeed, in that case each missing value is evaluated using a fixed number of rows (i.e., the k-nearest rows): it may occur that the result is biased, because of not having considered a sufficient number of relevant rows, or, even worse, by averaging rows that are completely unrelated. Conversely, in our approach each missing value is evaluated using a variable number of patterns, that depends on the given data set. A high value for the index $\sigma(a_{ij})$ indicates both a high relevance and a high number of patterns involved. As for flagged matrices, we will evaluate the relevance index for each element equal to '*'. Instead, when we are dealing with non-flagged missing values, we will evaluate the relevance of all the elements $a_{ij} \in A$ such that $a_{ij} = 0$.

In order to identify an algorithm that evaluates the relevance of missing values, we first make some considerations on the introduced indices. In particular, definitions 5.15 and 5.16 suggest a way to practically compute the relevance values. By simply combining the two indices, the following holds:

$$\sigma(a_{ij}) = \sum_{R \in MPR: a_{ij} \in R} \varrho(R) = \sum_{R \in MPR: a_{ij} \in R} \sum_{a_{\ell k} \in R} \gamma(a_{\ell k}, R).$$

Notice that elements which do not belong to R cannot generate it, thus we can replace R with the matrix A in the second sum. Moreover, only elements equal to 1 can be generators. Hence, we can rewrite the previous equation in the following way:

$$\sigma(a_{ij}) = \sum_{R \in MPR: a_{ij} \in R} \sum_{a_{\ell k} \in A: a_{\ell k}=1} \gamma(a_{\ell k}, R)$$

$$= \sum_{a_{\ell k} \in A: a_{\ell k}=1} \sum_{R \in MPR: a_{ij} \in R} \gamma(a_{\ell k}, R),$$

Since $\gamma(a_{\ell k}, R)$ holds true only when $a_{\ell k}$ generates R, the second sum has non-zero elements only when R is the maximal pseudo-role generated by $a_{\ell k}$, namely $R_{a_{\ell k}}$. Additionally, according to the second sum we have that a_{ij} must belong to maximal pseudo-roles $R_{a_{\ell k}}$. Formally:

$$\sigma(a_{ij}) = \sum_{a_{\ell k} \in A: a_{\ell k}=1} \delta(a_{ij}, R_{a_{\ell k}}) \tag{12.1}$$

where

$$\delta(a_{ij}, R_{a_{\ell k}}) = \begin{cases} 1, & a_{ij} \in R_{a_{\ell k}} \\ 0, & \text{otherwise.} \end{cases}$$

12.3   Algorithm Description $\star$

In this section we use Eq. (12.1) to define an algorithm referred to as ABꓱA (*Adaptive Bicluster-Based Approach*), that is described in Fig. 12.1. First, we calculate the set of all maximal pseudo-role by scanning all elements $a_{ij} \in A : a_{ij} = 1$. In turn, the relevance of missing values is determined by checking their membership to the generated maximal pseudo-role. In this way, all the identifiable data patterns that could have some relation with the missing value are involved in its imputation, according to their relevance. It is important to notice that the relevance can be also evaluated through the algorithm EXTRACT described in Sec. 5.3.4. It is also possible to normalize the value of each $\sigma(a_{ij})$ with respect to the maximal index found in the matrix A. In this way, the index value will range from 0 to 1. In the following, we will always consider this normalized version.

Fig. 1 is next described. The loop from Line 2 to Line 6 generates a maximal pseudo-role for each element $a_{ij} = 1$ of the matrix A. The loop from Line 3 to Line 5 increases the counter of each missing value contained in the maximal pseudo-role just created. Notice that the condition $a_{ij} = $ '*' in Line 3 assumes that we are dealing with a flagged matrix. If this is not the case, we can just replace this condition with $a_{ij} = 0$. At the end

```
 1: procedure EVALUATEMISSING(A)
 2:     for all aℓk ∈ A s.t. aℓk = 1 do
 3:         for all aij ∈ Raℓk s.t. aij = '∗' do
 4:             aij.count ← aij.count + 1
 5:         end for
 6:     end for
 7:     return A
 8: end procedure

 9: procedure BINARIZE(A, t)
10:     for all aij ∈ A s.t. aij.count > 0 do
11:         if aij.count > t then
12:             aij ← 1
13:         else
14:             aij ← 0
15:         end if
16:     end for
17:     return A
18: end procedure
```

Fig. 12.1: The algorithm AB8A

of the algorithm, each missing value (i.e., elements with $a_{ij} = $ '∗' in the flagged version, $a_{ij} = 0$ in the non-flagged version) will contain a value that corresponds to $\sigma(a_{ij})$ in its data field referred to as 'count'. Then, each counter can be optionally normalized with the maximum value found for the index. After having calculated the relevance through EVALUATEMISSING, the procedure BINARIZE can be called. It takes in input the matrix A and a threshold t for the relevance index, thus giving back the final binarized version of A.

The correctness of the algorithm in Fig. 12.1 is guaranteed by Eq. (12.1). As for its computational complexity, it is $\mathcal{O}(\mu |A|)$, where $|A|$ is the number of elements of the matrix A that are set to 1, and μ is the number of missing values. Indeed, the first loop is executed for each element of the matrix A that is equal to 1. The maximal pseudo-role can be determined in constant time, for example by using an hash table that gives all columns with 1's for a given row, and all rows with 1's for a given column—the hash table can be created in $\mathcal{O}(|A|)$. The internal loop is executed at most μ times, and the operation of Line 4 can be executed in constant time. The worst case is when $\mu = |A| = (nm/2)$, namely when half the matrix is filled by 1's half by '*' (in the flagged version) or 0's (in the non-flagged version). Yet, this seldom happens. When the number of missing values represents a small fraction of the data, or the matrix is sparse, our approach outperforms other algorithms such as KNN, that has a computational complexity $\mathcal{O}(n^2 m)$ [Troyanskaya *et al.* (2001)].

Finally, our approach can be considered a *multiple imputation method* [Rubin (1987)]. We refer to multiple imputation as a simulation technique that replaces each missing data with a set of $m > 1$ plausible values. The m versions of the complete data are analyzed by standard complete-data methods. In ABꓭA, we first impute missing values with the procedure EVALUATEMISSING described in Fig. 12.1. In turn, by changing a threshold t that does not require the complete re-imputation of missing data, it is possible to generate m versions of the dataset through the procedure BINARIZE. Each version can subsequently be analyzed by trying to find the one that better reaches the target function. The tuning of the threshold t depends on the final objective of the data analysis. First, a metric must be defined to measure how well the objective has been reached. Then, it is possible to use this metric to evaluate the imputed matrix. This can be an iterative process, executed several times with different thresholds, thus choosing the threshold value that provides the best result.

12.4   Testing ABꓭA

To test the quality of the results produced by ABꓭA, we now introduce a measure based on the Jaccard coefficient [Everitt (1993)] that has already been used in [Figueroa *et al.* (2003)] to compare the similarity of two matrices. Let n_{ij} be the number of entries on which two matrices A and R have values i and j, respectively. Thus, n_{11} is the number of detected mates, n_{00} is the number of non-mates, while n_{10} and n_{01} count the disagreements between the true and suggested solution. The Jaccard coefficient is defined as $n_{11}/(n_{11} + n_{10} + n_{01})$. It represents the proportion of the correctly identified mates to the sum of the correctly identified mates plus the total number of disagreements. Hence, the Jaccard coefficient should score one when all the missing values are correctly identified. Conversely, the closer this index is to zero, the less the two matrices can be considered similar.

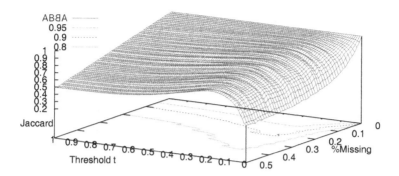

Fig. 12.2: Comparing the rebuilt matrix with the original one

12.4.1 *Testing on Synthetic Data*★

In the following simulations we first generate a matrix A then, uniformly at random, we introduce in A a fraction of missing values, generating a 0-1-'∗' matrix A'. In turn, A' is given as an input to our algorithm, which generates a matrix R. Using the Jaccard coefficient to measure the similarity of R (the rebuilt matrix) and A (the original matrix), we capture the quality of the rebuilt matrix, that is, how close it is to the original one (A).

To implement our experiments, we generated sample matrices composed by 600 rows and 100 columns. Each matrix has been generated with the next described procedure. First, 20 subsets of rows and columns have been randomly chosen. Each subset of rows, and each subset of columns, counts a number of elements that are proportional to MaxRows $\times x^y$ and MaxColumns $\times x^y$, where x is a random number uniformly chosen between 0 and 1, while y, MaxRows and MaxColumns are integer variables. The values used for MaxRows and MaxColumns are reported on Table 12.1. The elements of the matrix A that belongs to one of such subsets are set to 1, while the other ones are set to 0. The exponent y allows to change the number of small and large patterns created. Note that $y = 1$ corresponds to the uniform distribution. By increasing y we are able to generate a higher number of patterns of small dimension, and some of high dimension.

Fig. 12.2 reports the value of the Jaccard coefficient, considering the threshold t and the fraction of missing values introduced in A. To plot each point of the surface, 20 matrices have been generated according to the described method, with $y = 2$, MaxRows $= 60$ and MaxColumns $= 10$. Then, the average value of the Jaccard coefficients has been calculated. It can be seen that the threshold plays a fundamental role. Indeed, using a threshold

Table 12.1: Application of ABꓭA to synthetic data

MaxRows	MaxColumns	Missing rate	Jaccard
		0.1	0.914
		0.2	0.836
30	6	0.3	0.811
		0.4	0.724
		0.5	0.679
		0.1	0.949
		0.2	0.885
60	8	0.3	0.854
		0.4	0.750
		0.5	0.719
		0.1	0.949
		0.2	0.903
90	12	0.3	0.861
		0.4	0.811
		0.5	0.708
		0.1	0.949
		0.2	0.887
120	16	0.3	0.850
		0.4	0.756
		0.5	0.772
		0.1	0.959
		0.2	0.930
150	20	0.3	0.883
		0.4	0.783
		0.5	0.751
		0.1	0.952
		0.2	0.920
180	24	0.3	0.858
		0.4	0.812
		0.5	0.771

$t = 0$ means switching all the missing values that are involved in some patterns to 1, though it may be an unimportant one. Conversely, when the threshold is close to 1, a missing value is switched to 1 only if it is involved in a relevant pattern. As for the Jaccard coefficient, by analyzing Fig. 12.2 it is possible to note that the best results are obtained using a threshold between 0.1 and 0.2. Additionally, Fig. 12.2 shows that our algorithm is able to reach a Jaccard coefficient equal to 0.8 even if the missing values rate is equal to 0.4.

12.4.2 *Testing on Real Data*

As an application of our algorithm to discover non-flagged missing data, we have chosen to analyze a real dataset coming from an access control

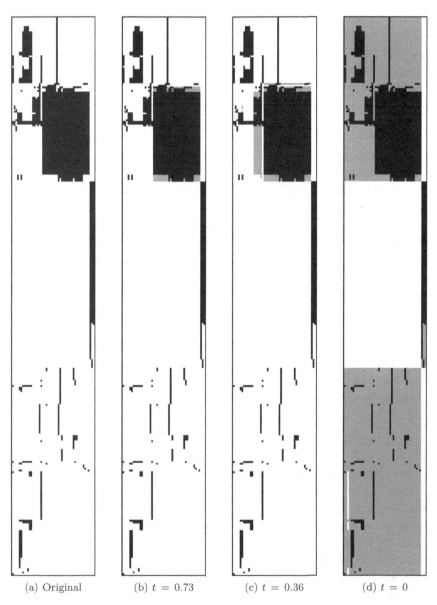

(a) Original   (b) $t = 0.73$ (c) $t = 0.36$ (d) $t = 0$

Fig. 12.3: An application of ABꓭA to non-flagged missing values

system. We evaluated the dataset using our algorithm with the target to discover data that are set to 0, but that could be set to 1. This operation, if carefully devised, can drastically reduce the number of automatically elicited roles that are needed to manage the access control system. The analyzed data involves a set of 323 users and 49 permissions related to a particular organization unit of a private company, counting a total of 2342 permissions granted—that correspond to almost 15% of cells set to 1. Figure 12.3 graphically shows the achieved results. Figure 12.3a is the original matrix, where black pixels corresponds to 1's (i.e., a permission granted to a user), while white pixels to 0's. Figure 12.3b shows the imputed matrix, where some of the initial 0-values have been switched to 1 according to a threshold $t = 0.73$ and highlighted in light blue. Figures 12.3c and 12.3d differs from Fig. 12.3b only for the used threshold, that is equal to 0.36 in the first case and 0 in the other one.

It is possible to see that the more the threshold t decreases, the larger the number of user-permission assignments switched to 1 are. Once we submitted these results to the system administrators, they recognized that the user-permissions assignments found using the threshold $t = 0.2$ are actually permissions that could be granted to the corresponding users. This means that only 96 out of 13,485 possible cells that were 0's have been switched to 1. The new access control scheme, that corresponds to the matrix rebuilt according to this threshold, contains 102 maximal roles, with respect to the 127 maximal roles that can be identified within the original access control scheme. This means that, for each user-permission assignment, the ambiguity of selecting the role needed to manage them is lower.

12.5 Final Remarks

In this chapter we proposed a solution for the missing values imputation problem in binary matrices. In particular, we proposed AB8A, an algorithm that leverages the underlying implicit relationships among data to address the issue. A thorough formal framework has been provided to justify the rationales behind our algorithm. Further, AB8A enjoys some relevant features when compared to similar approaches. In particular, its tuning is much easier and the computational complexity is reduced for a wide range of parameters. Finally, we applied our algorithm to a real problem in order to impute non-flagged missing values, also observing that our approach can improve the results achieved by a subsequent role mining task.

PART 5

The Risk of Unmanageable Roles

The last topic of this book is represented by the analysis of the *risk* derived from granting access to resources, and how RBAC allows to effectively manage such a risk. We point out that existing role mining techniques are not able to elicit roles with an associated clear business meaning. Hence, it is difficult to mitigate risk, to simplify business governance, and to ensure compliance throughout the enterprise. To elicit meaningful roles, we recall the methodology described in Chap. 8 where data to analyze are decomposed into smaller subsets according to the provided business information. We show how this leads to a decrease in the likelihood of making errors in role management, and consequently reduces the risk of role misuse. Additionally, we introduce an approach to highlight users and permissions that markedly deviate from others, and that might consequently be prone to error when roles are operating. By focusing on such users and permissions during the role definition process, it is possible to mitigate the risk of unauthorized accesses and role misuse.

Chapter 13

The Risk of Meaningless Roles

Role-based access control allows to effectively manage the risk derived from granting access to resources, provided that designed roles are business-driven. In Part 3 we pointed out that although role mining is an essential tool for role engineers, existing techniques are not able to elicit roles with an associated clear business meaning. Hence, it is difficult to mitigate risk, simplify business governance, and ensure compliance throughout the enterprise. To estimate the risk of eliciting meaningless roles, in this chapter we extend the divide-and-conquer methodology described in Chap. 10, where data to analyze are decomposed into smaller subsets according to the provided business information. Indeed, Chap. 10 demonstrated how the minability and similarity indices are estimates of the expected complexity to select roles within the role mining results. In this chapter we prove that they are also metrics for the likelihood of making administration errors when managing roles throughout their lifecycle.

13.1 Assessing Risky System Configurations

Security risk assessment is fundamental to the security of any organization [Humphrey (2008)]. It is aimed at ensuring that security controls and expenditure are fully commensurate with the risks to which the organization is exposed. The eventual goal is to create a system that encourages information sharing and prudent risk-taking behavior among its users. Hence, maximizing benefits to the organization while keeping users accountable for their actions and capping the expected damage an organization could suffer due to sensitive information disclosure. A systematic approach to risk assessment is necessary to identify organizational needs regarding information security requirements and to create an effective *information security management system* (ISMS) [ISO/IEC (2009)].

Among possible risks pertaining to organizational information, illegal access to data, as well as legal but incorrect use of permissions over data, are of utmost importance. Several frameworks have been proposed in literature for efficient access administration, but the most adopted is probably RBAC. Despite the widespread adoption of RBAC-oriented systems, organizations frequently implement them without due consideration of roles. To minimize deployment effort or to avoid project scope creep, organizations often neglect role definition in the initial part of the deployment project. Very often, organizations do not invest enough time to define roles in detail; rather, they define high-level roles that do not reflect actual business requirements. The result of this thoughtless role definition process is that deployed RBAC systems do not deliver the expected benefits.

One of the main drawback of having ill-defined roles is that resulting RBAC systems are prone to illegitimate access attempts via: (un)intentional incorrect use of already granted permission (i.e., "role abuse"); roles incorrectly assigned due to their unclear meaning, leading to toxic combination of permissions (i.e., "role misuse") [Celikel *et al.* (2009)]. Therefore, it is valuable to highlight potential risks through a proper *risk assessment* activity. However, none of the existing risk assessment methodologies are specifically tailored for access risk evaluation. Framework such as ISO/IEC 27005 [ISO/IEC (2008)], NIST SP800s [Stoneburner *et al.* (2002)], COBIT [ISACA/ITGI (2009)], PCI-DSS [Security Standards Council (2010)], etc., describes general approaches to risk assessment without providing specific guidelines for access control systems.

To address all the aforementioned issues, we leverage the methodology described in Chap. 10. In particular, we propose a role mining approach where access data to analyze is decomposed into smaller subsets that are homogeneous according to some business data. This eases the attribution of business meaning to automatically elicited roles and reduces the problem complexity, thus reducing the likelihood of security incidents related to illegal accesses. In order to select the best business information that mostly reduces the impact of having unmanageable roles produced by the subsequent role mining process, we propose two indices to estimate the expected risk pertaining elicited roles. Leveraging these indices allows for the identification of business information that best fits with the access control data, namely the information that induces a decomposition which increases the business meaning of the roles elicited in the role mining phase, focusing on the most critical business areas. This leads to a decrease in the likelihood of making errors in role management, and consequently reduces the risk pertaining to role misuse.

13.2 Risk Model

To better clarify the benefits introduced by the proposed approach, we first recall some *risk management* concepts. A typical risk management approach is made up of two key components: *risk analysis* (or *assessment*) and *risk control* [Humphrey (2008)]. During risk analysis we identify potential risks and assess probabilities of negative events together with their consequences. With risk control we establish the tolerable level of risk for the organization, hence providing controls for failure prevention as well as actions to reduce the likelihood of a negative event—such an activity is usually referred to as *risk mitigation*.

Plugging the previous concepts in a RBAC environment, three essential components should be considered: users, roles, and permissions. Among them, particular attention must be taken on risk incurred by users. Indeed, the main threat in an access control scenario is to allow a user to execute an illegitimate operation over an object or a resource. A system which is only supposed to be used by authorized users must attempt to detect and exclude unauthorized ones. Accesses are therefore usually controlled by insisting on an authentication procedure to determine with some established degree of confidence the identity of the user, hence granting permissions authorized to that identity. RBAC mitigate the risk of unauthorized accesses by restricting user's permission to predefined role definitions [O'Connor and Loomis (2010)].

In this scenario, and assuming that it is not possible to bypass the access control mechanism, the risk of illegitimate credentials is prevented by adopting a RBAC system. But, there is an important aspect that has not been considered so far: the role life-cycle. Roles are not static, but they follow the evolution of the organization: new users may join, existing users may leave or may change their job position, applications may be replaced with new ones, etc.. Hence, an important aspect to consider when evaluating the risks related to RBAC systems is the risk introduced by roles that are difficult to manage, mainly due to an unclear understanding of their meaning. Indeed, the more a role is intelligible and well designed, the less error prone it will be. *A comprehensive risk management approach should consider these aspects starting from the creation of roles.*

According to ISO/IEC 27005:2008, Section 8.1, we refer to risk assessment as the following:

> *Risk assessment determines the* value *of the* information assets, *identifies the* applicable threats *and* vulnerabilities *that exist (or could exist), identifies* existing controls *and their effect on the risk identified, determines the potential* consequences *and finally* prioritizes *the derived risks and ranks them against the risk evaluation criteria set in the context establishment.*

In other words, to perform a correct information security risk assessment, the owners of the objects to protect must identify possible threats and associated vulnerabilities. For each threat/vulnerability pair, the owners determine the severity of impact upon the asset's confidentiality, integrity, and availability, and determine the likelihood of the vulnerability exploit occurring given existing security controls.

More specifically, in a generic RBAC system, the aforementioned risk-related aspects can be detailed as follows:

- *Vulnerabilities.* They correspond to roles that are not meaningful enough from the administrator's perspective, namely roles that are difficult to manage and to maintain.
- *Threats.* They are errors and wrong administration actions, unintentionally committed while managing roles during their lifecycle.
- *Risks.* They correspond to allowing users to execute operations that are not permitted, or hampering their jobs by not granting required permissions. In both cases, the consequences could raise financial loss.

The product of the likelihood of occurrence and the impact severity results in the risk level for the system based on the exposure to the threat/vulnerability pair. To evaluate such risks, in this chapter we propose a general risk formula that involves multiple factors with different probabilities, namely [Colantonio *et al.* (2011a)]:

$$Risk = \sum_{i=1}^{n} P_i \times C_i, \qquad (13.1)$$

where P_i denotes the probability of each risk factor i (i.e., the threat/vulnerability pair affecting an asset), and C_i quantifies the consequences (or impact) of these risk factors.

In our model, risk factors are represented by homogeneous groups of users. Indeed, every user does not have the same degree of importance.

For example, there could be users in charge of activities that are critical for the main business of the organization, while other users could be assigned to roles that have a marginal importance for the business. In general, we need to assign various degree of importance to each risk factor by taking the consequence of its execution into consideration. This process requires a thorough analysis of the organization. We assume that the impact evaluation is provided by experts.

As for the probability of occurrence, in the following section we propose two metrics that are suitable to evaluate the likelihood that an administration error is made when managing roles. In such a way, we evaluate the risk of an error in role management, and subsequently we are able to drive the definition of roles that mitigate this risk.

Sorting risks by descending levels makes it possible to address the most critical risks first. In particular, compensatory controls are identified for each threat/vulnerability pair with moderate or high risk levels. After having implemented such recommended controls, the risk is re-evaluated to determine the remaining risk, or residual risk level.

13.3   Risk Metrics

When we have several business information at our disposal (e.g., organization units, job titles, applications, etc.), we have to select the one that induces a partition for access control data that minimizes the risk related to the elicitation of meaningless roles from each subset. The best partition can change depending on the organization needs. To guide the decomposition process, it is useful to have a metric that allows data analysts:

- To decide what business information most reduces the risk of a poor role definition and simplifies the subsequent mining steps.
- To predict whether splitting the problem into more sub-problems actually reduces the risk of having ill-defined roles. In particular, we can decide to iteratively decompose the data before executing the mining step, by applying a different decomposition at each iteration until given minability and similarity thresholds are reached for each subset.
- To verify that partitioning does not actually reduce the role mining complexity. If this is the case, access control information should thus be reviewed in order to improve their manageability.

In all previous cases, similarity and minability introduced in Chap. 10 are a possible means to estimate the risk related to the data being analyzed. In fact, since both indices express the likelihood of making bad administration decisions due to the unclear meaning of roles, they can be used in conjunction with the risk formula in Eq. (13.1). Depending on the kind of roles that role engineers are looking for (organizational or functional), the similarity or the minability value can be combined with the importance of each subset to evaluate the risk of incurring a poor role design, as shown in the following.

13.3.1   *Similarity- and Minability-Based Risks* ⋆

As mentioned before, the similarity and minability indices are good candidate to measure the likelihood of making administration errors. For instance, given a group of users, when the minability index equals 1 for user-permission assignments involved in the group, according to Theorem 10.2 there will be just one possible maximal equivalent role for managing those assignments. This means, for example, that new permissions introduced within the system will likely be assigned to all users of the group (via the single role) or to none of them, and new users that join such a group will likely be granted the same permissions of other users (namely, all the permissions contained within the single role). Moreover, the business meaning of the role is strictly related to business aspects that users within the group have in common. Therefore, the probability of making wrong access control decisions is low.

Therefore, the following indicators can support the partition selection problem [Colantonio *et al.* (2011a)]:

Definition 13.1 (Similarity-Based Risk). *Let USERS be a set of users to analyze, and PERMS, UP be the corresponding permissions and assignments. The* similarity-based risk *of USERS is defined as:*

$$Risk_S(USERS) = \big(1 - S(USERS)\big) \times C, \qquad (13.2)$$

where C is the importance of the user group USERS, while S(USERS) is the similarity value computed over the users belonging to USERS.

Definition 13.2 (Minability-Based Risk). *Let UP be a set of user-permission assignments between users in USERS and permissions in PERMS. The* minability-based risk *of UP is defined as:*

$$Risk_{\mathcal{M}}(UP) = \big(1 - \mathcal{M}(UP)\big) \times C, \qquad (13.3)$$

where C is the importance of the data represented by the assignment set UP, while $\mathcal{M}(UP)$ is the similarity value computed over the user-permission assignments belonging to UP.

The previous definitions offer an estimate for the risk pertaining to unmanageable roles for each subset. If the objective is to identify the best partition, we will compare the values obtained for similarity-based and/or minability-based risks on all subsets and choose the partition with the lowest "average" risk. Analogously, when we want to check if further decomposing the problem actually reduces the role mining complexity, we have to compare the "average" risk that we have with and without the decomposition. The following section shows a possible approach to summarize the risk related to a partition.

13.3.2 *Conditioned Indices* ⋆

Similar to Sec. 10.6, instead of analyzing the risk values calculated on each subset of a given partition, it is more advantageous to have a *conditioned* risk value that "summarizes" the simplification introduced by the partition. The conditioning concept will apply on both risk indices. We therefore speak of *conditioned similarity- or minability-based risk.*

Definition 10.4 at page 195 can be extended in order to take into account the importance of each subset. In particular, we provide the following definition [Colantonio *et al.* (2011a)]:

Definition 13.3 (Conditioned Similarity-Based Risk). *Given the k-partition $\Omega = \{\Omega_1, \ldots, \Omega_k\}$ of UP and the induced sets of users $\Upsilon_i = \{u \in USERS \mid \exists p \in PERMS, \langle u, p \rangle \in \Omega_i\}$, we define the similarity-based risk conditioned by Ω as*

$$Risk_{\mathcal{S}_\Omega}(USERS, \Omega) = \frac{\sum_{i=1}^{k} \left(1 - \mathcal{S}(\Upsilon_i)\right) C_i \left(\sigma_i + \binom{|\Upsilon_i|}{2}\right)}{\sum_{i=1}^{k} \left(\sigma_i + \binom{|\Upsilon_i|}{2}\right)}, \qquad (13.4)$$

where C_i is the importance of the user group Υ_i.

$Risk_{\mathcal{S}_\Omega}(USERS, \Omega)$ is a weighted average of the risks related to each subset, where the weights are proportional to the subset cardinalities.

Analogously, Definition 10.5 can be extended in order to take into account the importance of each subset. In particular, we provide the following definition:

Definition 13.4 (Conditioned Minability-Based Risk). *Given a k-partition $\Omega = \{\Omega_1, \ldots, \Omega_k\}$ of the set UP we define the minability-based risk conditioned by Ω as*

$$Risk_{\mathcal{M}_\Omega}(UP, \Omega) = \frac{\sum_{i=1}^{k} \left(1 - \mathcal{M}(\Omega_i)\right) C_i |\Omega_i|}{\sum_{i=1}^{k} |\Omega_i|}, \tag{13.5}$$

where C_i is the importance of the subset Ω_i.

$Risk_{\mathcal{M}_\Omega}(UP, \Omega)$ is a weighted average of the risks related to each subset, where the weights are represented by the subset cardinalities.

Figure 13.1 shows similarity- and minability-based risk values for the example introduced in Fig. 10.4 (see Sec. 10.6.3). In particular, it depicts a toy example with two different business information at our disposal: the organization unit the user belongs to, and the applications involved by the given permission set. Since the in this example does not use different importance for each partition, risk values agree with the results presented in Sec. 10.6.3.

13.3.3   *Fast Index Approximation* ⋆

Both similarity- and minability-based indices can be computed by simply applying the algorithms described in Sec. 10.3.2 (see Fig. 10.1 at page 186) and Sec. 10.4.3 (see Fig. 10.2 at page 191). We now demonstrate that the amount of approximation introduced by the proposed randomized algorithms, when applied to the calculation of conditioned indices, is comparable to the approximation of the non-conditioned indices [Colantonio *et al.* (2011a)].

Theorem 13.1. *Let $Risk_{\mathcal{S}_\Omega}(USERS, \Omega)$ and $Risk_{\mathcal{M}_\Omega}(UP, \Omega)$ be the exact indices conditioned by a given partition Ω according to definitions 13.3 and 13.4, respectively. Let $\widetilde{Risk}_{\mathcal{S}_\Omega}(USERS, \Omega, k)$ and $\widetilde{Risk}_{\mathcal{M}_\Omega}(UP, \Omega, k)$ be the corresponding approximated values computed by adopting the algorithms in Fig. 10.1 and Fig. 10.2 for each subset $\Omega_i \in \Omega$. Then:*

$$\Pr\left(\left|\widetilde{Risk}_{\mathcal{S}_\Omega}(USERS, \Omega, k) - Risk_{\mathcal{S}_\Omega}(USERS, \Omega)\right| \geq \varepsilon\right) \leq 2\exp\left(-2k\varepsilon^2\right),$$
$$\Pr\left(\left|\widetilde{Risk}_{\mathcal{M}_\Omega}(UP, \Omega, k) - Risk_{\mathcal{M}_\Omega}(UP, \Omega)\right| \geq \varepsilon\right) \leq 2\exp\left(-2k\varepsilon^2\right).$$

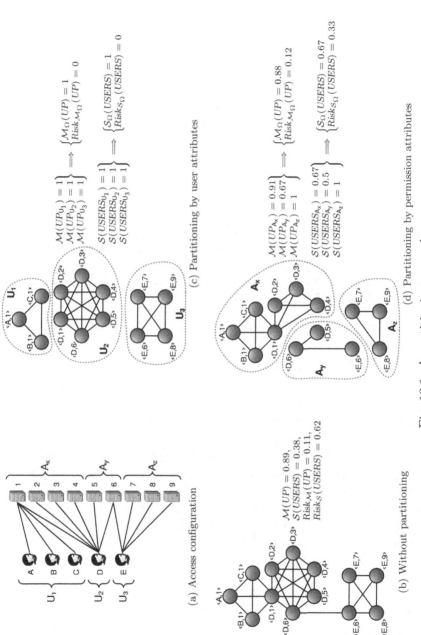

(a) Access configuration

(b) Without partitioning

(c) Partitioning by user attributes

(d) Partitioning by permission attributes

Fig. 13.1: A partitioning example

Table 13.1: Conditioned indices for the sample organization branch

Organization Unit Index Type	Similarity	Minability	Similarity-Based Risk	Minability-Based Risk	Roles	msec
Operations						
Manufacturing						
Not Conditioned	0.08	0.68	4.59	1.58	10,001	242
Conditioned by Alphabetical Groups	0.08	0.74	7.30	1.70	4,422	134
Conditioned by Organization Units	0.10	0.78	4.40	0.97	4,424	125
Conditioned by Job Titles	0.29	0.89	3.23	0.53	918	59
Product Development						
Not Conditioned	0.20	0.82	4.01	0.92	4,007	150
Conditioned by Alphabetical Groups	0.20	0.84	6.24	1.11	2,511	73
Conditioned by Organization Units	0.37	0.86	4.83	1.05	2,080	76
Conditioned by Job Titles	0.38	0.90	5.63	0.64	818	36
Material Management						
Not Conditioned	0.28	0.76	0.72	0.24	36,620	276
Conditioned by Alphabetical Groups	0.28	0.80	5.58	1.28	3,504	48
Conditioned by Organization Units	0.33	0.85	0.69	0.17	1,224	25
Conditioned by Job Titles	0.28	0.82	0.72	0.21	21,614	105
Sales						
Not Conditioned	0.07	0.63	4.64	1.85	61,933	471
Conditioned by Alphabetical Groups	0.08	0.72	8.15	2.23	11,659	81
Conditioned by Organization Units	0.11	0.67	1.63	1.39	50,314	301
Conditioned by Job Titles	0.11	0.80	4.21	0.73	1,757	30
Quality						
Not Conditioned	0.08	0.89	4.61	0.57	40	2
Conditioned by Alphabetical Groups	0.08	0.94	8.35	0.58	36	1
Conditioned by Organization Units	0.12	0.94	5.92	0.45	24	2
Conditioned by Job Titles	0.21	0.96	3.61	0.22	25	1
Logistics						
Not Conditioned	0.24	0.71	3.78	1.43	1,677	19
Conditioned by Alphabetical Groups	0.24	0.80	6.47	1.60	642	13
Conditioned by Organization Units	0.33	0.80	3.35	0.87	854	16
Conditioned by Job Titles	0.64	0.83	0.59	0.45	357	12

13.4   Analysis of a Real Case

This section completes the real-case application described in Sec. 10.7. Following the selection of the best business information of Sec. 10.7.2, we first decomposed the problem by using the first OU level. As required by Definition 13.3 and Definition 13.4, for both OUs and job titles we estimated the impact of harmful administration actions for each potential group of users—due to the large number of involved job titles, in Table 13.2 we only report the impact classification for OUs. Each group of users had been classified as "Low", "Medium", or "High" impact. Adopting a three-point scale made it easier to reach consensus among administrators. The values assigned to those impact classes were conventionally set by administrators to 1, 5, and 10, respectively.

For each index, the best values among all available partitions is highlighted in gray in Table 13.1. In addition to Sec. 10.7.2, the following observations can be made:

• The unit Sales shows a configuration where the minability and similarity

Table 13.2: Further decomposition of the sample organization branch

Organization Unit	Users	Permissions	User-Perms Assignments	Impact	Similarity	Minability	Similarity-Based Risk	Minability-Based Risk	Roles	msec
Operations	946	3,647	56,905	Medium	0.07	0.65	4.63	1.73	219,086	3,637
Manufacturing	379	1,810	20,400	Medium	0.08	0.68	4.59	1.58	10,001	242
Parent	1	64	64	Low	1.00	1.00	0.00	0.00	1	0
Technology	49	323	2,342	Low	0.35	0.92	0.65	0.08	127	6
Control	26	577	2,396	Low	0.30	0.81	0.70	0.19	254	7
Test & Quality	8	226	301	Low	0.09	0.92	0.91	0.08	17	1
Production	288	1,452	15,226	Medium	0.09	0.75	4.54	1.26	4,013	111
Plants	7	39	71	Low	0.12	0.83	0.88	0.17	12	0
Product Development	319	1,341	14,222	Medium	0.20	0.82	4.01	0.92	4,007	150
Parent	2	32	33	Low	0.03	0.98	0.97	0.02	3	0
Engineering	77	559	2,898	Medium	0.36	0.82	3.22	0.90	564	16
Design #1	88	361	3,275	Medium	0.41	0.84	2.94	0.80	10	1
Design #2	121	739	6,965	High	0.35	0.87	6.48	1.34	232	10
Design #3	6	115	214	Medium	0.14	0.93	4.28	0.36	1,205	47
Marketing	17	404	663	Medium	0.08	0.91	4.58	0.45	57	2
Innovation	8	92	174	Medium	0.23	0.97	3.85	0.16	9	0
Material Management	58	1,038	8,670	Low	0.28	0.76	0.72	0.24	36,620	276
Parent	3	286	368	Low	0.17	0.95	0.83	0.05	6	1
Purchase Dept #1	23	549	3,043	Low	0.27	0.80	0.73	0.20	745	10
Purchase Dept #2	13	407	2,136	Low	0.49	0.89	0.51	0.11	382	6
Purchase Dept #3	7	406	1,054	Low	0.29	0.77	0.71	0.23	56	3
Purchase Dept #4	5	311	972	Low	0.69	0.91	0.31	0.09	15	2
Saving Control	3	203	303	Medium	0.32	0.86	3.40	0.70	7	1
Analysis & Reporting	4	376	794	Low	0.35	0.87	0.65	0.13	13	2
Sales	100	1,531	9,483	Medium	0.07	0.63	4.64	1.85	61,933	471
Parent	1	68	68	Low	1.00	1.00	0.00	0.00	1	0
Logistics	36	1,142	6,836	Medium	0.24	0.63	3.78	1.84	49,256	279
Support	63	795	2,579	Low	0.07	0.76	0.93	0.24	1,057	22
Quality	16	272	697	Medium	0.08	0.89	4.61	0.57	40	2
Parent	1	20	20	Low	1.00	1.00	0.00	0.00	1	0
Certification	2	40	46	Low	0.15	0.92	0.85	0.08	3	0
Audit	6	188	352	High	0.20	0.94	8.00	0.60	7	1
Quality Center	7	151	279	Medium	0.07	0.93	4.67	0.36	13	1
Logistics	73	1,078	3,432	Medium	0.24	0.71	3.78	1.43	1,677	19
Parent	0	0	0	Low	-	1.00	1.00	1.00	0	0
Methodologies	2	350	549	Low	0.57	0.92	0.43	0.08	3	1
Planning	7	311	682	Low	0.41	0.88	0.59	0.12	38	2
Distribution #1	62	464	1,780	Medium	0.32	0.70	3.38	1.52	810	12
Distribution #2	2	351	421	Medium	0.20	0.93	4.00	0.37	3	1

indices suggest to partition by job title, but the risk indices promote
the OU information. This happens because the unit Logistics contains
many users that have a medium impact, and such users are not as similar
among them as those having job titles with medium impact.

- Partitioning is *not* always advantageous. For instance, all users within
  the unit Product Development have some commonalities in their permissions that will be lost when decomposing—as a matter of fact, users
  within Marketing have a medium impact and are not similar among them.
  Thus, if the role engineering objective is to find organizational roles for
  Product Development, it is better to analyze the unit as a whole.

The previous examples also demonstrate that, in general, the choice of
the best index to use (similarity, minability, similarity-based risk index,
or minability-based risk index) depends on the main objective of the role
engineering task.

As for drilling down (see Sec. 10.7.3), Table 13.2 highlights the behavior
with respect to minability, similarity, minability-based risk, and similarity-
based risk. For example, although the unit Audit has higher values for
minability and similarity than the parent unit Quality, the high impact of
the tasks performed by involved users compels a careful role design. According to this example, decomposing is a possible way to highlight data that
requires particular attention from a risk management perspective. Another
aspect to take into account is the required granularity for the partition.
The most sensible approach is probably to stop decomposing when the risk
indices do not increase or even increase slightly. For example, as shown
in Table 13.1, by partitioning Product Development according to its sub-
units, the similarity-based risk index increases from 4.01 to 4.83, while the
minability-based risk index grows from 0.92 to 1.05, reducing the gain in
performing sub-unit driven analysis.

13.5   Final Remarks

This chapter described a methodology that helps role engineers leverage
business information during the role mining process in order to reduce the
risk of having unmanageable roles. In particular, we demonstrated that by
applying the divide-and-conquer strategy of Chap. 10, that is dividing data
to analyze into smaller, more homogeneous subsets, it practically leads to
more meaningful roles from a business perspective, hence decreasing the
risk to make errors in managing them.

Several examples, developed on real data, illustrate how to apply the tools that implement the proposed methodology, as well as its practical implications. Achieved results support the quality and the viability of the proposal.

Chapter 14

Ranking Users and Permissions

In this chapter, we introduce a risk analysis framework that allows to evaluate the risk incurred when managing users and permissions through RBAC. A distinguishing feature of the proposed approach is that it can be used without having already defined roles, namely in a pre-engineering phase. By evaluating the risk level of a single user or a single permission, we make it possible to produce a ranking of users and permissions, highlighting those that most deviate from others in comparison to available user-permission relationships. Consequently, we are able to identify those users and permissions that represent the most (likely) dangerous and error prone ones from an administration point of view. Having this ranking available during the role engineering phase allows data analysts and role engineers to highlight users and permissions that are more prone to error and misuse when designed roles will be operating.

14.1 Stability ⋆

We now extend some of the concepts introduced in Chap. 11 and further described in [Colantonio *et al.* (2010b)].

Definition 14.1 (Role Weight). *Given a role* $r \in ROLES$, *let* U_r *and* P_r *be the sets of users and permissions associated to* r, *that is* $U_r = \{u \in USERS \mid \langle u, r \rangle \in UA\}$ *and* $P_r = \{p \in PERMS \mid \langle p, r \rangle \in PA\}$. *We indicate with* $w \colon ROLES \to \mathbb{N}$ *the weight function of roles, defined as* $w(r) = |U_r| \times |P_r|$.

Definition 14.2 (*t*-stability). *Let* Σ_{UP} *be the set of all RBAC states that cover the user-permission assignments of* UP, *that is all states*

$\langle ROLES, UA, PA \rangle \in \Sigma_{UP}$ *such that* $\forall \langle u, p \rangle \in UP \implies \exists r \in$ $ROLES : \langle u, r \rangle \in UA, \langle p, r \rangle \in PA.$ *Given* $\langle u, p \rangle \in UP,$ *let* $\mathcal{R}: UP \to 2^{\left(\bigcup_{(ROLES, UA, PA) \in \Sigma_{UP}} ROLES \right)}$ *be the function that identifies the roles which could be used to manage* $\langle u, p \rangle,$ *that is:*

$$\mathcal{R}(\langle u, p \rangle) = \bigcup_{\langle ROLES, UA, PA \rangle \in \Sigma_{UP}} \{ r \in ROLES \mid \langle u, r \rangle \in UA, \ \langle p, r \rangle \in PA \}.$$

We say that $\langle u, p \rangle$ *is* t*-stable if it can be managed with at least one role* r *with weight* $w(r) \geq t,$ *namely* $\exists r \in \mathcal{R}(\langle u, p \rangle) : w(r) \geq t.$

If an assignment $\langle u, p \rangle \in UP$ is t-stable, it is also $(t - i)$-stable for each $i = 1, \ldots, t.$ We are thus interested in the maximal stability of a given assignment, namely the maximum t that verifies the t-stability condition:

Definition 14.3 (Maximal Stability). *The* maximal stability *of an assignment* $\langle u, p \rangle \in UP$ *is the maximum* t *such that the assignment is* t-*stable. It is identified by the function* $t^*: UP \to \mathbb{N}$ *such that* $t^*(\langle u, p \rangle) = \max_{r \in \mathcal{R}(\langle u, p \rangle)} w(r).$

The rational behind the introduction of the *stability* concept is that if an assignment can only be managed by roles with a limited weight, it represents an outlier—see also Chap. 11. Indeed, only few users and permissions are involved in a role together with that assignment. System administrators are willing to manage roles with high weights—that is, which involve many users and many permissions—for several reasons. First, the benefits of using RBAC increase because there are fewer user-role and role-permission relationships to manage. Second, these roles represent relevant portions of the whole access control system of the company. Because of this relevance, they have a greater meaning for system administrators. Conversely, when an assignment cannot be managed with a high-weight role, it represents a portion of data which appears to be inconsistent with the remainder of that dataset. It might not be an error, but from the system administrator point of view, it is riskier than others. In other words, the risk of making mistakes when managing roles with a limited weight is higher: they are roles that are not used frequently, and are in some way obscure to administrators.

The following Lemma relates $\mathcal{B}(\cdot)$ (see Eq. (5.2) at page 5.2) with the t-stability concept [Colantonio *et al.* (2010b)]:

Lemma 14.1. *Given an assignment* $\omega = \langle u, p \rangle \in UP,$ *then* $|\mathcal{B}(\omega)|$ *is an upper bound for* $t^*(\omega).$

The joint usage of Lemma 14.1 and the algorithms described in Chap. 10 makes it possible to practically find an upper-bound for the maximal stability of each assignment belonging to *UP*. In the next section, we will show how to leverage this information to assign a risk level to a particular user or a particular permission.

14.2 Framework Description ★

In this section we adapt the risk model of Sec. 13.2. In particular, we use the t-stability concept to give to each user-permission assignment a probability of occurrence for each risk factor. In particular, given the assignment $\omega = \langle u, p \rangle \in UP$, we define the risk probability of ω as:

Definition 14.4 (Risk Probability of an Assignment). *Given an assignment $\langle u, p \rangle \in UP$, the risk probability of $\langle u, p \rangle$ is a function ass_risk: $UP \to [0,1]$ such that:*

$$\text{ass\_risk}(\langle u, p \rangle) = 1 - \frac{t^*(\langle u, p \rangle)}{|UP|}.$$

The rationale behind the risk probability function is the following: The more $t^*(\langle u, p \rangle)$ is close to $|UP|$, the more the risk level of the assignment ω is close to 0. Indeed, if an assignment can be managed by a single role that covers almost all assignments in *UP*, the user-permission assignment reflects a permission granted to the majority of the users in the dataset. Note that we are not assuming the presence of such a role among those used in the RBAC configuration, but we are only saying that such a role can exist. This consideration allows us to use our risk model in a pre-mining phase, when roles have not yet been decided on.

According to Lemma 14.1, we can quickly estimate an upper bound for $t^*(\langle u, p \rangle)$, and therefore a lower bound for the risk function [Colantonio *et al.* (2010b)]:

Lemma 14.2 (Lower-Bound for Risk Probability of an Assignment). *Given an assignment $\langle u, p \rangle \in UP$, then*

$$\text{ass\_risk}(\langle u, p \rangle) \leq 1 - \frac{|\mathcal{B}(\langle u, p \rangle)|}{|UP|}.$$

By leveraging the above concepts, we can evaluate the risk probability for users and permissions in the following way:

Definition 14.5 (Risk Probability of a User). *Given an user* $u \in$ *USERS, the risk probability of* u *is a function* user_risk: *USERS* $\rightarrow [0,1]$ *defined as:*

$$user\_risk(u) = \sqrt{\frac{\sum_{p \in perms(u)} ass\_risk^2(\langle u, p \rangle)}{|perms(u)|}}. \qquad (14.1)$$

Definition 14.6 (Risk Probability of a Permission). *Given a permission* $p \in$ *PERMS, the risk probability of* p *is a function* perm_risk: *PERMS* $\rightarrow [0,1]$ *defined as:*

$$perm\_risk(p) = \sqrt{\frac{\sum_{u \in users(p)} ass\_risk^2(\langle u, p \rangle)}{|users(p)|}}. \qquad (14.2)$$

By considering the root mean square instead of the arithmetic mean we give more importance to high risk values.

14.3   Experimental Results

We now show an application of our risk framework to a set of real data. Our case study has been carried out on a large private organization. We only report on a representative organization branch that contains 17 users and 72 permissions, counting 560 assignments.

Fig. 14.1a depicts user-permission assignments in a matrix form (see Chap. 9), where each row represents a user, each column represents a permission, and a black cell indicates a user with a granted permission. Figure 14.1b depicts the same access control configuration, but the assignments colors indicate the corresponding risk probabilities. In particular, the cell color goes from a dark color to white: Darker cells means that the pertaining assignment has a high risk level when managed through RBAC; white means that it has a low risk level. Histograms on columns and rows borders respectively report the risk probability of managing permissions and users. Note that there are 6 users that are likely to be risky, mainly because they have a set of granted permissions that the majority of the other users do not have. This set is easily identifiable by looking at the permission histograms: Almost all the first half of the permissions are risky to manage. It is also possible to note that among the high risk users, two users have a slightly minor risk level compared to the other four. Indeed, these two users have similar permissions granted, and this is recognized as a kind of pattern within the data that reduces the overall risk.

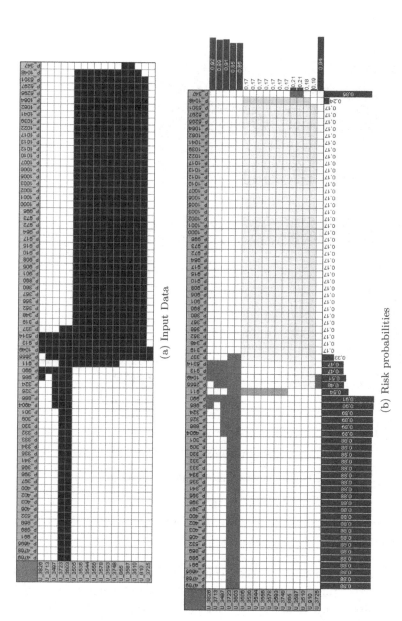

(a) Input Data

(b) Risk probabilities

Fig. 14.1: Risk probability of users and permissions in UP

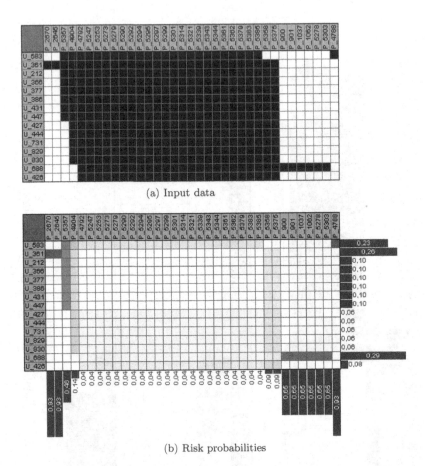

(a) Input data

(b) Risk probabilities

Fig. 14.2: Low risk users and permissions

Fig. 14.2a depicts another access control configuration relative to a different branch of the same organization, while Fig. 14.2b depicts the result of our risk function applied to this branch. Here, the risk levels of all the users are lower than 0.30. It means that, when adopting RBAC, the risk level is generally lower than in the previous example. In other words, role administration should make less mistakes in this second branch than in the first one.

14.4 Final Remarks

The risk management framework introduced in this chapter allows role engineers and system administrators of an RBAC system to highlight those users and permissions that are more prone to error and misuse when roles are operating. A distinguishing feature of our proposal, other than that of being rooted on sound theory, is that role definition is not an input parameter for the risk analysis to be performed; indeed, our model only needs to know the access control configuration of the organization, optionally enriched with other business information. Finally, it has been applied on a real case, and results obtained showed the usefulness and viability of the proposal.

Bibliography

Agrawal, R., Imieliński, T. and Swami, A. (1993). Mining association rules between sets of items in large databases, *SIGMOD Record* **22**, 2, pp. 207–216.

Agrawal, R. and Srikant, R. (1994). Fast algorithms for mining association rules, in *Proceedings of the 20th International Conference on Very Large Data Bases, VLDB*, pp. 487–499.

Aho, A. V., Garey, M. R. and Ullman, J. D. (1972). The transitive reduction of a directed graph, *SIAM Journal on Computing* **1**, 2, pp. 131–137.

ANSI/INCITS (2004). ANSI/INCITS 359-2004, Information Technology – Role Based Access Control, standard specifications.

Armin, E. H., Schmitt, A. O., Lange, J., Meier-ewert, S., Lehrach, H. and Shamir, R. (2000). An algorithm for clustering DNA fingerprints, *Genomics* **66**, pp. 249–256.

Bell, D. E. and LaPadula, L. J. (1976). Secure computer system: Unified exposition and multics interpretation, Electronic Systems Division, Air Force Systems Command, Hanscom Field, Bedford, MA, 01731, ESD-TR-75-306, Rev. 1.

Bertino, E., Bettini, C., Ferrari, E. and Samarati, P. (1998). An access control model supporting periodicity constraints and temporal reasoning, *ACM Transactions on Database Systems* **23**, 3, pp. 231–285.

Biba, K. J. (1977). Integrity considerations for secure computer systems, Tech. Rep. ADA039324, The Mitre Corporation.

Bollobás, B. (1988). The chromatic number of random graphs, *Combinatorica* **8**, 1, pp. 49–55.

Celikel, E., Kantarcioglu, M., Thuraisingham, B. and Bertino, E. (2009). A risk management approach to RBAC, *Risk and Decision Analysis* **1**, 2, pp. 21–33, IOS Press.

Chen, C. (2005). Top 10 unsolved information visualization problems, *IEEE Transactions on Computer Graphics and Applications* **25**, 4, pp. 12–16.

Chierichetti, F., Kumar, R., Pandey, S. and Vassilvitskii, S. (2010). Finding the Jaccard median, in *Proceedings of the 21st annual ACM-SIAM Symposium on Discrete algorithms Conference on Knowledge Discovery and Data Mining, SODA '10*, pp. 293–311.

Cios, K. J., Pedrycz, W., Swiniarski, R. W. and Kurgan, L. A. (2007). *Data Mining: A Knowledge Discovery Approach* (Springer-Verlag).

Colantonio, A. and Di Pietro, R. (2010). CONCISE: COmpressed 'N' Composable Integer SEt, *Information Processing Letters* **110**, pp. 644–650.

Colantonio, A., Di Pietro, R. and Ocello, A. (2008a). An activity-based model for separation of duty, *CoRR* **abs/0810.5351**, URL http://arxiv.org/abs/0810.5351.

Colantonio, A., Di Pietro, R. and Ocello, A. (2008b). A cost-driven approach to role engineering, in *Proceedings of the 23rd ACM Symposium on Applied Computing, SAC '08*, pp. 2129–2136.

Colantonio, A., Di Pietro, R. and Ocello, A. (2008c). Leveraging lattices to improve role mining, in *Proceedings of the IFIP TC 11 23rd International Information Security Conference, SEC '08*, pp. 333–347.

Colantonio, A., Di Pietro, R., Ocello, A. and Verde, N. V. (2009a). A formal framework to elicit roles with business meaning in RBAC systems, in *Proceedings of the 14th ACM Symposium on Access Control Models and Technologies, SACMAT '09*, pp. 85–94.

Colantonio, A., Di Pietro, R., Ocello, A. and Verde, N. V. (2009b). Mining stable roles in RBAC, in *Proceedings of the IFIP TC 11 24th International Information Security Conference, SEC '09*, pp. 259–269.

Colantonio, A., Di Pietro, R., Ocello, A. and Verde, N. V. (2009c). A probabilistic bound on the basic role mining problem and its applications, in *Proceedings of the IFIP TC 11 24th International Information Security Conference, SEC '09*, pp. 376–386.

Colantonio, A., Di Pietro, R., Ocello, A. and Verde, N. V. (2010a). ABBA: Adaptive bicluster-based approach to impute missing values in binary matrices, in *Proceedings of the 25th ACM Symposium on Applied Computing, SAC '10*, pp. 1027–1034.

Colantonio, A., Di Pietro, R., Ocello, A. and Verde, N. V. (2010b). Evaluating the risk of adopting RBAC roles, in *Proceedings of the 24th Annual IFIP WG 11.3 Working Conference on Data and Applications Security, DBSec '10*, pp. 303–310.

Colantonio, A., Di Pietro, R., Ocello, A. and Verde, N. V. (2010c). Mining business-relevant RBAC states through decomposition, in *Proceedings of the IFIP TC 11 25th International Information Security Conference, SEC '10*, pp. 19–30.

Colantonio, A., Di Pietro, R., Ocello, A. and Verde, N. V. (2010d). Taming role mining complexity in RBAC, *Computers & Security* **29**, pp. 548–564, Special Issue on "Challenges for Security, Privacy & Trust".

Colantonio, A., Di Pietro, R., Ocello, A. and Verde, N. V. (2011a). A new role mining framework to elicit business roles and to mitigate enterprise risk, *Decision Support Systems* **50**, pp. 715–731, Special Issue on "Enterprise Risk and Security Management: Data, Text and Web Mining".

Colantonio, A., Di Pietro, R., Ocello, A. and Verde, N. V. (2011b). Visual role mining: A picture is worth a thousand roles, *IEEE Transactions on Knowledge and Data Engineering (TKDE)* In press.

Cormen, T. H., Leiserson, C. E., Rivest, R. L. and Stein, C. (2009). *Introduction to Algorithms* (MIT Press and McGraw-Hill).

Coyne, E. J. (1995). Role-engineering, in *Proceedings of the 1ˢᵗ ACM Workshop on Role-Based Access Control, RBAC '95*, pp. 15–16.

Coyne, E. J. and Davis, J. M. (2007). *Role Engineering for Enterprise Security Management* (Artech House).

Crook, R., Ince, D. and Nuseibeh, B. (2002). Towards an analytical role modelling framework for security requirements, in *Proceedings of the 8ᵗʰ International Workshop on Requirements Engineering: Foundation for Software Quality, REFSQ '02*, pp. 9–10.

Davey, B. A. and Priestley, H. A. (2002). *Introduction to Lattices and Order*, 2nd edn. (Cambridge University Press).

De Capitani Di Vimercati, S., Foresti, S., Samarati, P. and Jajodia, S. (2007). Access control policies and languages, *International Journal of Computational Science and Engineering (IJCSE)* **3**, 2, pp. 94–102.

Deb, K. (2001). *Multi-Objective Optimization Using Evolutionary Algorithms* (John Wiley & Sons, Inc.).

Diestel, R. (2005). *Graph Theory*, 3rd edn. (Springer-Verlag).

Ene, A., Horne, W., Milosavljevic, N., Rao, P., Schreiber, R. and Tarjan, R. E. (2008). Fast exact and heuristic methods for role minimization problems, in *Proceedings of the 13ᵗʰ ACM Symposium on Access Control Models and Technologies, SACMAT '08*, pp. 1–10.

Epstein, P. and Sandhu, R. S. (2001). Engineering of role/permission assignments, in *Proceedings of the 17ᵗʰ Annual Computer Security Applications Conference, ACSAC 2001*, pp. 127–136.

Everitt, B. S. (1993). *Cluster Analysis* (Edward Arnold and Halsted Press).

Federal Financial Institutions Examination Council (2005). Authentication in an internet banking environment, http://www.ffiec.gov/pdf/authentication_guidance.pdf, retrieved April 2011.

Fekete, J.-D., Wijk, J. J., Stasko, J. T. and North, C. (2008). The value of information visualization, in *Information Visualization: Human-Centered Issues and Perspectives*, pp. 1–18.

Fernandez, E. B. and Hawkins, J. C. (1997). Determining role rights from use cases, in *Proceedings of the 2ⁿᵈ ACM Workshop on Role-Based Access Control, RBAC '97*, pp. 121–125.

Ferraiolo, D., Sandhu, R. S., Gavrila, S., Kuhn, R. and Chandramouli., R. (2001). Proposed NIST standard for role-based access control, *ACM Transactions on Information and System Security (TISSEC)* .

Ferraiolo, D. F., Kuhn, D. R. and Chandramouli, R. (2007). *Role-Based Access Control*, 2nd edn. (Artech House).

Ferraiolo, D. F. and Kuhn, R. (1992). Role-based access controls, in *Proceedings of the 15ᵗʰ NIST-NSA National Computer Security Conference*, pp. 554–563.

Figueroa, A., Borneman, J. and Jiang, T. (2003). Clustering binary fingerprint vectors with missing values for DNA array data analysis, in *CSB '03: Proceedings of the IEEE Computer Society Conference on Bioinformatics*, pp. 38–47.

Frank, M., Basin, D. and Buhmann, J. M. (2008). A class of probabilistic models for role engineering, in *Proceedings of the 15ᵗʰ ACM Conference on Computer and Communications Security, CCS '08*, pp. 299–310.

Frank, M., Buhmann, J. M. and Basin, D. (2010). On the definition of role mining, in *Proceedings of the 15ᵗʰ ACM Symposium on Access Control Models and Technologies, SACMAT '10*, pp. 35–44.

Frank, M., Streich, A. P., Basin, D. and Buhmann, J. M. (2009). A probabilistic approach to hybrid role mining, in *Proceedings of the 16ᵗʰ ACM Conference on Computer and Communications Security, CCS '09*, pp. 101–111.

Gallaher, M. P., O'Connor, A. and Kropp, B. (2002). The economic impact of role-based access control, Tech. rep., Planning report 02-1, National Institute of Standards and Technology (NIST).

Ganter, B. and Wille, R. (1999). *Formal Concept Analysis* (Springer-Verlag).

Geerts, F., Goethals, B. and Mielikäinen, T. (2004). Tiling databases, in *Discovery Science*, pp. 278–289.

Giblin, C., Graf, M., Karjoth, G., Wespi, A., Molloy, I., Lobo, J. and Calo, S. (2010). Towards an integrated approach to role engineering, in *Proceedings of the 3ʳᵈ ACM workshop on Assurable and usable security configuration*, SafeConfig '10, pp. 63–70.

Gramm, W. P., Leach, J. A. S. and Bliley, T. J. (1999). Gramm-Leach-Bliley Financial Services Modernization Act, URL http://en.wikipedia.org/wiki/Gramm-Leach-Bliley_Act, act of the United States Congress. Pub. L. No. 106-102, 113 Stat. 1338. Also known as the "Gramm-Leach-Bliley Act".

Guo, Q., Vaidya, J. and Atluri, V. (2008). The role hierarchy mining problem: Discovery of optimal role hierarchies, in *Proceedings of the 24ᵗʰ Annual Computer Security Applications Conference, ACSAC 2008*, pp. 237–246.

Gupta, R., Fang, G., Field, B., Steinbach, M. and Kumar, V. (2008). Quantitative evaluation of approximate frequent pattern mining algorithms, in *Proceedings of the 14ᵗʰ ACM SIGKDD International Conference on Knowledge Discovery and Data Mining, KDD '08*, pp. 301–309.

Hamrouni, T., Denden, I., Ben Yahia, S. and Mephu Nguifo, E. (2008). An experimental study of concise representations for frequent patterns, Tech. Rep. 1, Tunis (Tunisie) – Lens (France).

Han, J. and Kamber, M. (2006). *Data Mining: Concepts and Techniques*, 2nd edn. (Morgan Kaufmann).

Hu, V. C., Ferraiolo, D. F. and Kuhn, D. R. (2006). Assessment of access control systems, Tech. rep., National Institute of Standards and Technology (NIST).

Humphrey, E. (2008). *Implementing the ISO/IEC 27001 Information Security Management System Standard*, 1st edn. (Artech House).

ISACA/ITGI (2009). *Control Objectives for Information and related Technology (COBIT)*.

ISO/IEC (2008). *ISO/IEC 27005:2008(E): Information technology – Security techniques – Information security management*.

ISO/IEC (2009). *ISO/IEC 27000:2009(E): Information technology – Security* techniques – *Information security management systems – Overview and vocabulary*.

Jaccard, P. (1901). Etude comparative de la distribution florale dans une portion des Alpes et des Jura, *Bulletin del la Société Vaudoise des Sciences Naturelles* **37**, pp. 547–579.

Jin, R., Xiang, Y., Fuhry, D. and Dragan, F. F. (2008). Overlapping matrix pattern visualization: A hypergraph approach, in *Proceedings of the 8th IEEE International Conference on Data Mining, ICDM '08*, pp. 313–322.

Kampman, K. (2007). Understanding role management applications: No pain, no gain, Tech. rep., Burton Group.

Kampman, K. and Purdue, H. (2006). The business of roles, The Burton Group.

Keim, D. A., Andrienko, G., Fekete, J.-D., Görg, C., Kohlhammer, J. and Melançon, G. (2008). Visual analytics: Definition, process, and challenges, in *Information Visualization: Human-Centered Issues and Perspectives*, pp. 154–175.

Kennedy, E. and Kassebaum, N. (1996). US Health Insurance Portability and Accountability Act (HIPAA), URL http://en.wikipedia.org/wiki/Health_Insurance_Portability_and_Accountability_Act, act of the United States Congress.

Kern, A., Kuhlmann, M., Schaad, A. and Moffett, J. (2002). Observations on the role life-cycle in the context of enterprise security management, in *Proceedings of the 7th ACM Symposium on Access Control Models and Technologies, SACMAT '02*, pp. 43–51.

Kim, H., Golub, G. H. and Park, H. (2005). Missing value estimation for DNA microarray gene expression data: local least squares imputation, *Bioinformatics* **21**, 2, pp. 187–198.

Kim, S., Dougherty, E. R., Chen, Y., Sivakumar, K., Meltzer, P., Trent, J. M. and Bittner, M. (2000). Multivariate measurement of gene expression relationships, *Genomics* **67**, pp. 201–209.

Koutsonikola, V. and Vakali, A. (2004). Ldap: Framework, practices, and trends, *IEEE Internet Computing* **8**, pp. 66–72.

Kryszkiewicz, M. (2002). Concise representations of association rules, in *Pattern Detection and Discovery*, pp. 92–109.

Kuhlmann, M., Shohat, D. and Schimpf, G. (2003). Role mining – revealing business roles for security administration using data mining technology, in *Proceedings of the 8th ACM Symposium on Access Control Models and Technologies, SACMAT '03*, pp. 179–186.

Kuhn, D. R., Coyne, E. J. and Weil, T. R. (2010). Adding attributes to role-based access control, *Computer* **43**, pp. 79–81.

Li, N., Byun, J.-W. and Bertino, E. (2007). A critique of the ANSI standard on role-based access control, *IEEE Security & Privacy* **5**, 6, pp. 41–49.

Linares, M. (2005). Identity and access management solution, SANS InfoSec Reading Room, http://www.sans.org/reading_room/whitepapers/services/identity-access-management-solution_1640.

Little, R. J. A. and Rubin, D. B. (1987). *Statistical Analysis with Missing Data*, 1st edn., Wiley Series in Probability and Statistics (Wiley).

Liu, J., Paulsen, S., Sun, X., Wang, W., Nobel, A. B. and Prins, J. (2006). Mining approximate frequent itemsets in the presence of noise: Algorithm and analysis, in *Proceedings of the 6th SIAM International Conference on Data Mining*, pp. 405–416.

Liu, J., Paulsen, S., Wang, W., Nobel, A. and Prins, J. (2005). Mining approximate frequent itemsets from noisy data, in *Proceedings of the 5th IEEE International Conference on Data Mining, ICDM '05*, pp. 721–724.

Lu, H., Vaidya, J. and Atluri, V. (2008). Optimal boolean matrix decomposition: Application to role engineering, in *Proceedings of the 24th IEEE International Conferene on Data Engineering, ICDE '08*, pp. 297–306.

Lucchese, C., Orlando, S. and Perego, R. (2006). Fast and memory efficient mining of frequent closed itemsets, *IEEE Transactions on Knowledge and Data Engineering (TKDE)* **18**, 1, pp. 21–36.

Łuczak, T. (1991). The chromatic number of random graphs, *Combinatorica* **11**, 1, pp. 45–54.

Mahfouz, M. A. and Ismail, M. A. (2009). BIDENS: Iterative density based biclustering algorithm with application to gene expression analysis, in *Proceedings of World Academy of Science, Engineering and Technology, PWASET*, Vol. 37, pp. 342–348.

Matys, V., Fischer-Hbner, S., Cvrcek, D. and Svenda, P. (2009). *The Future of Identity in the Information Society (FIDIS)*, 1st edn. (Springer-Verlag).

McDiarmid, C. J. H. (1989). On the method of bounded differences, in *Surveys in Combinatorics: Invited Chapters at the 12th British Combinatorial Conference*, 141 in London Mathematical Society Lecture Notes Series, pp. 148–188.

Mitzenmacher, M. and Upfal, E. (2005). *Probability and Computing: Randomized Algorithms and Probabilistic Analysis* (Cambridge University Press).

Molloy, I., Chen, H., Li, T., Wang, Q., Li, N., Bertino, E., Calo, S. and Lobo, J. (2008). Mining roles with semantic meanings, in *Proceedings of the 13th ACM Symposium on Access Control Models and Technologies, SACMAT '08*, pp. 21–30.

Molloy, I., Chen, H., Li, T., Wang, Q., Li, N., Bertino, E., Calo, S. and Lobo, J. (2010). Mining roles with multiple objectives, *ACM Transactions on Information and System Security (TISSEC)* **13**, 36, pp. 1–35.

Molloy, I., Li, N., Li, T., Mao, Z., Wang, Q. and Lobo, J. (2009). Evaluating role mining algorithms, in *Proceedings of the 14th ACM Symposium on Access Control Models and Technologies, SACMAT '09*, pp. 95–104.

Neumann, G. and Strembeck, M. (2002). A scenario-driven role engineering process for functional RBAC roles, in *Proceedings of the 7th ACM Symposium on Access Control Models and Technologies, SACMAT '02*, pp. 33–42.

Ni, Q., Bertino, E., Lobo, J., Brodie, C., Karat, C.-M., Karat, J. and Trombeta, A. (2010). Privacy-aware role-based access control, *TISSEC* **13**, 24, pp. 1–31.

Oba, S., Sato, M.-A., Takemasa, I., Monden, M., Matsubara, K.-I. and Ishii, S. (2003). A bayesian missing value estimation method for gene expression profile data, *Bioinformatics* **19**, 16, pp. 2088–2096.

O'Connor, A. C. and Loomis, R. J. (2010). 2010 economic analysis of role-based access control, Tech. rep., National Institute of Standards and Technology (NIST).

Oh, S. and Park, S. (2003). Task-role-based access control model, *Information Systems* **28**, 6, pp. 533–562.

Oh, S., Sandhu, R. S. and Zhang, X. (2006). An effective role administration model using organization structure, *ACM Transactions on Information and System Security (TISSEC)* **9**, 2, pp. 113–137.

Pasquier, N., Bastide, Y., Taouil, R. and Lakhal, L. (1999). Efficient mining of association rules using closed itemset lattices, *Inf. Syst.* **24**, pp. 25–46.

Perwaiz, N. and Sommerville, I. (2001). Structured management of role-permission relationships, in *Proceedings of the 6th ACM Symposium on Access Control Models and Technologies, SACMAT '01*, pp. 163–169.

PriceWaterhouseCoopers (2008). Société Générale: Summary of PwC Diagnosis and Analysis of the Action Plan, http://www.societegenerale.com/sites/default/files/documents/pricewatercooper.pdf.

Puolamäki, K., Fortelius, M. and Mannila, H. (2006). Seriation in paleontological data using Markov Chain Monte Carlo methods. *PLoS Computational Biology* **2**, 2.

Reilly, S. (2010). Despite WikiLeaks, Joint Chiefs Vice Chairman Endorses Information Sharing, Federal Times, http://www.federaltimes.com/article/20101208/DEPARTMENTS01/12080301/.

Röckle, H., Schimpf, G. and Weidinger, R. (2000). Process-oriented approach for role-finding to implement role-based security administration in a large industrial organization, in *Proceedings of the 5th ACM Workshop on Role-Based Access Control, RBAC 2000*, pp. 103–110.

Rubin, D. B. (1976). Inference and missing data, *Biometrika* **63**, 3, pp. 581–592.

Rubin, D. B. (1987). *Multiple imputation for nonresponse in surveys* (Wiley).

Rymon, R. (2003). Method and apparatus for role grouping by shared resource utilization, United States Patent Application 20030172161.

Saltzer, J. H. and Schroeder, M. D. (1975). The protection of information in computer systems, *Proceedings of the IEEE* **63**, 9, pp. 1278–1308.

Sandhu, R. S., Coyne, E. J., Feinstein, H. L. and Youman, C. E. (1996). Role-based access control models, *IEEE Computer* **29**, 2, pp. 38–47.

Santamaria, R., Theron, R. and Quintales, L. (2008). BicOverlapper: A tool for bicluster visualization, *Bioinformatics* **24**, 9, pp. 1212–1213.

Sarbanes, P. S. and Oxley, M. G. (2002). Sarbanes-Oxley Act, URL http://en.wikipedia.org/wiki/Sarbanes_oxley, united States federal law. Pub. L. No. 107–204, 116 Stat. 745. Also known as the "Public Company Accounting Reform and Investor Protection Act".

Schafer, J. (1997). *Analysis of Incomplete Multivariate Data*, no. 72 in Monographs on Statistics and Applied Probability (Chapman Hall/CRC).

Schafer, J. and Graham, J. (2002). Missing data: Our view of the state of the art, *Psychological Methods* **7**, 2, pp. 147–177.

Schank, T. and Wagner, D. (2005). Approximating clustering coefficient and transitivity, *Journal of Graph Algorithms and Applications* **9**.

Schlegelmilch, J. and Steffens, U. (2005). Role mining with ORCA, in *Proceedings of the 10th ACM Symposium on Access Control Models and Technologies, SACMAT '05*, pp. 168–176.

Security Standards Council (2010). *PCI DSS Quick Reference Guide.*

Shekofteh, M. (2010). A survey of algorithms in FCIM, in *Proceedings of the International Conference on Data Storage and Data Engineering (DSDE)*, pp. 29–33.

Shin, D., Ahn, G.-J., Cho, S. and Jin, S. (2003). On modeling system-centric information for role engineering, in *Proceedings of the 8th ACM Symposium on Access Control Models and Technologies, SACMAT '03*, pp. 169–178.

Shmulevich, I. and Zhang, W. (2002). Binary analysis and optimization-based normalization of gene expression data, *Bioinformatics* **18**, 4, pp. 555–565.

Siewert, D. J. (2000). *Biclique Covers and Partitions of Bipartite Graphs and Digraphs and Related Matrix Ranks of $\{0, 1\}$ Matrices*, Ph.D. thesis, The University of Colorado at Denver.

Sinclair, S. and Smith, S. W. (2008). Preventative directions for insider threat mitigation via access control, in *Insider Attack and Cyber Security, Advances in Information Security*, Vol. 39, pp. 165–194.

Stoneburner, G., Goguen, A. and Feringa, A. (2002). *Special Publication 800-30: Risk Management Guide for Information Technology Systems*, National Institute of Standards and Technology (NIST).

Streich, A., Frank, M., Basin, D. and Buhmann, J. M. (2009). Multi-assignment clustering for boolean data, in *Proceedings of the 26th International Conference on Machine Learning, ICML 2009*, pp. 969–976.

Strembeck, M. (2010). Scenario-driven role engineering, *IEEE Security and Privacy* **8**, 1, pp. 28–35.

Takabi, H. and Joshi, J. B. (2010). Stateminer: an efficient similarity-based approach for optimal mining of role hierarchy, in *Proceedings of the 15th ACM Symposium on Access Control Models and Technologies, SACMAT '10*, pp. 55–64.

Tan, P. N., Steinbach, M. and Kumar, V. (2006). *Introduction to Data Mining* (Pearson Education).

Tarantino, A. G. (2008). *Governance, Risk, and Compliance Handbook* (John Wiley & Sons, Inc.).

Tolone, W., Ahn, G.-J., Pai, T. and Hong, S.-P. (2005). Access control in collaborative systems, *ACM Computing Surveys (CSUR)* **37**, pp. 29–41.

Troyanskaya, O. G., Cantor, M., Sherlock, G., Brown, P. O., Hastie, T., Tibshirani, R., Botstein, D. and Altman, R. B. (2001). Missing value estimation methods for DNA microarrays. *Bioinformatics* **17**, 6, pp. 520–525.

Tuikkala, J., Elo, L. L., Nevalainen, O. S. and Aittokallio, T. (2008). Missing value imputation improves clustering and interpretation of gene expression microarray data, *BMC Bioinformatics* **9**, 202.

United States DoD (1983). Trusted Computer System Evaluation Criteria (TC-SEC), Orange Book, DoD 5200.28-STD.

Vaidya, J., Atluri, V. and Guo, Q. (2007). The role mining problem: finding a minimal descriptive set of roles, in *Proceedings of the 12th ACM Symposium* *on Access Control Models and Technologies, SACMAT '07*, pp. 175–184.

Vaidya, J., Atluri, V. and Guo, Q. (2010). The role mining problem: A formal perspective, *ACM Transactions on Information and System Security (TIS-SEC)* **13**, 27, pp. 1–31.

Vaidya, J., Atluri, V., Guo, Q. and Adam, N. (2008). Migrating to optimal RBAC with minimal perturbation, in *Proceedings of the 13th ACM Symposium on Access Control Models and Technologies, SACMAT '08*, pp. 11–20.

Vaidya, J., Atluri, V. and Warner, J. (2006). RoleMiner: mining roles using subset enumeration, in *Proceedings of the 13th ACM Conference on Computer and Communications Security, CCS '06*, pp. 144–153.

Wasserman, S. and Faust, K. (1994). *Social Network Analysis*, chap. 5 (Cambridge University Press), pp. 169–219.

Watts, D. J. and Strogatz, S. H. (1998). Collective dynamics of 'small-world' networks. *Nature* **393**, 6684, pp. 440–442.

Williams, D. (1991). *Probability with Martingales* (Cambridge University Press).

Yahia, S. B., Hamrouni, T. and Nguifo, E. M. (2006). Frequent closed itemset based algorithms: A thorough structural and analytical survey, *SIGKDD Explorations Newsletter* **8**, pp. 93–104.

Yang, G. (2006). Computational aspects of mining maximal frequent patterns, *Theoretical Computer Science* **362**, 1, pp. 63–85.

Zaki, M. J. and Hsiao, C.-J. (2005). Efficient algorithms for mining closed itemsets and their lattice structure, *IEEE Transactions on Knowledge and Data Engineering (TKDE)* **17**, 4, pp. 462–478.

Zaki, M. J. and Ogihara, M. (1998). Theoretical foundations of association rules, in *In 3rd ACM SIGMOD Workshop on Research Issues in Data Mining and Knowledge Discovery*, pp. 1–8.

Zhang, D., Ramamohanarao, K. and Ebringer, T. (2007). Role engineering using graph optimisation, in *Proceedings of the 12th ACM Symposium on Access Control Models and Technologies, SACMAT '07*, pp. 139–144.

Index